Knowing our World

George F. Luger

Knowing our World

An Artificial Intelligence Perspective

 Springer

George F. Luger
Department of Computer Science
University of New Mexico
Albuquerque, NM, USA

ISBN 978-3-030-71875-6   ISBN 978-3-030-71873-2   (eBook)
https://doi.org/10.1007/978-3-030-71873-2

This Springer imprint is published by the registered company Springer Nature Switzerland AG
The registered company address is: Gewerbestrasse 11, 6330 Cham, Switzerland

For Kate

Preface

*like the geometer who strives to square the circle and cannot
find by thinking the principle needed, was I at that new sight...*

—DANTE, *Paradiso*

Why Write This Book?

Like many of us, I was born a *naïve realist*, believing that our senses provide us with direct awareness of and access to objects as they really are. Psychologists and philosophers, including Jean Piaget, Tom Bower, Alison Gopnik, and Clark Glymour, have chronicled the developmental processes that normal children take toward knowing themselves and their world. Through experimentation, exploration, and just being alive, we discover that objects still exist when they disappear from sight, that intention, desires, and emotion are important, and that throwing food off a high-chair can teach us about parents' frustration levels as well as simple physics, for example, that some things bounce!

Being brought up in a religious environment was also a component of coming to know the world. The deity, accepted myths, saints, all of these were part of what was "real." And importantly, these beliefs carried me through my early formative years. And the supporting love of family and a close circle of friends sustained my maturing worldview.

At some time, however, the critical questions come to a necessary focus, almost like fruit ripening: How do you know what is real? How can you make judgments about alternate truths? How can you explain the disparate "true beliefs" of others in a complex world? If a person is to live a mature life, does it require being committed to something? Plato has suggested that the unexamined life is not worth living.

Some of the maturational cracks came while taking mathematics courses. What exactly IS the square root of 2? Or pi? It can easily be shown that the square root of 2 is not a rational number, i.e., a fraction. (Suppose the root of 2 is a fraction and is represented by the integers p/q, where p and q have no common factors. Then squaring both sides gives $2 = p^2/q^2$ or $2 * q^2 = p^2$, or q^2 is $\frac{1}{2}$ of p^2, which contradicts the no common factors assumption). If the square root of 2 is not a fraction, what is it? Why are fractions called "rational" anyway? Does "irrational" mean that we cannot understand what the number is? It turns out the square root of 2 is a very important abstraction. We created this abstraction because it is useful.

Philosophy courses, during more than a decade of Jesuit education, were also an important component of coming to understand the world. Reading Plato and Aristotle was great fun; after Plato's cave *gadanken experiment* in the seventh book of *The Republic*, rationalism was an obvious worldview to espouse. But there were always the haunting viewpoints of the Skeptics and Epicureans as part of the background noise. Augustine, Aquinas, and Descartes only confirmed a rationalist perspective, with a God playing an essential role in the mind/body composition of the human persona.

The enlightenment was just that. It started off comfortably with Descartes' *Meditations*, the *cogito ergo sum*, and an assumption of a benevolent God who made a coherent world possible. But Berkeley, Hume, Spinoza, and Kant soon changed the entire philosophical discourse. Of course, any perspective on the world must come through the senses, even seeing and touching are mediated by the physiological and emotional constraints of the human system as noted by Maturana and Verala. Perhaps conditioning over time makes some associations linking perceptions possible? What is there "outside" of us and how could we know it? The concurring question, of course, is what is there "inside" of us and how could we possibly know that either? Hume's arguments demolished the naive understanding of causality as well as any possible coherent proofs for the existence of a God.

Heidegger, Husserl, and the existentialist tradition proposed self-creation through actualizing oneself in space and time. As Sartre proposed, *existence precedes essence*, which means that first of all we are individuals, independently acting, and responsible agents. We are always beings in process, starting from a state of disorientation and confusion and moving toward freedom and authenticity. In important ways, these many philosophical positions, along with a growing experience of love, responsibility, and the embrace of society, began to open up a possible path toward intellectual and emotional maturity.

American pragmatists also played a central role. Although lacking any epistemic foundation other than *what was useful*, pragmatists point out that life, learning, and judgments are always *about* something. As William James suggests, religion is good if it produces a better life for those practicing it. The pragmatist offers important constraints for a rationalist view of the world: Are pure and distinct ideas a good in themselves, or must they be seen as components of some useful purpose?

But utility in itself is a very slippery criterion for judging the real, and one person's useful goals can easily contradict those of others. Among the pragmatist writers, C.S. Peirce stands out, especially his discussions about abductive inference or "reasoning to the best explanation." Although Peirce himself was not very coherent about what algorithms might support abduction, Bayesian inference and the insights of Judea Pearl, as we see in Chaps. 7 and 8, offer a cogent beginning.

There were important challenges here. The existentialist tradition, along with American pragmatism's lack of what I considered epistemic grounding, supported a postmodern and poststructuralist skepticism. On this viewpoint, the very bedrock on which Western cultures had based their ideas of knowledge, truth, and meaning are brought under scrutiny. A nihilist relativism seemed to permeate the ideas and promise of humanism and the enlightenment.

At the same time, the logical positivist tradition of Carnap, Russell, Frege, and others emerged. This tradition supported building foundations for logic and philosophy. Besides the mathematical components of logical positivism, there was the proposal by philosophers including Popper and Kuhn of the utility and critical importance of the scientific method as a medium for coming to understand ourselves and the world.

While finishing a graduate program in mathematics, I happened on Norbert Weiner's book *Cybernetics*, and although I did not fully appreciate it at the time, I was headed toward a computational vision of the world. I began my PhD work at the University of Pennsylvania soon afterword and was very pleased to be in an interdisciplinary program in the School of Arts and Sciences. My interest areas included mathematics, computer science, linguists, and psychology, and I worked with my advisors to select a PhD committee and an interdisciplinary program of study.

A favorite graduate student book was Thomas Kuhn's *The Structure of Scientific Revolutions*. We students explored Kuhn's ideas, not just because, with the energy of youth and ideas, we might be part of such a revolution, but more importantly because Kuhn clearly delineated the processes of science. Besides my education at Penn, I was a fan of Herbert Simon and Allen Newell's research projects at Carnegie Mellon University that focused on using computational techniques to better understand human problem-solving performance. Their book, *Human Problem Solving*, is still on my shelf. I also was fortunate to be able to visit their research labs several times during my early research years. My own dissertation involved using the state-space technology, taken from representations used in computing, to describe aspects of human problem-solving behavior.

The University of Pennsylvania as well as the Newell and Simon research launched me fully into the domain of artificial intelligence. In 1974, I obtained a four-and-a-half-year postdoctoral research position in the Department of Artificial Intelligence at the University of Edinburgh in Scotland. Edinburgh was at that time, and still is, at the heart of AI research in Europe. A strength of the University of Edinburgh's AI Department was its interdisciplinary flavor. I was able to work actively with faculty and graduate students in the Departments of Psychology, Linguistics, and Epistemics, as well as with colleagues in the world class Department of Artificial Intelligence.

In 1979, we moved to Albuquerque, where I became a professor of computer science at the University of New Mexico, with joint appointments in the Departments of Linguistics and Psychology. In the early 1980s, Peder Johnson, a professor of psychology, and I began the Cognitive Science graduate program at UNM. In the mid-1990s, Caroline Smith, a professor of linguistics, and I began the graduate program in Computational Linguistics at UNM. Our interdisciplinary studies included lectures from the UNM Neuroscience and Psychology Departments in a seminar called Cognitive and Computational Neuroscience.

One of the exciting by-products of a faculty position at UNM has been the opportunity to take graduate courses in the Physics Department on neuroimaging, in the Psychology Department on issues related to neuroscience, and in the Philosophy Department with seminars on Ludwig Wittgenstein, Richard Rorty, and other topics in modern epistemology.

I am now professor emeritus at the University of New Mexico. My resume is available at https://www.cs.unm.edu/~luger/. My consulting is in natural language processing, building web agents, and in using deep learning technologies that analyze information in very large collections of data.

The Story

The book is divided into three parts, each containing three chapters. Chapter 1 introduces the art of programming, Alan Turing's machine, and the foundations of computing, and asks the question of how best to represent complex world situations to a machine.

Chapter 2 describes the philosophical background that supports the scientific method, modern epistemology, and the foundations for modern computing and artificial intelligence. These topics are essential for contemplating a modern epistemic outlook.

Chapter 3 describes the 1956 Dartmouth Summer Workshop that marked the beginning of the artificial intelligence enterprise. Chapter 3 also describes early AI research and the origins of the Cognitive Science research community. These first three chapters also discuss the nature of AI programming as iterative refinement and present the very-high-level language tools that support AI application building.

Part II, Chaps. 4, 5, and 6, introduces three of the four main paradigms that have supported research and development in the artificial intelligence community over the past sixty plus years: the symbol-based, the neural network or connectionist, and the genetic or emergent. Each of these chapters present introductory "programs" and describe their applications. These examples are included to demonstrate each different representational approach to AI. The chapters also describe several of the more recent research and advanced projects in each of these areas. Each chapter ends with a critique of the strengths and the limitations of that paradigm.

Part III, the final three chapters, is the raison d'être for the book and presents the fourth emphasis in current AI: probabilistic reasoning and dynamic modeling. In Chap. 7, a philosophical rapprochement is proposed between the different approaches AI has taken, which are seen as founded within the rationalist, empiricist, and pragmatist philosophical traditions. Based on this constructivist synthesis, the chapter ends with a set of assumptions and follow-on conjectures that offer a basis both for current AI research and for a modern epistemology.

Chapter 8 presents Bayes' theorem along with a proof in a simple situation. The primary reason for introducing Bayes, and the follow-on technology of Bayesian belief networks and hidden Markov models, is to demonstrate a mathematics-based linkage between the *a priori* knowledge of the human subject and *a posteriori* information perceived at any particular time. We see this cognitive quest for equilibrium as a foundation for knowing and operating in the world. The last half of Chap. 8 describes a number of programs, supported by the Bayesian tradition, that capture and display these epistemic insights.

Chapter 9 summarizes our project and describes building and adapting models of the world through active exploration in the world. We describe the promising future of AI as it continues to use the scientific tradition to expand its horizons, explore our evolving environment, and build intelligent artifacts. We consider the contemporary pragmatist thinking of Wittgenstein, Putnam, Kuhn, and Rorty, and insights from cognitive neuroscience all exploring the nature of knowledge, meaning, and truth. The book concludes with a critique of postmodern relativism and proposes an epistemic stance called *an active, pragmatic, model-revising realism.*

1 December 2020   George F. Luger
Albuquerque, NM

Acknowledgments

A main theme of this book is how individuals and society create symbols, associations, and sets of relationships that later become parts of a belief system, through a consistent and survival-based dialectic with the environment. This has certainly been true with my own intellectual life and the insights that support the creation of this book. It is often impossible to separate oneself from the web of both intellectual and social support enjoyed over the years. My task here is to attempt to acknowledge this debt.

First, of course, my gratitude is for my wife of more than fifty years, Kathleen Kelly Luger, and my children, Sarah, David, and Peter. I have always been fortunate in the unconditioned support of family and friends.

At Penn my advisor was Gerald A. Goldin, a Physics PhD from Princeton. Also advising me was John W. Carr III, an early practitioner in the field of artificial intelligence. As already noted, I owe a huge debt to Allen Newell and Herbert A. Simon, then at CMU.

In the Artificial Intelligence Department at the University of Edinburgh, I worked under Bernard Meltzer and Alan Bundy. I am also indebted to Donald Michie and Rod Burstall for their friendship and support during those years. Other colleagues during the Edinburgh years included Mike Bauer, Tom Bower, Danny Kopek, Bob Kowalski, David MacQueen, Brendon McGonigle, Tim O'Shea, Martha Palmer, Fernando Pereira, Gordon Plotkin, Michael Steen, David Warren, Jennifer Wishart, and Richard Young. Important research visitors during that time included Michael Arbib, George Lakoff, Alan Robinson, and Yorick Wilks.

At the University of New Mexico, where much of the AI research presented in this book took place, I am indebted to my PhD graduate students, including Chayan Chakrabarti, Paul DePalma, Sunny Fugate, Ben Gordon, Kshanti Greene, Bill Klein, Joseph Lewis, Linda Means, Dan Pless, Roshan Rammohan, Nakita Sakhanenko, Jim Skinner, Carl Stern, and Bill Stubblefield. Chayan, Carl, and Bill have been especially important coauthors of my books and papers as well as long-time friends.

I thank my friend, internationally recognized artist Thomas Barrow, for his cover art. Several colleagues and friends read early versions of this manuscript. These include Bertram (Chip) Bruce, Thomas Caudell, Chayan Chakrabarti, Russell Goodman, David MacQueen, Keith Phillips, Don Vogt, and Lance Williams. I am indebted to them all for their criticisms, suggestions, and encouragement. Thanks to Matt Alexander and Ray Yuen for their excellent assistance in graphics design. Thanks also to my Springer editor, Paul Drougas, for his support in bringing this effort to completion. Finally, thanks to Daniel Kelly for many years of advice and support.

The material for this book comes from various sources. Many of the figures and programs come from my very early teaching and were used in my AI textbook, *Artificial Intelligence: Structures and Strategies for Complex Problem Solving*, now in its 6th edition. Some of the material describing the philosophical support for modern AI comes from my book, *Cognitive Science: The Science of Intelligent Systems*. Many of the projects presented are from my own research group and from collaborations with colleagues. These projects are a direct result of talented and hard-working graduate students. I am truly thankful for their effort, skills, and friendships.

Contents

Part I
In the Beginning…

Part I contains three chapters. Chapter 1 introduces the reader to the art of programming, Alan Turing's machine, and the foundations of computing, and asks the question of how best to represent complex world situations on a machine.

Chapter 2 describes the philosophical background that supports the scientific method, modern epistemology, and the foundations for computing and artificial intelligence. These topics are essential for the support of a modern epistemic stance.

Chapter 3 describes the 1956 Dartmouth Summer Workshop that marked the beginning of the artificial intelligence enterprise. Chapter 3 also describes early AI research and the origins of the Cognitive Science research community. The first three chapters also discuss the nature of AI programming as iterative refinement and present the very-high-level language tools that support AI application building.

Chapter 1
Creating Computer Programs: An Epistemic Commitment

Everything must have a beginning, to speak in Sanchean phrase; and that beginning must be linked to something that went before. Hindus give the world an elephant to support it, but they make the elephant stand upon a tortoise. Invention, it must be humbly admitted, does not consist in creating out of void, but out of chaos; the materials must, in the first place, be afforded...

—*MARY SHELLEY, Frankenstein*

Contents

1.1   Introduction and Focus of Our Story

There are already a number of excellent books available on the history of automating human intelligent behavior. Their writers, often pointing out the similar actions of computers and brains, employ the techniques of computer science and artificial intelligence to both better understand many of the mental activities that the human brain supports and to create programs critical to human progress.

This book is different. We describe the successful use of the methodologies of science and computation to explore how we humans come to understand and operate in our world. While humankind's history of articulating ideas and building machines that can replicate the activity of the human brain is impressive, we focus on understanding and modeling the practices that accomplishes these goals.

This book explores the nature of knowledge, meaning, and truth through reviewing the history of science and the human creativity required to produce computer

© Springer Nature Switzerland AG 2021

G. F. Luger, *Knowing our World*, https://doi.org/10.1007/978-3-030-71873-2_1

programs that support intelligent responses. This quest is within the domain and purview of the study of *epistemology.*

Epistemology. What is this field of study? Why is it important? How does epistemology relate to artificial intelligence? How does the creation of artificial intelligence relate to epistemology? These questions and their answers make up the foundation of this book and will be introduced in this first chapter.

Epistemology is the study of how we humans know our world. The word "epistemology," like "psychology" or "anthropology," has its origin in Greek language. There are two roots to the word, $\varepsilon\pi\iota\sigma\tau\varepsilon\mu\varepsilon$, meaning "knowledge" or "understanding," and $\lambda o\gamma os$ meaning "exploration" or "the study of." Thus, epistemology can be described as the study of human understanding, knowledge, and meaning. The Stanford Encyclopedia of Philosophy describes epistemology:

> Defined narrowly, epistemology is the study of knowledge and justified belief. As the study of knowledge, epistemology is concerned with the following questions: What are the necessary and sufficient conditions of knowledge? What are its sources? What is its structure, and what are its limits? As the study of justified belief, epistemology aims to answer questions such as: How are we to understand the concept of justification? What makes justified beliefs justified? Is justification internal or external to one's own mind? Understood more broadly, epistemology is about issues having to do with the creation and dissemination of knowledge in particular areas of enquiry.

Interestingly, the Greek $\lambda o\gamma o\sigma$ and its Latin translation *verbum* also mean the "rational principle that governs and develops the universe." On this viewpoint, epistemology takes on deeper and more important implications: the study of knowledge, meaning, purpose, and truth.

What would a science of epistemology look like? Would there be some basic assumptions upon which further conclusions could be constructed? What would these assumptions be? Perhaps the negation or the change of an assumption would support an alternative epistemology, as we see in modern geometries. Does human purpose or pragmatic intent shape meaning? What is truth, and can there be multiple truths? What is causality and how can the search for explanations justify beliefs? Is a coherent epistemic policy possible or are we condemned to a postmodern position of skepticism, subjectivity, and contingency? Before addressing these issues, we present an epistemic perspective on computer-based problem-solving in general and artificial intelligence in particular.

How does epistemology relate to artificial intelligence? Knowledge, meaning, and purpose are certainly critical to building a computer program that, when run, results in "intelligent" performance. The important juncture of epistemology and building programs that produce intelligent results is a major theme of this book. Further, we contend that reflecting on the art of programming a computer offers insight into how we humans explore and come to understand the natural world.

Creating any program for a computer requires selecting symbols and program instructions, called *algorithms*, to "capture" the task at hand. There is also a continuing process of refining the program until the result produces the desired solution. We will call this task-driven selection of symbols and programming instructions an *epistemic commitment* or *stance*. When this program is intended to reflect aspects of human intelligence, the program's implicit epistemic stance becomes critical. We contend that making explicit this program/epistemic stance relationship offers considerable insight into how we humans discover, explore, and survive in our world.

Besides choosing symbols and algorithms, program designers also choose "containers," called *data structures*, for organizing these symbols; the program's algorithms will manipulate both the symbols and the data structures. For example, the symbol C_n might represent the cost of an item numbered n from a particular inventory of items for sale; N_n might reflect the number of the items n remaining in inventory. Similarly, ST might represent the current percentage of sales tax for all the inventory items.

In this example, the symbols can be contained in an *array*, a numbered list that describes all the parts in the inventory. Each element of the array would be a *record*. The data structure, an *array of records*, could then be used to index, give the current cost, and the number of each item currently in the inventory. This record could even provide reorder information. Finally, a sequence of instructions, the algorithm, is needed to identify the desired item in inventory (does the algorithm go to each element of the array in order to check if it is the desired item or can it go directly to the appropriate array element?) The algorithm will then need to decrease by one the number of the items remaining in the inventory and calculate for the customer the cost of the item, including the sales tax.

Engineering quality software often requires a progressive approximation of the desired solution with continuing program revision that better meets task goals. For example, when our proposed program attempts to remove an item from the inventory, it must be told that, if there are no items remaining in inventory, it cannot sell one to the customer, nor can it ever allow a negative number to represent the quantity of an item in inventory. A continuing refinement to the inventory algorithm might put these two "guards" in the customer cost program and might also add instructions to use the supplier information to automatically reorder items when the inventory reaches a certain value. The key point here is that as a program is used, its limitations are better understood with a newly revised and refined program able to better accomplish tasks.

Most programs, especially AI programs, are more complex than this simple inventory maintenance example, and most problems discovered in running programs, sometimes referred to as *bugs*, are harder to determine than having a negative number that represents an item in an inventory. Nonetheless, selection of symbols, structures for data, and program instructions, as well as the iterative program refinement process, remains constant across successful program building.

Writing programs for computers is an exercise of representational and algorithmic choice, and the programming experience must be viewed from this perspective. It follows that selection of the symbols, data structures, and algorithms is an *epistemic experiment* and *commitment*. These choices can explain both the strengths and the limitations of most programming endeavors. From this perspective, we contend that exploring this experience of building successful computational artifacts provides an important perspective on the nature of epistemology itself. We explore this theme further in Parts II and III.

Selecting symbols, data structures, and algorithms in an effort to capture aspects of reality can also be seen as the programmers' challenge. The steady evolution of newer computer languages and structures for data with associated control algorithms is a steady progression toward better capturing and manipulating useful components of the environment. The larger story of AI algorithms and data structures, including the use of logic, rule systems, semantic and object-oriented networks, structures for deep learning, and tools for stochastic modeling, are all components of successful programming. These AI tools and techniques are described in detail in Parts II and III.

In the remainder of this chapter, we address several fundamental issues including, in Sect. 1.2, asking what it means to compute. We then discuss, in Sect. 1.3, the role of computer languages and how we represent information and human knowledge for computation. The answers to these questions lead us to discussions in Parts II and III of computational models and their roles in AI and science.

1.2   The Foundation for Computation

As we see in Chap. 2, the goal of building mechanical systems that tell time, automate arithmetic operations, mimic the operations of the solar system, and even attempt to calculate the full array of attributes of a god were important for mathematicians, engineers, and even philosophers from the beginning of recorded time.

The notion of building such "intelligent" artifacts has a long tradition found primarily in efforts to improve the human condition. The Chinese built early water clocks, and of course, the wheel was used to support moving heavy objects. An early reference to building robot automatons was that the Greek god Hephaestus was said to have fashioned tripods that could walk to and from Mount Olympus and could serve nectar and ambrosia to the gods. Later, Aristotle mentioned that if these automatons were indeed possible, slavery would not be justified!

There is also a cultural phobia of "stealing knowledge belonging only to the gods" that has followed on the building of intelligent machines. Prometheus stole fire from Hephaestus and also medicinal treatments for humans and, as a result of his daring, Aeschylus leaves him bound to a boulder being eternally bitten by birds. Humans' daring to understand and create algorithms reflecting knowledge and the nature of human intelligence and then building these into computational devices is still seen by many as a threat to and diminution of specifically human or divine attributes.

Challenging the domain of the deities notwithstanding, throughout history, this automation of aspects of human intelligence continued with the building of clocks, astronomical instruments, arithmetic calculators, and much more. The early nineteenth century produced some flexibly programmed devices including, in 1804, the Jacquard loom that was controlled by a sequence of punched cards that produced different weaving patterns.

Charles Babbage was one of the first to ask if a general-purpose calculating machine could be built and reconfigured to solve any number of different algebraic problems. In 1822, Babbage proposed and began building his *Difference Engine* a machine that, through a method of *finite differences*, was intended to find values for polynomial functions. The engineering technology of that period did not support Babbage's desire to build an even more general-purpose computing device, called the *Analytic Engine*. Fortunately, Babbage and his staff, including the nineteenth-century mathematician and writer Ada Lovelace (1961), produced detailed drawings of these different engines. We discuss Babbage's technology and goals further in Sect. 2.9.

It remained for the mathematicians of the early twentieth century to finally specify what was meant by the notion of a general-purpose computing machine. In the 1930–1950 time period, Gödel (1930), Turing (1936, 1948), Church (1941), Post (1943), and others created abstract specifications for universal computing. These specifications included Post-style production systems, general recursive functions, the predicate calculus, and Alan Turing's finite state machine that read from and wrote to a movable memory tape. Turing's creation (1936) was called the *Turing machine* (TM), and his extension of that machine, with its program encoded as part of its tape, was called the *universal Turing machine* (UTM). We next present the TM and will describe it as an instance of what we call an *automated formal system*.

1.2.1   The Turing Machine

The components of a Turing machine, Fig. 1.1, are a set of tokens or symbols, a set of rules for manipulating these tokens, and an algorithm that uses the symbols and rules to actually manipulate the symbols. The tokens are discrete entities in that they can be uniquely identified, counted, and configured with other tokens into patterns of tokens. The distinctness of the tokens allows for comparing them and looking for equivalences in patterns of tokens. The token patterns are such that tokens are next to each other in some ordering on a memory device: the data structure for Turing is the moveable tape. The set of rules for operating on token patterns include adding, deleting, or, in any well-defined manner, changing the patterns of these tokens on the tape.

For this automated formal system to solve a problem, a commitment had to be made for a set of symbols to represent that problem as well as for instructions to manipulate these symbols in solving the problem. Although a more complete description of the evolution of symbol representations and search algorithms for computing will follow in Sect. 1.3, we next give an example of a representation scheme and an algorithm for solving a problem using a Turing machine.

Turing machine "descriptions" have taken several forms over the years, all of them equivalent. For us, a Turing machine will be made up of three components. A

Fig. 1.1 A Turing machine, including a controller that itself has a "state," a head that can read and write symbols and move along a potentially infinite tape

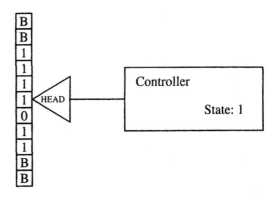

potentially infinite tape for encoding symbols: The symbols in our example are 1, 0, and B, or *blank*, for a space on the tape with no symbol at all. The Turing machine will also have a programmed set of instructions, and, finally, a mechanism called a "controller" for applying the program's rules to the symbols on the tape. This Turing machine can be visualized in Fig. 1.1. The set of instructions or program is presented in Table 1.1. The finite-state controller will itself have a state, in our example, an integer from 1 to 4 and "halt," which stops the computation.

We next consider a simple problem called *unary subtraction*. An example of unary subtraction is having two piles of things such as coins or pencils. The problem's task is to see which pile is larger and by how much. A simple algorithm for doing this, which we implement on the Turing machine, is to remove one item at a time from each pile until one of the piles is exhausted. In our example, consider a left pile, above the 0 in Fig. 1.1, and a right pile, below the 0. We want to determine which pile contains more pencils. The B is used before and after the sets of 1 s that are separated by the 0 to delimit the problem on the tape.

We will simplify the unary subtraction problem in three ways. First, we put the larger number of items in the left pile or above the 0 on the tape of Fig. 1.1. Second, we will begin the problem assuming the controller's "head" is over the leftmost 1, the topmost 1 on the tape of Fig. 1.1. Finally, we will not count the number of items remaining in the piles when the machine halts. All of these constraints could be replaced by another more complex program for the Turing machine, but the goal of this example is to understand the operation of the Turing machine rather than to write a rather more complex program.

After the program's rules (the algorithm) are applied to take away an equal number of 1 s from each side of the 0, the result is the answer to the problem. Three examples of the results of the Turing machine running its program:

BB1111011BB produces BBBB11BBBB and the left pile has two more items.
BB111101BB produces BBB111BBBB and the left pile has three more items.
BB11011BB produces BBBBBBBBB and the piles are equal.

As just noted, the program does not count the number of items (the 1 s) left when the program halts.

Table 1.1 The program for the Turing machine of Fig. 1.1 is represented as a list, left to right by row, of instructions

State	Reading	Write	Move	Next State
1	1	1	R	1
1	0	0	R	1
1	B	B	L	2
2	1	B	L	3
2	0	B	N	Halt
3	0	0	L	3
3	1	1	L	3
3	B	B	R	4
4	1	B	R	1

A representation for the set of rules, sometimes called the finite state machine, that make up the program for unary subtraction is described next, and the full program is given in Table 1.1. Each rule, a row in Table 1.1, consists of an ordered list of five symbols:

1. The current state of the finite state machine: 1, 2, 3, 4, or halt;
2. The current symbol, 1, 0, or B, seen by the *head* or reading device on the tape;
3. The new symbol, 1, 0, or B, to be written on the tape;
4. The instruction for moving the head to the next position on the tape: to the left, L, or right, R, or no move, N, which happens when the machine halts; and
5. The new state of the finite state machine, again, 1, 2, 3, 4, or halt.

In Table 1.1, each instruction is presented in a list, left to right in each row, telling the machine what to do. When the first two symbols in each list (row) are matched, the final three instructions are performed. For example, the top row of Table 1.1 says that if the controller is in state 1 and sees a 1 at the tape location it is viewing, then it writes a 1 at that location, moves one position to the right on the tape, and makes the next (new) state of the controller to be 1.

A trace of the running program is presented in Table 1.2. The string of characters on the top row, BB1111011BB, reflects that the machine starts seeing the leftmost 1 of the sequence where the "_" indicates the character that the head currently sees on the tape. The Turing machine instructions of Table 1.1 will eventually produce, see Table 1.2, the pattern BBBB11BBBBB from the pattern BB1111011BB.

As we see with unary subtraction, and again in later chapters, the representation for a problem situation is coupled with rules for manipulating that representation. This relationship between representational structures for problem situations and the related "search" algorithms is a critical component of the success of the AI, or in fact any programming enterprise.

We make several points here. First, as presented in this example, the program or finite state machine was independent of the tape. The machine's rules were applied to produce new results recorded both on the tape and in the state machine. This limitation was addressed when Turing (1936) created his *Universal Turing Machine* (UTM), where the program itself, Table 1.1, was placed on the tape along with the data. Thus, after an instruction was executed, the read/write head would move to

Table 1.2 A trace of the moves of the Turing machine in Fig. 1.1 using the programmed instructions of Table 1.1

State	Tape
1	BB111011BB
1	BB111011BB
1	BB111011BB
1	BB111011BB
1	BB111011BB
1	BB111011BB
1	BB111011BB
1	BB111011BB
2	BB111011BB
3	BB111101BBB
3	BB111101BBB
3	BB111101BBB
3	BB111101BBB
3	BB111101BBB
3	BB111101BBB
3	BB111101BBB
4	BB111101BBB
1	BBB11101BBB
1	BBB11101BBB
1	BBB11101BBB
1	BBB11101BBB
1	BBB11101BBB
1	BBB11101BBB
2	BBB11101BBB
3	BBB1110BBBB
3	BBB1110BBBB
3	BBB1110BBBB
3	BBB1110BBBB
3	BBB1110BBBB
4	BBB1110BBBB
1	BBBB110BBBB
1	BBBB110BBBB
1	BBBB110BBBB
1	BBBB110BBBB
2	BBBB110BBBB
hall	BBBB11BBBBB

"State" gives the current state of the controller

that area of the tape, where the set of instructions, the program for calculating the next operation, was located. It would determine the next instruction and return to the data portion of the tape to execute that instruction.

A final issue for Turing machines is the idea, and technical impossibility, of having an "infinite tape." There are two answers to this: First, every computer is in fact a *finite* state machine, and periodically programmers, often because of incorrect programs or faulty thinking about a problem, have received a message that the computer is out of memory. Second, the actual requirement for the Turing machine, or for any other computer, is that there only needs to be sufficient memory for the machine to run its current program. For modern computing, the automatic reclaiming of already used but no longer needed memory helps address the issue of computation on a finite state machine. This real-time reclamation of memory is often called *garbage collection*.

1.2.2 The Post Production System and Unary Subtraction

We next consider the unary subtraction problem from another representational and machine instruction viewpoint. Suppose our two "piles of objects" are represented as two lists of 1 s. Rather than putting them sequentially on a tape separated by a symbol, we will leave them as two lists considered in parallel. The list will be a structure delimited by brackets, "[ ]," containing a 1 to represent each element in the pile.

The list representing the left pile is on the top with the right pile below it as shown in the next examples. The algorithm for this example will let either pile have more items in it. Unary subtraction examples now look like these:

> [1111]
> [11]
> Produces [11] on top, and the left pile has 11 more
> [11]
> [11]
> Produces two []s, and determines that the two piles are even
> [11]
> [111]
> Produces [1] on the bottom, and the right pile has 1 more

Next, we make a set of rules to manipulate these lists. We describe the rules as pattern → action pairs and present them as four "if → then" rules:

1. If there is a 1 as the left-most element of each list, then remove both 1 s.
2. If there is a 1 as the left-most element of the top list and the bottom list is empty, [ ], then write: "The left pile has this many more:", write out the 1 s of the top list, and halt.
3. If the top list is empty, [ ], and a 1 as the left-most element of the bottom list, then write: "The right pile has this many more:" write out the 1 s of the bottom list, and halt.
4. If the top list is empty and the bottom list is empty, then write: "The two piles are even," and halt.

We now create another type of finite state machine, called a *Post Production System*, to process these patterns. Figure 1.2 presents a schematic for this production system. There are three components. The first is the *production memory* that contains the rules for processing the patterns that are contained in the second component, the *working memory*. Finally, there is a *recognize-act* control cycle that takes the patterns contained in working memory and presents them to the set of rules in

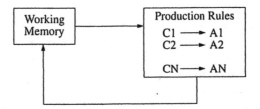

Fig. 1.2 A Post Production System made up of three components: a production memory containing the rules, a working memory containing the pattern representing the current state of the problem, and a recognize-act cycle, the arrows

Table 1.3 The trace of a production system solution to the unary subtraction problem with four items in the right pile and two in the left

The problem starts with the working memory pattern:
[1111]
[11]
Rule 1 is activated to produce the new working memory pattern:
[111]
[1]
Rule 1 is activated again to produce the new working memory pattern:
[11]
[ ]
Rule 2 is activated to produce the new working memory pattern:
The left pile has this many more: 11 and halt

production memory. The result of applying a rule is then returned as part of the new working memory.

The recognize-act cycle continues until no pattern matches or, as in our case, a particular rule, causes the cycling to halt. For our example, we will assume the rules are tested in order, although obviously, for very large sets of rules and complex patterns, trying each rule in order could be very inefficient. A trace of the production system solution for the unary subtraction problem, where there are four items in the left pile, the top list, and two in the right pile, the bottom list, can be seen in Table 1.3.

We have just shown the unary subtraction problem with two different representations and solved by two different computing machines. As noted previously, in the 1930–1950 time period, a number of mathematicians provided abstract specifications for what it meant to compute, including Alan Turing whose TM we described,

Emil Post (1943) whose production system machine we just considered, Alonzo Church using the lambda-calculus, Andrei Markov, Kurt Gödel, and others.

Alonzo Church (1935) conjectured that any possible computable function could be translated into a Turing machine computation. Later, the Church-Turing thesis demonstrated that all of the then known models for computation were in fact equivalent and equally powerful. The proof methodology was to build each of the abstract machines using the technology of the other machines. Church-Turing also conjectured that any of these machines could compute whatever it might be possible to compute (Davis 1965).

In Chapters 5 and 6, we consider two more specifications for computing, neural or connectionist networks and finite-state automata. Researchers (Siegelman and Sontag 1991) have shown that recurrent neural networks are computationally complete, that is, equivalent to the class of Turing Machines. This Turing equivalence extends earlier results: Kolmogorov (1957) showed that for any continuous function there exists a neural network that computes that function. It has also been shown that a one hidden-layer backpropagation network can approximate any of a more restricted class of continuous functions (Hecht-Nielsen 1989). Similarly, we see in Chap. 6 that von Neumann created finite-state automata that were Turing complete. Thus, connectionist networks and finite state automata appear to be but two more classes of machines capable of computing virtually any computable function.

In the recent years, more exciting new models for computation have emerged, including molecular or DNA computing, proposed by Leonard Adleman (1994) and quantum computing, a concept originally suggested by Richard Feynman (1982) in the late 1950s. These approaches to computation offer interesting and more flexible representations as well as faster algorithms; it remains to be seen, however, whether they can compute anything not computable by a Turing machine. Finally, cognitive scientists (Luger 1995) often ask whether the human mind, seen as a computational device, can compute any result outside of what Church-Turing hypothesizes as computable.

Alan Turing (1936) and others also demonstrated algorithms that had no computable solution. An example of this class of computations is the *halting problem*, where it is asked whether a computer can always determine whether or not any program sent to it will complete or finish its computation.

Turing's halting problem proof is an example of an *incompleteness* proof. Incompleteness indicates the inherent limitations of formal systems. For any formal system at least as powerful as arithmetic, there will always be statements about the system that are true but are not provable within the system itself. There is a history of these proofs in mathematics going back through Turing, Gödel, and Cantor to David Hilbert.

Turing's proof supposed that there existed a program, call it *quit*, that could determine whether any program given to it would actually complete its computation and halt. Then, Turing created a second program that did the opposite of the *quit* program, for example, directing the new program that if the program *quit* actually halts then the second program should keep running. The program *quit* is then given as data to be run by the second program.

The commitment of computer engineers and program designers to different models for computation supports different pragmatic as well as epistemic stances. For example, cognitive scientists often followed Post's approach, where they see the production system's rule memory as representative of human long-term memory and the working memory as human short-term memory or attention, a property of the human prefrontal cortex. The production system control algorithm then presents the current contents of working memory to the knowledge and procedures found in long-term memory (Newell and Simon 1972, 1976). According to this model, learning is seen as forming new rules for permanent memory through a form of reinforcement learning based on the interactions between the working and the long-term memories (Newell 1990; Laird 2012). The production system as a model for human problem-solving is discussed further in Sect. 3.4.3 on Cognitive Science.

1.3   Computer Languages, Representations, and Search

Fortunately, modern programmers do not need to use the Turing or Post machines to accomplish their tasks. Although computers, at the machine level, do operate with 0/1 or on/off processing, a great deal of energy in the years since the first computers were created has gone into the development of higher level languages for programming. This effort by generations of computer scientists and engineers has produced our contemporary programming languages, where high-level language instructions result in producing appropriate machine-level executions.

There are several other reasons for creating these higher level languages for computation. One is to make a language for addressing the computer that is more like a human language, where the programmer can more easily build solution strategies, such as to "take the largest element from a list and see if it is a possible solution." The more the computer language can reflect human thinking, the more useful it tends to be. We will see this point again in discussing representations.

A further task for high-level languages is to protect the programmer from having to do memory management on the computer itself. Of course, the skilled programmer will not abuse the memory limitations of the finite state machine by creating data structures or algorithms unsuited for either the task at hand or the limitations of the machine. But from the opposite viewpoint, the quality programmer should not have to worry about what particular memory register she is using but rather should focus on building algorithms reflecting the thought processes used in problem-solving. The high-level language implementation itself should handle the memory management necessary to support her efforts.

Current high-level computer languages can be seen as belonging to two groups. The first group of languages, sometimes referred to as *applicative*, offers efficient tools for manipulating data structures on the traditional computer architecture. This approach can be visualized as separating data elements from control algorithms, where the goal of the programming endeavor is to use the command-based control language to manipulate the data in a step-by-step fashion, telling the computer to call specific algorithms on a particular data set. The running program applies the program-based instructions to the data. Currently, languages such as Java, Python, and C# are in this group.

The second group of languages, both *declarative* and *functional*, offers programmers the opportunity of solving problems with mathematics-based support systems. The idea of having a mathematical foundation for programming is that the language and the algorithms afforded by the language can help control unintended errors and side effects in the resulting programs. An example would be trying to multiply a number by a string of letters. Using a mathematical system can also assist in demonstrating that the answer of a program is mathematically (logically) correct and not just some random result that the computer produced. The two main classes of mathematically based languages are those based on the predicate calculus, such as Prolog, an instance of a *declarative* language, and languages based on *functional* mathematics such as the lambda calculus; Lisp, Scheme, ML, Haskell, and OCaml are in this group.

Any choice of a particular language, however, will have its limitations, both in the ease of expressing complex relationships for the computer, sometimes referred to as a language's *expressive power* and in its ability to capture appropriate relationships and interactions in the application domain. Finally, a programming language is indeed a language. In computer-based problem-solving, the language offers communication links with the machine itself. It also offers a medium for interacting with other programmers assisting with the problem-solving task, augmenting an earlier solution, or simply maintaining the completed program.

As noted previously, when solving a problem, the programmer selects symbols and data structures to represent salient aspects of the problem. The function of any such representational scheme is to capture, often by *abstracting out,* the critical features of a problem domain to make that information accessible to an algorithm. *Abstraction* is an essential tool for managing complexity as well as an important factor in assuring that the resulting programs are computationally efficient.

Expressiveness, the transparency of the abstracted features, and *efficiency,* the computational complexity of the algorithms used on the abstracted features, are major dimensions for evaluating languages for representing information. Sometimes, expressiveness must be sacrificed to improve an algorithm's efficiency. This must be done without limiting the representation's ability to capture essential problem-solving knowledge. Optimizing the trade-off between efficiency and expressiveness is a major task for designers of intelligent programs. We next present several example representations and demonstrate how they assist the program designer in capturing critical components for solving specific problems.

Table 1.4 presents different representations for the number π. The real number π is a useful abstraction: the relationship between the diameter of a circle and its circumference. There is no finite sequence of decimal digits that describes π, so it cannot be exactly represented on a finite state device. One answer to this dilemma, called the *floating-point* representation, is to represent the number in two pieces: its most important digits and the location within these digits of the decimal point.

Table 1.4 Different representations for the real number π

The real number:	π
The decimal equivalent:	3.1415927…
The floating-point representation:	Exponent: 1; Mantissa: 31416
Representation in computer memory:	11100010…

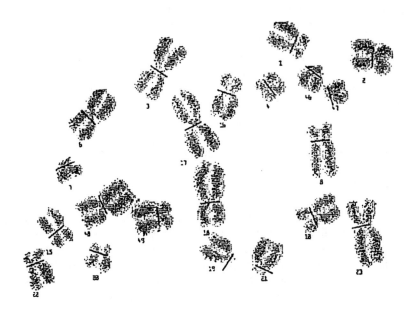

Fig. 1.3 The digitized image of human chromosomes in metaphase

Although not exactly π, this convention makes it possible to compute with π in practical applications.

Floating-point representation thus sacrifices full expressive power to make the representation both efficient and possible. This representation also supports algorithms for *multiple-precision* arithmetic, giving effectively infinite precision by limiting the approximation error, called *round-off*, to be less than any prespecified value. As in all representations, the result is only an abstraction, a pattern of symbols that designates a desired entity. It is NOT the entity itself.

The array is another representational structure common in computer science. For many problems, it is both natural and efficient. An example where the array representation works well is the inventory problem presented at the beginning of this chapter. To represent the inventory, we created an array of records. Our record contained four components: the part number, the price of the part, the number of parts currently in inventory, and the company address for reordering. The record could be extended to carry even more data.

A second example of using an array is for image processing. Figure 1.3 is a digitized image of human chromosomes in a stage called *metaphase*. The goal of this image processing was to identify chromosome damage from radiation exposure. The image is processed to determine the number and structure of the chromosomes, looking for breaks, missing pieces, and other abnormalities.

The visual scene is made up of a number of picture points. Each picture point, or *pixel*, has both a location and a number representing its intensity or *gray level*. It is natural, then, to collect the entire scene into a two-dimensional array, where the row and column address give the location of a pixel, the X and Y coordinates, and the content of the array element is the gray level of the image at that point.

Algorithms are then designed to perform operations on these gray-scale images. These include looking for isolated points to remove noise from the image and finding threshold values for determining objects and their edges. Algorithms can also sum up contiguous elements of a chromosome to determine its size and, in various other ways, transform the picture point data into understandable information. FORTRAN and related languages are efficient for array processing. This task would be cumbersome using other representations, such as the predicate calculus, records, or assembly code.

When we represent this image as an array of pixel points, we often sacrifice the quality of resolution; as an example, compare a photo in a newspaper to the original print of the same picture. In addition, pixel arrays cannot express the deeper semantic relationships of the image, such as representing the organization of chromosomes in a single cell nucleus, their genetic function, or the role of metaphase in cell division. This knowledge is more easily captured using representations such as the predicate calculus or semantic network, discussed later. In summary, a representation should support a natural scheme for expressing all information required for solving the problem as well as for efficient computation.

Often, the problems that the AI community addresses do not lend themselves to the representations offered by more traditional formalisms such as records and arrays. Artificial intelligence is usually more concerned with qualitative relationships rather than quantitative measures, with purpose-oriented reasoning rather than numeric calculation, and with organizing large and varied amounts of knowledge rather than implementing a single, well-defined algorithm.

Consider, for example, Fig. 1.4, the arrangement of blocks on a table. In early AI, this domain was called a *blocks world*. Suppose we wish to capture the properties and relations required to control a robot arm. We must determine which blocks are stacked on other blocks and which blocks are clear on top so that they can be picked up. The *predicate calculus* offers a medium to capture this descriptive information. The first word of each predicate expression, e.g., on, ontable, clear, etc., is a *predicate* denoting some property or relationship among its *arguments,* the names of the objects in parentheses.

$$\text{clear}(c), \text{clear}(a), \text{ontable}(a), \text{ontable}(b),$$

$$\text{on}(c,b), \text{cube}(b), \text{cube}(a), \text{pyramid}(c).$$

Fig. 1.4 A configuration
of blocks for robot
manipulation and a set of
predicates describing the
blocks. Cubes a and b rest
on a table, while pyramid c
is on top of cube b

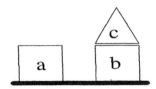

clear(c), clear(a), ontable(a), ontable(b),
on(c, b), cube(b), cube(a), pyramid(c).

Predicate calculus provides artificial intelligence programmers with a well-defined language for describing and reasoning about qualitative aspects of a system. Suppose in the example of Fig. 1.4 that we want to define a test to determine whether a block is clear on top, that is, has nothing stacked on top of it. This is important if the robot hand is to pick it up or stack another block on top of it. We can define a general rule:

$$\forall X \neg \exists Y \, on(Y,X) \Rightarrow clear(X).$$

This rule is read: "for all objects X, $\forall$ X, object X is clear if there does not exist an object Y, $\neg \exists$ Y, such that Y is on top of X." This general rule can be applied to a variety of situations by substituting different block's names, a, b, c, etc., for X and Y. By supporting such general reasoning rules, the predicate calculus allows economy of representation as well as the possibility of designing systems that are flexible and general enough to respond intelligently to a wide range of situations. There is further discussion of predicate calculus planning for robot solutions in Sect. 4.1.2.

The predicate calculus can also be used to represent the properties of individual items and groups. It is often not sufficient, for example, to describe a car by simply listing its component parts; we may want to describe the ways in which those parts are combined and the interactions between them. This view of structure is essential to a range of situations, including taxonomic information, such as the classification of plants by genus and species, or a description of complex objects, such as a diesel engine or a human body in terms of their constituent parts. For example, a simple description of a bluebird might be "a bluebird is a small blue-colored bird" and "a bird is a feathered flying vertebrate," which may be represented as the set of logical predicates:

hassize(bluebird,small), hascovering(bird,feathers), hascolor(bluebird,blue),
hasproperty(bird,flies), isa(bluebird,bird), isa(bird,vertebrate)

This predicate description can be represented graphically by using the *arcs*, or *links*, in a graph instead of predicates to indicate relationships as seen in Fig. 1.5. This *semantic network* is a technique for representing the meanings of relationships.

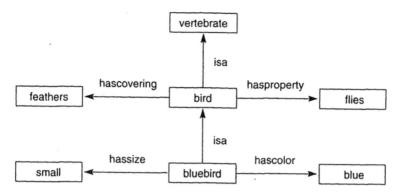

Fig. 1.5 A semantic network description of a bluebird and its properties

Because relationships are explicitly denoted in the semantic network, an algorithm for reasoning about a problem situation can make relevant associations by following the links. In the bluebird illustration, for example, the program needs to only follow one link to see that a bluebird flies and two links to determine that a bluebird is a vertebrate. Perhaps the most important application for semantic networks is to represent meanings for programs intended to understand human languages. When it is necessary to comprehend a child's story, the details of a journal article, or the contents of a web page, semantic networks may be used to encode the information and relationships that reflect the knowledge. We have further discussion of semantic network representations in Sect. 5.1.2.

Another example representation is the probabilistic network. Suppose you know traffic patterns on a route you travel often. You are aware that if there is road construction, it will likely slow down traffic about 30% of the time and traffic would keep moving, as usual, 20% of the time. If there is no construction, you still might have slow-moving traffic about 10% of the time. Finally, there will probably be no construction and no bad traffic about 40% of the time. You are also aware of similar sets of likelihoods for accidents, including flashing police or ambulance warning lights, and the presence of orange traffic control barrels on the highway.

A *Bayesian belief network* (BBN), as shown in Fig. 1.6, is an appropriate representation for this traffic situation. The BBN is a *directed* graph without *cycles*. A graph is directed, as seen in Fig. 1.6, where the heads of the arrows indicate the connection between the states. The directed arrows are intended to reflect a causal relationship between the situations, for example, construction, C, sometimes, 0.4, causes bad traffic, T. Further, no state may have cycles where a dependency arrow refers back to that state itself. The BBN representation is on the left in Fig. 1.6, while the table representing a subset of the probability relationships is on the right. In the table, true is T, false is F, and probability is p. Each row presents one of the probabilistic situations just described.

The BBN just described can be made dynamic to reflect the changes in the world across time periods. For example, if at some point while driving you see flashing lights, then L becomes true and the rest of the probabilities must change to reflect

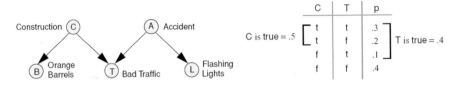

Fig. 1.6 A Bayesian belief network (BBN) representing a driving example. The BBN is on the left and a partial table of probabilities for the network is at the right

this new fact, making the possibility of an accident, A, more likely, as well as construction, C, less likely. This belief network that changes over time is called a *dynamic Bayesian network* or DBN, which we will demonstrate further in Chap. 8.

We have only briefly touched on network representation systems that support much of the current effort in artificial intelligence. Among those we have not yet considered are neural and deep learning networks, seen in Chap. 5, and structures for genetic algorithms and artificial life described in Chap. 6.

Complementing each representation chosen for intelligent problem-solving is a *search algorithm*. Humans generally consider a number of strategies in solving a problem. A chess player reviews alternative moves, selecting the "best" according to criteria such as the opponent's possible responses or the degree to which various moves support some global game strategy. A player also considers short-term gain, such as taking an opponent's knight, opportunities to sacrifice a piece for positional advantage, or to support conjectures about the opponent's psychological makeup and level of skill. This aspect of intelligent behavior underlies the representational technique called *state-space search*.

Consider, for example, the game of tic-tac-toe, the British *naughts-and-crosses*. In most board situations, e.g., Fig. 1.7, there are only a finite number of moves for a player. Starting with an empty board, the first player puts an X in any of nine places. Each move yields a different board that allows the opponent eight possible responses, and so on. We represent this collection of possible moves and responses by regarding each board configuration as a *node* or *state* in a graph. The *links* between the nodes of the graph represent legal moves from one board position to another. The resulting structure is described with the *state-space graph* of Fig. 1.7.

The state-space representation supports treating all possible games of tic-tac-toe as different paths through the state space. Given this representation, an effective game strategy searches through the space for paths that lead to the most likely wins and fewest losses, playing in a way that always tries to force the game along one of these optimal paths. We present further techniques that build search strategies for graphs in Chap. 4 and demonstrate computer learning using graph search in Sect. 4.2.

As an example of how search is used to solve a more complicated problem, consider the task of diagnosing a mechanical fault in an automobile. Although this problem does not initially seem to lend itself to state-space search as easily as tic-tac-toe or chess, it actually fits this situation quite well. Instead of letting each node of the graph represent a board state, we let it represent a state of partial knowledge about the automobile's mechanical problems. The state space for diagnostic search

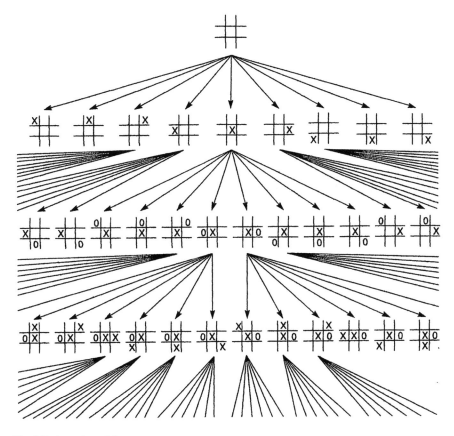

Fig. 1.7 A portion of the state space for playing tic-tac-toe

is often produced dynamically, as we see with rule-based expert systems in Sect. 4.1.3.

The process of examining the symptoms of possible faults and figuring out their causes may be thought of as searching through states of increasing knowledge. The starting node of the graph is empty, indicating that nothing is known about the cause of the problem. The first question a mechanic might ask the customer is what car component, engine, transmission, steering, brakes, etc., seems to be causing the trouble. This is represented by a collection of arcs from the start state to states that indicate a focus on different subsystems of the automobile, as in Fig. 1.8.

Each of the states in the graph has arcs representing different diagnostic checks that then lead to states describing further accumulations of knowledge in the process of diagnosis. For example, the "engine trouble" node has arcs to nodes labeled "engine starts" and "engine won't start." From the "engine won't start" node, we move to nodes labeled "turns over" and "won't turn over." The "won't turn over" node has arcs to nodes labeled "battery dead" and "battery ok" as seen in Fig. 1.8. A problem solver can diagnose car trouble by searching for a path through this

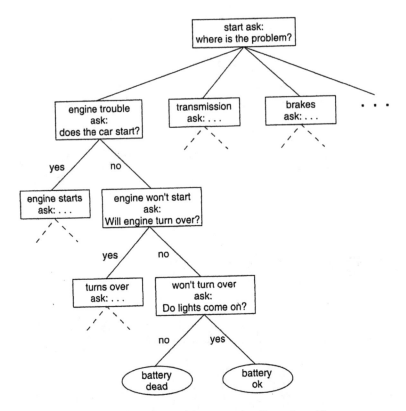

Fig. 1.8 A state-space description of part of the automotive diagnosis problem

graph that is consistent with the symptoms of a particular defective car. Although this problem is very different from that of finding an optimal way to play tic-tac-toe or chess, it is equally amenable to solution by state-space search as we see in Sect. 4.1.3.

Despite this apparent universality, state-space search is not, by itself, sufficient for automating intelligent problem-solving behavior; rather it is an important tool for the design of intelligent programs. If state-space search were sufficient, it would be fairly simple to write a program that plays chess or go by searching through the entire space of possible moves for that sequence of moves that brings a victory, a method known as *exhaustive search*.

Although exhaustive search can be applied to any state space, the overwhelming size of the space for many interesting problems makes this approach a practical impossibility. Chess, for example, has approximately 10^{120} different board states. This is a larger number than molecules in the universe or the number of nanoseconds that have passed since the *big bang*. Search of this space is beyond the capabilities of any computing device, whose dimensions must be confined to the known universe and whose execution must be completed before the universe succumbs to the ravages of entropy.

Humans use intelligent search: A game player considers a number of possible moves, a doctor focuses on several possible diagnoses, and a computer scientist entertains different designs before beginning to write a program. Humans usually do not use exhaustive search: the chess player examines only moves that experience has shown to be effective, and the doctor need not require tests that are not indicated by the symptoms at hand. Human problem-solving seems to be based on judgmental rules that guide search to those portions of the state space that seem most promising.

These human judgment rules are known as *heuristics* taken from the Greek verb 'ευρισκο' meaning *to discover*. They constitute one of the central topics of AI research. The heuristic is a strategy used for selectively searching a problem space. It guides searching along lines that have a high probability of success while avoiding moves to states that a human expert would call wasted or not supporting a winning opportunity.

State-space search algorithms give the programmer a means of formalizing the problem-solving process and heuristics that allow her to search that formalism intelligently. Heuristic techniques make up an important component of modern AI. In summary, state-space search is a representational formalism, independent of particular problems or search strategies, that is used as a launch point for many different implementations of intelligent problem-solving. Heuristic search is described in detail in Sect. 4.1.2.

Chapter 2 offers a brief history of the philosophical precursors of modern epistemology and artificial intelligence. Chapter 3 describes the early research efforts and successes of the AI community. Part II, Chaps. 4–6, describes three of the major approaches to problem-solving that the AI community has taken across its brief history. Part III describes probabilistic techniques for AI problem-solving. Many of the AI representations and programming techniques presented in the remainder of this book also offer sufficient models for both understanding important components of human problem-solving and suggesting constraints for a science of epistemology.

1.4   In Summary

A computer program that solves tasks makes an epistemic commitment to understanding its application domain: symbols stand for entities in the application, structures of symbols capture relationships in the domain, and search strategies find solutions. In the example early in this chapter, the array of records represents the numbers and costs of all items in an inventory, and the search strategy produces the desired result of the customer cost for an item as well as an updated inventory.

We saw that computation was not a single machine or language applied to a machine; but an abstraction, represented by different, but equivalent, definitions of finite state machines. Computing is not a particular architecture: not Turing's, Post's, von Neumann's, or the sophisticated use of tinker toys, but a finite state system with a certain level of complexity. This leaves us open to using different models of computation to capture differing aspects of human problem-solving as we will see in later chapters.

In this first chapter, we also considered several representational schemes and search algorithms as an introduction to the model building and model revision process that embodies the commitment of the AI programmer. These will be developed further in later chapters. As computer scientists see the limitations of their current programs and revise them, they also revise their model of and expectations for understanding our changing world.

Further Thoughts and Readings The creation of both computer-based representations and novel search algorithms for capturing intelligence is sometimes seen as the fundamental definition of AI.

In a 2016 paper, *From Alan Turing to Modern AI: Practical Solutions and an Implicit Epistemic Stance*, in the Springer journal *AI and Society*, Luger and Chakrabarti go into deeper detail describing how epistemic issues support and limit the success of AI research projects.

Wikipedia has descriptions of many of the computability issues discussed in this chapter. For further detail visit topics including:

Theory of Computation,
Turing and Post-production Machines,
The Church-Turing Thesis, and
Computability Theory.

Several examples of this chapter were taken from my textbook *Artificial Intelligence: Structures and Strategies for Complex Problem Solving, sixth edition* (Luger 2009a). The Turing Machine and Post-production examples were taken from *Cognitive Science: The Science of Intelligent Systems* (Luger 1995).

Chapter 2
Historical Foundations

Hear the rest, and you will marvel even more at the crafts and resources I have contrived. Greatest was this: in the former times if a man fell sick he had no defense against the sickness, neither healing food nor drink, nor unguent; but through the lack of drugs men wasted away, until I showed them the blending of mild simples wherewith they drive out all manner of diseases....

It was I who made visible to men's eyes the flaming signs of the sky that were before dim. So much for these. Beneath the earth, man's hidden blessing, copper, iron, silver, and gold—will anyone claim to have discovered these before I did? No one, I am very sure, who wants to speak truly and to the purpose. One brief word will tell the whole story: all arts that mortals have come from Prometheus.

—AESCHYLUS, Prometheus Bound.

All people by nature desire to know...
—ARISTOTLE, Opening sentence of his Metaphysics.

Contents

This chapter traces the origins of epistemology, modern science, and the scientific method within the evolution of Western thought. This evolution is organic and seamless, as the perspectives of philosophers, scientists, and engineers over the past three millennia come together to produce both the specifications for computation, as we saw in Sect. 1.2, and the mathematical systems that have supported and expanded its use. This tradition also produced the cognitive sciences, see Sect. 3.5, and offers a foundation for a modern epistemology, Part III.

There are several important themes within the evolution of Western thought and culture; first, an attempt at what can be called *model building* with continuing *model refinement*. This can be seen in early Greek thinkers who proposed ideas such as *everything is water*, as water could be "transformed" under different conditions. Later thinkers proposed that *all reality is made up of the four basic elements of water, earth, fire, and air*. Although such thoughts may now seem rather naive, what is important to our story is the process of actually proposing explanations (models) of reality, and then, as new observations no longer fit the data, revising these models as better explanations are required.

A second theme constant in the evolution of Western thought is the various forms of skepticism that are interwoven with the philosophical and scientific processes. We discuss two different forms of skepticism, the first is questioning the veridicality of human perceptions and observations. The second form of skepticism is questioning the ability to establish, conclusively, any form of what might be called *truth*. We see this disposition even today when coping with postmodernism's relative truths and values. We consider skepticism again in Sects. 7.4 and 9.5.

This chapter begins by discussing Aesculus and the Promethean gifts to humanity, introduced in Sect. 1.2, and the most important gift of intelligent exploration of our world. Sections 2.2–2.8, describe the evolution of Western thought that has brought us to our current understanding of science as well as supported the birth of computation. The final three sections describe the mathematical basis for computing, the Turing test of intelligence, and the emergence of artificial intelligence.

2.1 Mary Shelley, Frankenstein, and Prometheus

Prometheus speaks of the fruits of his transgression against the gods of Olympus: His purpose was not merely to steal fire for the human race but also to enlighten humanity through the gift of intelligence or *nous*: the *rational mind*. This intelligence forms the foundation for all human technology and ultimately all human civilization.

The work of the classical Greek dramatist Aeschylus illustrates a deep and ancient awareness of the extraordinary power of knowledge. Artificial intelligence, in its very direct concern for Prometheus's gift, has been applied to all the areas of his legacy—medicine, psychology, biology, astronomy, geology—and many areas of scientific endeavor that Aeschylus could not have imagined. Although Prometheus's action began to free humanity from the sickness of ignorance, it also earned him the wrath of Zeus. Outraged over this theft of knowledge that previously belonged only to the gods of Olympus, Zeus commanded that Prometheus be chained to a rock to suffer for eternity.

The notion that human efforts to gain knowledge constitute a transgression against the laws of god or nature is deeply ingrained in Western thought. It is the basis of the story of Eden and appears in the work of Dante and Milton. Both Shakespeare and the ancient Greek tragedians portrayed intellectual ambition as a cause of disaster. The belief that the desire for knowledge must ultimately lead to perdition has persisted throughout history, enduring the Renaissance, the Age of Enlightenment, and even challenges current scientific, philosophical, and political advances. We should not be surprised that the idea of an "artificial" intelligence provokes so much controversy in both academic and popular circles.

Indeed, rather than dispelling this ancient fear of the consequences of intellectual ambition, modern technology has only made those consequences seem likely, even imminent. The legends of Prometheus, Eve, and Faustus have been retold in the language of a technological society. In her introduction to *Frankenstein,* subtitled, not surprisingly, *The Modern Prometheus*, Mary Shelley writes:

> Many and long were the conversations between Lord Byron and Shelley to which I was a devout and silent listener. During one of these, various philosophical doctrines were discussed, and among others the nature of the principle of life, and whether there was any probability of its ever being discovered and communicated. They talked of the experiments of Dr. Darwin (I speak not of what the doctor really did or said that he did, but, as more to my purpose, of what was then spoken of as having been done by him), who preserved a piece of vermicelli in a glass case till by some extraordinary means it began to move with a voluntary motion. Not thus, after all, would life be given. Perhaps a corpse would be reanimated; galvanism had given token of such things: perhaps the component parts of a creature might be manufactured, brought together, and endued with vital warmth.

Mary Shelley shows us the extent to which scientific advances including the works of Darwin and the discovery of electricity had convinced even nonscientists that the workings of nature were not divine secrets but could be broken down and understood. Frankenstein's monster is not the product of shamanistic incantations or unspeakable transactions with the underworld: It is assembled from separately "manufactured" components and infused with the vital force of electricity. Although nineteenth-century science was inadequate to realize the goal of understanding and creating a fully intelligent agent, it affirmed the notion that the mysteries of life and intellect might be brought into the light of scientific analysis.

2.2 Early Greek Thought

By the time Mary Shelley combined modern science with the Promethean myth, the philosophical foundations for understanding our world had been developing for several thousand years. Western philosophy began in the eastern Mediterranean around the sixth century BCE. The Greek inhabitants of the Ionian Islands were located along major trade routes placing them in contact with a variety of cultures and civilizations, including the Babylonian, Persian, Indian, Egyptian, and Cretan. These contacts involved an exchange of ideas as well as trade. Amidst this diversity of cultural perspectives, intelligent people could no longer assume the correctness of their own inherited belief systems. The first philosophers were challenged to discover a source of knowledge more universal than that of their own personal, cultural, or religious perspectives.

These early philosophers were strongly influenced by their observations of natural processes and astronomical events. Thales of Miletus, in about 585 BCE, is said to have successfully predicted a solar eclipse. He proposed the theory that *everything is water* and that the diversity of phenomena can be explained by the variety of forms that water takes in different situations. His followers, Anaximander, and Anaximenes of Miletus also studied astronomy and developed geometric models of remarkable clarity and precision. Like Thales, they also constructed explanations of the physical universe based on a few simple principles such as the separation of hot and cold and the condensation of air. The point is not that they got many of their answers wrong but rather that they were beginning a scientific tradition of observation, generation of explanations, and revision of explanations in the light of further observation.

Pythagoras, Heraclitus, and Parmenides rejected the explanation of phenomena proposed by the Milesian school. Each of them proposed theories that interpreted the changing phenomena of nature as superficial or illusory. Pythagoras of Samos, about 570 BCE, saw in mathematics and music the sources of ultimate revelation. He held that music and mathematics reveal the unchangeable harmony of the cosmos, a mystery hidden below the surface of perceptual phenomena.

Heraclitus of Ephesus, about 500 BCE, held that the flux of appearance is governed by a hidden structure or *logos*, which is only accessible to those who have trained themselves to "listen." An important aspect of this structure is the unity of opposites, where opposites require one another and continually flow into and replace each other. Parmenides of Elea, in about 450 BCE, argued that being is one and unchangeable and that multiplicity and change are illusory. His student Zeno developed a set of arguments or paradoxes designed to demonstrate that the concept of motion is self-contradictory. A common thread throughout this period is the conjectured split between appearances and reality: the former characterized by diversity and change and the latter by unity and permanence.

A different response to this clash of theories came from the skeptics and sophists. The lesson drawn by the skeptics from this diversity of opinions was that truth was unknowable. Xenophanes of Colophon, around 575 BCE, argued that even if the truth were fully stated, it could not be known. That is, if the truth were ever to appear among the spectrum of diverse opinions, there would be nothing to distinguish it from other views and therefore no reason to choose it.

Sextus Empiricus, a later codifier of skepticism, elaborated Xenophanes' claim into an argument known as the *criteriological regress*. Suppose you present a proposition that you claim to be true. I can then ask you by what criterion should I judge this to be true. If you provide me with a criterion of truth, I can then ask you to provide a criterion by which I should judge your criterion of truth. If you provide me a criterion for judging that criterion for truth, I can ask again why I should accept it. By what criterion is it a valid criterion? And so on. You will run out of criteria before I run out of questions. Therefore, if one ever accepts a proposition as true, that acceptance can never rest on a valid epistemological foundation.

2.3 The Later Greeks: Plato, Euclid, and Aristotle

Socrates and his student Plato acknowledged the force of this skeptical argument but contested its ultimate conclusion. Socrates agreed with the skeptics that knowledge of the cosmos and the ultimate nature of things is unattainable. Wisdom, he argued, consists precisely in attaining an accurate view of our own ignorance along with a critical ability to deconstruct false beliefs in others and in ourselves. Socrates suggests *know thyself*, or in Greek, γνoθι σε αυτoυ. This critical self-penetrating self-knowledge, he claimed, would lead to the pursuit of virtue. A deep recognition of our own ignorance regarding the outcome of material goals leaves only virtue as an end worth pursuing in itself.

Plato (1961, translation) acknowledged the problem of truth validation as defined by the skeptics. But, by turning the skeptics' arguments back against them, Plato agreed that learning or the acquisition of new knowledge was impossible. If we did not already know that a proposition presented to us was true, we would have no reason to accept it; it could be acquired, at best, as a belief held on the authority of another.

But learning in some sense is possible. In his dialogue, the *Meno*, we are presented with the example of a student, a slave of Meno, who is lead through the proof of a theorem in geometry. Meno starts the discussion as a skeptic, asking:

> And how can you inquire, Socrates, into that which you do not already know? What will you put forth as the subject of the inquiry? And if you find out what you want, how will you ever know that this is what you did not know?

As a result of answering a series of well-chosen questions, Meno's slave ends up learning the geometry theorem. He has not merely memorized it, but he has recognized its truth beyond doubt. Given the problem of truth validation, how is this possible?

Plato's answer is that it is only possible in the case of a certain kind of knowledge: the knowledge of formal properties of *essences*. With such knowledge, we have, under the right conditions, the experience of a luminous self-evidence. This can only be explained, Plato continues, if learning is actually recollection: a remembrance of knowledge that we already dimly possess. If this is the nature of learning, then the problem of truth validation is solved.

The theory of learning as recollection has extraordinary consequences: When did we originally acquire this knowledge that is now recollected? Since it was not in this lifetime, it must have been in a previous existence. Furthermore, it must have been in a different kind of existence; otherwise, the same problem of truth validation would have made learning impossible. Based on this and related arguments, Plato hypothesizes that each of us has a soul distinct from our body, a soul that survives from lifetime to lifetime. Plato does not say that knowledge is unattainable but that during each lifetime we continue to struggle to attain it.

To explain the process of recollection, we must acknowledge that the soul was at one time in direct contact with a world of *forms* or *essences*. Indeed, Plato argues, only these forms or essences can be truly known and only they have true being. The world of our knowing through our senses is "a shadowy world," a world in which the forms are only dimly reflected. Even the beauty perceived in our lover is but a shadowy reflection of the form of beauty itself. (This imagery—shadowy, dimly—is taken from the cave scene in Plato's Republic).

Plato's rejection of the veridicality of sense objects and his attribution of ultimate reality to forms or essences is called *idealism*. His dismissal of sense perception and his identification of mathematics and formal reasoning as the primary sources of knowledge is called *rationalism*. His identification of the soul as a separate entity, distinct from and independent of its physical embodiment, is called *dualism*. Although Plato's versions of these positions may seem extreme and implausible to our modern mind, each position has repeatedly reappeared in differing forms and guises throughout the history of Western thought.

In Egypt, Euclid of Alexandria, a mathematician who is said to have worked with several students of Plato, described in about 290 BCE, what was to be called his *Elements*. The Elements was perhaps the first creation of a mathematical system based on a set of axioms or assumptions about phenomena in the world. Euclid then used these axioms to support a complex mathematical system of theorems and proofs that we now call *Euclidian Geometry*. In the nineteenth century, other mathematicians created new geometries, often called *non-Euclidean*, from different sets of foundational axioms. Euclid's axiom/theorem approach to building mathematical systems was a critical addition to the growth of modern mathematics.

Aristotle was Plato's student but rejected Plato's postulation of a world of perfect forms. Aristotle's epistemology is a blend of the rationalist and empiricist positions. As an empiricist, Aristotle attributes to perception and observation an essential role in the acquisition of knowledge. However, Aristotle's emphasis on the role of rational methods, such as mathematics and logic in organizing and interpreting observations, makes his position a highly sophisticated form of empiricism.

Aristotle argued that knowledge could not have arisen from the senses alone. Some perceptions, such as rainbows and mirages, are deceptive and misleading. If knowledge depended on perception alone, what could we do when perceptions conflict? How would we recognize which perception is veridical? This problem is similar to Xenophanes' and Plato's skeptical conundrum: if the truth were in fact presented, how would we recognize it? How could it be distinguished from the full spectrum of opinions?

The development of systematic knowledge, $\varepsilon\pi\iota\sigma\tau\varepsilon\mu\varepsilon$, or science, requires the contribution of reason. Aristotle proposed a scientific method: the organized gathering of observations and measurements followed by the creation of a relational network or "taxonomic" classification. Rational methods, including categorization, interpretation, and reasoning followed after the data were appropriately classified. Through the use of logic particular concepts and laws are subsumed under more general ones, while their content or consequences can still be recovered through deduction.

Aristotle taught that physical objects had both a matter and a form. Thus, a marble statue might have the form of some ruler. The artist gives form to the material substance of the statue. Only the form is knowable, but the form requires matter for its embodiment. Through perception, the form of the object is delivered into our sense organs; it becomes literally present in these organs. This matter/form distinction provides a philosophical basis for modern notions such as symbolic computing and data abstraction.

In computing, we are manipulating patterns that are the forms of electromagnetic material, with the changes in form of this material representing aspects of the solution process. Abstracting the form from the medium of its representation not only allows these forms to be manipulated computationally but also provides the promise of a theory of data structures, the heart of modern computer science, and as we will see, supports the creation of an "artificial" intelligence.

In his *Metaphysics*, beginning with the statement that *all people by nature desire to know*, Aristotle developed a science of things that never change, including his cosmology and theology. In his *Logic*, Aristotle referred to deductive reasoning as his instrument, *organon*, because he felt that the study of thought itself was at the basis of all knowledge.

Aristotle investigated whether certain propositions can be said to be "true" because they are related to other things that are known to be "true." For example, if we know that "all men are mortal" and that "Socrates is a man," then we can conclude: "Socrates is mortal." This argument is an example of what Aristotle referred to as a syllogism using the deductive form *modus ponens*. Although the full formal axiomatization of logical reasoning needed another 2000 years for its flowering in the works of Gottlob Frege, Bertrand Russell, Kurt Gödel, Alan Turing, Alfred Tarski, and others, its roots may be traced back to Aristotle.

Finally, Aristotle's empiricist compromise contains lingering residues of rationalism and dualism. Aristotle's ontology, his science of existing things, presents the notion of a chain of being, ranging in perfection from our world, the most material, least perfect, and changeable to that of the non-material divine, the most perfect, and unchangeable. Aristotle's cosmology reflected this ontology, ranging from the earth and human realm outwards through a sequence of concentric spheres, to a fifth sphere, the *quintessence*, the realm of pure being: thought thinking itself, form without matter.

2.4   Post-medieval or Modern Philosophy

Renaissance thought, building on the Greek tradition, continued the evolution of the scientific tradition. The hypothesis-test-revise methodology proved a powerful way of thinking about humanity and its relation to the natural world. Science began to flourish in chemistry, biology, medicine, physics, astronomy, and more: the scientific revolution had begun! Most of the modern social and physical sciences found their origin in the notion that processes, whether natural or artificial, could be mathematically analyzed and understood. In particular, scientists and philosophers realized that even thought and how knowledge was represented and manipulated in the human mind was a difficult but essential subject for scientific study.

Perhaps the major event in the development of the modern worldview was the Copernican revolution, the replacement of the ancient Earth-centered model of the universe with the idea that the Earth and other planets are actually in orbits around the sun. After centuries of an "obvious" order, in which the scientific explanation of the nature of the cosmos was consistent with the teachings of religion and common sense, a drastically different and not at all obvious model was proposed to explain the motions of heavenly bodies. Again, as suggested by many earlier philosophers, *our ideas about the world were seen as fundamentally distinct from that world's appearance.*

This split between the human mind and its surrounding reality, between ideas about things and things themselves, is essential to the modern study of the mind and its organization. This breach was widened by the writings of Galileo whose scientific observations further contradicted the "obvious" truths about the natural world. Galileo's development of mathematics as a tool for describing that world emphasized the distinction between the world and our ideas about it. It is out of this breach that the modern notion of the mind evolved: introspection became a common motif in the literature, and mathematics and the systematic application of the scientific method rivaled the senses as tools for human understanding of the world.

In 1620, Francis Bacon's *Novum Organun* offered a set of search techniques for this emerging scientific methodology. Based on the Aristotelian and Platonic idea that the form of an entity was equivalent to the sum of its necessary and sufficient features, Bacon articulated an algorithm for determining the essence of an entity. First, he made an organized collection of all instances of the entity, enumerating the features of each in a table. Then, he collected a similar list of negative instances of the entity, focusing especially on near instances, that is, those that deviated from the form of the entity by single features. Then, Bacon attempts—this step is not totally clear—to make a systematic list of all the features essential to the entity, that is, those that are common to all positive instances of the entity and missing from the negative instances.

Although the Chinese created the first calculating machine, the abacus, in the twenty-sixth century BCE, further mechanization of algebraic processes awaited the skills of the seventeenth-century Europeans. In 1614, the Scots mathematician, John Napier, created logarithms. These mathematical transformations allowed multiplication and the use of exponents to be reduced to addition and multiplication. Napier also created his *bones* that were used to represent *overflow* or "carry" values for arithmetic operations. Wilhelm Schickard (1592–1635), a mathematician and clergyman of Tübingen Germany, used Napier's *bones* in his invention of a *Calculating Clock* for performing addition and subtraction. This machine recorded the overflow from its calculations by the chiming of a clock.

Another famous calculating machine was the *Pascaline* that Blaise Pascal, the French philosopher and mathematician, created in 1642. Although the mechanisms of Schickard and Pascal were limited to addition and subtraction—including carries and borrows—they showed that processes that previously were thought to require human thought and skill could be fully automated. As Pascal later stated in his *Pensees* (1670), "The arithmetical machine produces effects which approach nearer to thought than all the actions of animals."

Pascal's successes with calculating machines inspired Gottfried Wilhelm von Leibniz in 1694 to complete a working machine that became known as the *Leibniz Wheel*. It integrated a moveable carriage and hand crank to drive wheels and cylinders that performed the more complex operations of multiplication and division. Leibniz was also fascinated by the possibility of an automated logic for the mechanical proofs of propositions.

Using Francis Bacon's earlier entity specification algorithm, where concepts were characterized as the collection of their necessary and sufficient features, Leibniz conjectured the creation of a machine that could calculate with these features to produce logically correct concepts. Leibniz (1887) also envisioned a machine, reflecting modern ideas of deductive inference and proof, by which the production of scientific knowledge could become automated, the creation of a calculus for reasoning.

René Descartes (1680), often called the father of modern philosophy, was a mathematician, and like Plato, a rationalist. For Descartes, only mathematical concepts, his *clear and distinct ideas*, were considered veridical and acceptable as a basis for understanding reality.

Descartes published his *Meditations* in 1637, wherein he established the modern epistemological project: to reconstruct the foundations of knowledge starting from his *epoche*, or doubt, and the full suspension of judgment. Descartes asks: How can I know that my beliefs about the world are true? There is an important difference between Descartes' *epoche* and doubt regarding a particular belief. Making further observations or bringing to bear additional evidence often resolves a particular doubt. General doubt, the *epoche*, calls into question the value of all evidence, both perceptual and rational. Descartes invites us to envision a clever but evil god who deceives us at every turn. Given this possibility, is there any belief or insight about which we could not be mistaken?

Descartes asks the questions: In accepting systematic doubt, what can I hold onto? What cannot be doubted? His answer is that only his own existence cannot be questioned. *Cogito ergo sum*. A consequence of this epistemic retreat, however, is that the only existence that he is aware of is a disembodied thinking being. Only this aspect of existence is presented and verified in his self-consciousness.

From this minimalist foundation, Descartes attempts to reconstruct all knowledge and reality. His reconstruction is implausible, however, and depends on a series of "proofs" for the existence of god. Descartes' proofs are deductive but circular, with his notion of *clear and distinct* ideas used in the proof of the veridicality of clear and distinct ideas. With god's existence established, Descartes appeals to the benevolence and veracity of the deity to save a portion of his former beliefs. A benevolent deity, he argues, would not allow him to be mistaken about ideas that, like those of mathematics, are perceived clearly and distinctly. Thus, finally, Descartes' belief in an external world is reconstituted through the ideas of mathematics and analytic geometry.

For Descartes, as for Plato, rationalism leads to dualism. Descartes thinking being, his *res cogitans*, is disembodied and cut off from interaction with an external and physical world, the *res extensa*. His problem, then, is to reestablish the possibility of a mental/physical interaction. Descartes posited this "connection" as somehow involving the *pituitary gland*, a part of the cortex whose functions at that time were little understood. An important component of the study of philosophy since Descartes has focused on how to put the material and immaterial parts of the human system back together.

We can make two observations here: first, the schism between the mind and the physical world had become so complete that the process of thinking could be discussed in isolation from any specific sensory input or worldly subject matter. Second, the connection between the mind and the physical world was so tenuous that it required the intervention of a benign god to support reliable knowledge of the physical world.

Why have we included this mind/body discussion in a book analyzing epistemology from an artificial intelligence perspective? There are (at least) three consequences essential to our enterprise:

1. By separating the mind from the physical world, Descartes and related thinkers conjectured that the structure of ideas about the world was not necessarily the same as the structure of their subject matter. This schism underlies the methodologies of many AI practitioners, epistemologists, and psychologists, as well as much of modern literature. According to Descartes, mental processes have an existence of their own, obey their own laws, and can be studied in and of themselves.
2. Once the mind and the body are separated, philosophers found it necessary to find ways to reconnect the two. Interaction between Descartes' *res cogitans* and *res extensa* is essential for human existence. This is an important concern for programs that intend to reflect "intelligence."
3. The Cartesian mind/body assumption also supports the disengagement of the cognitive subject from the community of knowers and separates the individual from the social milieu. In this sense, the individual is seen as "watching" reality move by understanding and criticizing as a detached observer. As we note in Chap. 7, the very concepts with which thoughts are framed and rooted are part of a shared language and tradition. The individual cannot escape intersubjective and societal aspects of knowledge and truth.

Gottfried Wilhelm von Leibniz represents the extreme position in a rationalist world view. Like Descartes before him, Leibniz takes mathematics as the sole model and ideal for knowledge. He was the co-inventor of calculus along with Isaac Newton. Leibniz proposed a *universal characteristic*, a language of primitives from which, he suggested, all concepts and properties could be defined. Leibniz further proposed a mathematical calculus for constructing true propositions from this language. Interestingly, several AI researchers, including Roger Schank (1980), have adopted similar semantic, or meaning, systems for understanding human language.

Like Descartes, Leibniz questions the reality of physical causality and the interaction of objects in the world. The ultimate description of world events is in terms of noninteracting monads: each monad governed solely by its own internal laws of development. Interaction is explained and supported by the veracity and benevolence of the creator god. Once again, divine intervention is required to support an embodied world. Leibniz described this linkage as the principle of *preestablished harmony*.

The most widely accepted response to the problems implicit in the rationalist enterprise, and the one that provides an essential foundation for the study of AI, is that the mind and the body are not fundamentally different entities at all. From this view, mental processes are indeed achieved by physical systems such as brains or computers. Mental processes, like physical processes, can be characterized through formal specifications. As stated in the *Leviathan* by the seventeenth-century English philosopher Thomas Hobbes (1651), "By ratiocination, I mean computation."

2.5   The British Empiricists: Hobbes, Locke, and Hume

The British empiricists, beginning with John Locke's (1689) *Essay Concerning Human Understanding*, rejected rationalism as a theory of knowledge. Differing from Descartes and Leibniz, Locke argues that we are born with no innate ideas, a *tabula rasa*. Locke then argues that all ideas come through our experiences in the world. The empiricist tradition holds that knowledge must be explained through introspective but empirical psychology. Empiricists distinguish two different types of mental phenomena: direct perceptual experience, on the one hand, and thought, memory, and imagination on the other. Each empiricist thinker, of course, uses slightly different terms for this distinction.

The eighteenth-century Scottish philosopher David Hume, for example, distinguishes between *impressions* and *ideas*. Impressions are lively and vivid and not subject to voluntary control. This involuntary character suggests that they may in some way reflect the effect of an external object on the subject's awareness. Ideas, on the other hand, are less vivid and detailed and more amenable to the subject's voluntary control.

Given this distinction between impressions and ideas, how then does knowledge arise? For Hobbes, Locke, and Hume, the basic explanatory mechanism is *association*. Certain properties are repeatedly experienced together in our impressions. This repeated association creates a disposition in the mind to associate their corresponding ideas. The fundamental limitation of this account of knowledge is revealed by David Hume's skepticism. Hume's purely descriptive account of the origin of ideas cannot, by his own admission, justify his belief in causality. Indeed, even the use of logic and induction cannot be rationally supported in this empiricist epistemology.

The characterization of knowledge as association plays a significant role in modern theories of human memory organization. We will see this in AI research that created semantic networks, models for memory organization, data structures for human language understanding, and more (Chap. 5). The associational approach to machine learning may be seen in different architectures for neural networks and algorithms supporting deep learning. The empiricists' attempt to interpret knowledge as habitual associations based on the repetition of certain elements of experience also influenced the behaviorist tradition in psychology.

2.6 Bridging the Empiricist/Rationalist Chasm: Baruch Spinoza

In 1632, Baruch Spinoza was born into the Jewish community of Amsterdam. This group had left Portugal and Spain because of the fifteenth-century expulsion of the Jews and the subsequent Inquisition. In the decade of Spinoza's birth, John Locke and Isaac Newton were also born, Descartes was writing his Meditations, and Galileo was placed under house arrest for his views on cosmology. Although a rationalist inspired by Descartes, Spinoza disagreed with Descartes' mind–body dualism. He felt that *God* or *Nature* was a being of infinite attributes and that *thought* and *extension* were only two of these. Spinoza felt that the physical and mental worlds were causally interrelated and the attributes of one substance.

Spinoza, whose philosophical approach is called *neutral monism*, was thus one of the earliest of modern thinkers to blend together components of the empiricist and rationalist traditions. Spinoza rejected the existence and immortality of the human soul. Thought and body, Descartes' *res cogitans* and *res extensa*, had to collaborate and interact; in fact, he suggested, they were causally interconnected components of one unified system. Spinoza extended his theory of substance with a pantheistic god, not ruling over the world by providence or changeable through prayer or sacrifice. Rather, God is the deterministic system of which everything in nature is a component.

Spinoza's *Tractatus Theologico-Politicus,* published in 1670, proposed that the study of philosophy and its epistemic foundations supported piety and peaceful coexistence. He condemned the current political establishments that used ignorance and religious superstition to control the body politic. For these opinions, as well as his contention that the bible was nothing more than the creation of humans, Spinoza was both excommunicated from the Jewish community and condemned by the Christian. Most of his works were published posthumously.

Perhaps Spinoza's most important philosophical work, his *Ethics*, was published in 1677. The Ethics was written as a set of axioms that offered a foundation for his philosophical stance along with sets of follow-on theorems and corollaries that this axiom base supported. We take a similar approach in Chap. 7, proposing sets of assumptions and conjectures as a foundation for a modern epistemology.

2.7 Bridging the Empiricist/Rationalist Chasm: Immanuel Kant

Immanuel Kant, a German philosopher trained in the rationalist tradition, was strongly influenced by the British empiricists. Reading David Hume, Kant (1781/1964) remarked, awakened him from his *dogmatic slumbers*. In response to Hume, Kant developed his critical philosophy: an attempted synthesis of rationalism and empiricism. Knowledge contains two components for Kant, an *a priori* component coming from previous experience and understanding and an *a posteriori* component arising from the present. Experience itself is meaningful to a subject only through the active contribution of the subject. Without a unifying form imposed by the subject, the world would offer nothing more than passing sensations.

For Kant, the subject's contribution begins at the sensory level. Space and time, Kant argues, are forms of experience that unify perceptual representations and give them meaningful relationships with each other. The framework of space and time could not have been learned from experience, since this framework is a condition for the possibility of experience.

According to Kant, the human subject makes a second contribution at the level of judgment. Passing images or representations are bound together and taken as diverse appearances of an object. Without the active synthesis of representations, the experience of objects would not be possible. This synthesis that transforms passing sensations into appearances of an object gives mental life its intentional character. It makes representations more than mere affectations of the mind; it allows them to refer to an object outside the mind. For example, Kant says:

> Suppose a person is walking toward me, approaching from a distance. I experience a series of images growing increasingly large. First, perhaps, I recognize the age and gender of this person. Then, when they are close enough, I see their hair and eye color. Finally, I recognize this person, an occasional acquaintance.

What is required to turn this series of images into the experience of a person with whom I am acquainted? Kant believes that what is required is that they all be taken as images of the same re-identifiable object, an object which perhaps I experienced yesterday and could potentially experience tomorrow. Note that this synthesis requires work and an active constructive judgment. The same object actually changes in appearance due to perceptual factors, such as distance, profile, and lighting, and also changes over a longer period of time as a result, for example, of a haircut, glasses, a change in emotional state, or even aging.

Kant argues against pure empiricism and for an *a priori* component to experience. The framework of space and time, the concept of reidentifiable objects and properties could not have been learned from experience, since they are preconditions of experience. Meaningful experience would not be possible without these unifying structures.

According to Kant, understanding utilizes the synthesis required to construct the experience of objects. Understanding enables the higher level synthesis of knowledge, constructing generalizations across objects and domains, generating scientific laws, and the structure of scientific theories. Reason contributes the *a priori* form of these syntheses, while their matter comes from experience. Both reason and understanding ultimately rely on the same *a priori* principles.

Kant notes that perceptual experience is an a priori experience of objects in space and time, without any voluntary act or conscious intervention of the subject. He explains this by arguing that the same *a priori* principles of synthesis that inform understanding at the level of conscious reflection must also operate in perception at an unconscious level. He attributes this to the work of the transcendental imagination, an active faculty governed by what he called *schemata*, that is, by *a priori* patterns that determine how perceptual elements are brought together and organized.

Kant's concept of an active subject whose *schemata* organize experience has had an important influence on twentieth- and twenty-first-century thought. Philosophers, including Peirce, Husserl, Kuhn, and others, and psychologists, such as Bartlett and Piaget, have been influenced by Kant's notion of an active epistemic subject. They agree with Kant that experience is constructed in accordance with certain organizing forms or *schemata* and that this constructive activity takes place below the level of conscious awareness.

Those modern thinkers depart from Kant on the question of whether the form of this constructive process is fixed. For Kant, only one set of organizing forms or *schemata* is possible, and its nature is determined by a transcendental logic. For modern thinkers, alternative schemata are possible, and their forms can be compared, at least to some extent, with respect to their effectiveness in organizing an individual or a community's practices and interactions with the natural and social environment.

Kant's a priori schemata and a posteriori perception of information will offer important content to our later presentation. In Chap. 8, we describe Bayes' and Pearl's models of probabilistic reasoning, specifically how a human's current understanding of the world enables their interpretation of new information. As we will see, Bayes' representation with Pearl's algorithms offers a sufficient epistemic model of how new information can be interpreted, both in the present and dynamically, across time, in the context of a world of a priori expectations.

2.8 American Pragmatism: Peirce, James, and Dewey

Pragmatism may be described as a philosophy that assesses the truth or meaning of theories or beliefs in terms of the success of their practical application. American pragmatism, as proposed by William James (1902) and Charles Sanders Peirce (1931–1958), expands the parameters needed to constitute an epistemology.

Empiricism and rationalism can be seen as self-based characterizations of knowing, particularly as epistemology seems to be the product of internalized thought experiments. Pragmatism asks what an action or stance will "effect" or "do" in a specific situation. In short, pragmatism asserts that the meaning, as well as an ethical valence of a word or action is dependent on its externalization in an active and situated world.

In Pragmatism, James (1981) contends that "27" may mean "one dollar too few" or equally "a board one inch too long" … He asserts:

> What shall we call a thing anyhow? It seems quite arbitrary, for we carve out everything, just as we carve out constellations, to suit our human purposes.

Further, James claims:

> We break the flux of sensible reality into things, then, at our will. We create the subjects of our true as well as of our false propositions. We create our predicates also. Many of the predicates of things express only the relations of the things to us and to our feelings. Such predicates, of course, are human additions.

Peirce (1931–1958, vol. 1, paragraph 132), in *How to Make our Ideas Clear*, describes his *Pragmatic Maxim* as:

> Consider what effects, which might conceivably have practical bearings, we conceive the object of our conception to have. Then our conception of these effects is the whole of our conception of the object.

Further, in *How to Make our Ideas Clear*, Peirce (1931–1958, vol. 1, paragraph 138) clarifies what he means by truth and reality:

> The opinion which is fated to be ultimately agreed to by all who investigate, is what we mean by the truth, and the object represented in this opinion is the real. This is the way I would explain reality.

James (1909) has a similar conception of truth:

> Ideas … become true just in so far as they help us to get into satisfactory relation with other parts of our experience.

Pragmatism, then, purports to ground all thoughts, words, and actions in their expected consequences. An example of this epistemological stance, from James' (1902) *Varieties of Religious Experience*, is that the *truth*, as well as any imputed *value* of a particular religious stance, is what that stance does for an individual's life. For example, does the disposition help with an addiction problem or encourage the performance of charitable acts?

This form of pragmatism allows little critique, however, as one person's religious values can directly contradict those of others. For instance, various "inquisitions" or "fundamentalist actions" are often justified in the name of some religion. An important consequence of the pragmatist philosophy was John Dewey's (1916), writings that had an important impact on twentieth-century education in both the US and worldwide.

American Pragmatism offers an important critique of epistemology as well as of modern AI. For epistemology:

1. The rationalist and empiricist epistemic traditions tend to be matters of individual, or self, accountability; for example, how do my ideas relate to my perceptions? What is (my) truth? The pragmatist forces meaning and truth to require an external dimension, to be a function of results in an interpreting context.
2. The weak side of pragmatism is that there is no universally accepted notion of meaning or truth within this external interpretive context. One agent's action can have multiple effects depending on its contexts, and multiple agents can have differing interpretations for a single action.

Many aspects of modern AI have a pragmatic focus: intelligent programs are about what they can do in their situated environment. Stuart Russell (2019), in his discussion on the nature of intelligence claims:

> Before we can understand how to create intelligence it helps to understand what it is. The answer is not to be found in IQ tests, or even in Turing tests, but in a simple relationship between what we perceive, what we want, and what we do. Roughly speaking, an entity is intelligent to the extent that what it does is likely to achieve what it wants, given what it has perceived.

The Russell description of intelligence falls within the scope of point 2, above. When the "success" of a running AI program is the main measure of its "quality," other important aspects are easily overlooked: How does the AI program generalize to new, related situations? Is there any quantitative measure of success for the program's results, such as a mathematical guarantee of optimal convergence? Did the response of the program address all its user's concerns?

Computer programs meant to communicate with humans demonstrate the difficulty reflecting a pragmatist stance, namely, understanding why the human requests specific information. When asking a web bot sponsored by an airline company "Do you go to Seattle?" the intelligent answer is not simply "yes." A more appropriate response might be "What day do you want to fly to Seattle?" Full "success" for the inquirer likely includes the purchase of an airline ticket.

When interacting with human users, the program must come to understand the pragmatic intent of the conversation. Many question-answering bots are coming to have such sophisticated understanding of customers' queries, as, for example, bots for airlines' ticket sales and for a bank's wealth management services. IBM's Watson, once company-specific information is added to its knowledge base, can also perform goal-oriented transactions. In Sect. 8.3, we demonstrate how such a conversation system can work using probabilistic finite state machine technology.

American pragmatism, with its commitment to actions having "meaning" by how their results are externalized in some context, also captures the spirit of the European existentialist tradition of Kierkegaard, Nietzshe, and Sartre. From this perspective, a person "actualizes" himself or herself in internal and external activities. There is a direct statement of this in James' 1902 Varieties of Religious Experience:

> In our cognitive as well as our active life we are creative… The world stands really malleable, waiting to receive its final touches at our hands. Like the kingdom of heaven, it suffers human violence willingly. Man engenders truths upon it.

Driven by existentialist standards and lack of commonly accepted "objective" constraints, pragmatism approaches a postmodern version of contingency, skepticism, and relativism. Our own conjectures on knowledge, meaning, and truth, presented in Sects. 7.3 and 7.4, are extensions of the pragmatists' approach to these issues. American Pragmatism has seen a strong revival near the end of the twentieth century, with philosophers including Hilary Putnam, W.V.O. Quine, and Richard Rorty. We take up the pragmatist tradition again in Sect. 9.5.

2.9   The Mathematical Foundations for Computation

Logical positivism, sometimes called "scientific philosophy," is another tradition that emerged in Europe in the late nineteenth and the early decades of the twentieth century. Logical positivism, influenced by Wittgenstein's (1922) *Tractatus Logico-Philosophicus*, Carnap's (1928) *The Logical Structure of the World*, and others, produced many of the philosophers and mathematicians who provided a foundation for the sciences of computation and artificial intelligence. These include Russell, Whitehead, Frege, Gödel, Tarski, Post, and Turing.

Once thinking had come to be regarded as a form of computation (Hobbes), its formalization and eventual mechanization were obvious next steps. As already noted, Gottfried Wilhelm von Leibniz (1887) in his *Calculus Philosophicus*, introduced, after Aristotle, the first system of formal logic. Leibniz also proposed a machine for automating its tasks. The steps and stages of this mechanical solution can be represented as movement through the states of a tree or graph. Leonhard Euler (1735), with his analysis of the bridges joining the riverbanks and islands of the city of Königsberg, introduced graph theory, a representation that can capture many structures and relationships in the world.

The formalization of graph theory also supported the possibility of *state-space search*, a major conceptual tool of artificial intelligence. The nodes of a *state-space graph* represent possible stages of a problem solution and the arcs of the graph represent decisions, moves in a game, or other steps within a solution, as we saw in Sect. 1.3. By describing the entire space of problem solutions, state-space graphs provide a powerful tool for measuring the structure and complexity of problems and analyzing the efficiency, correctness, as well as generality of solution strategies. For an introduction to graph theory and state-space search, including Euler's solution of the Königsberg bridge problem, see Sect. 4.1.

Charles Babbage, the nineteenth-century mathematician first introduced in Sect. 1.2, was one of the originators of the science of operations research as well as the designer of the first programmable mechanical computing machines. Babbage may also be considered an early practitioner of artificial intelligence (Morrison and Morrison 1961). Babbage's *difference engine* was a special-purpose machine for computing the values of certain polynomial functions and was the forerunner of his *analytical engine*. The analytical engine, designed but not successfully constructed during his lifetime, was a general-purpose programmable computing machine that presaged many of the architectural assumptions underlying the modern computer.

Ada Lovelace (1961), Babbage's friend, supporter, and collaborator, described the analytical engine:

> We may say most aptly that the Analytical Engine weaves algebraical patterns just as the Jacquard loom weaves flowers and leaves. Here, it seems to us, resides much more of originality than the difference engine can be fairly entitled to claim.

Babbage's inspiration was his desire to apply the technology of his day to liberate humans from the drudgery of making arithmetic calculations. In this sentiment, as well as with his conception of computers as mechanical devices, Babbage was thinking in purely nineteenth-century terms. His analytical engine, however, also included many modern notions, such as the separation of memory and processor, the *store* and the *mill* in Babbage's terms, the concept of a digital rather than an analog machine, and programmability based on the execution of a series of operations encoded on punched pasteboard cards.

The most striking feature of Ada Lovelace's description, and Babbage's work in general, is its treatment of the "patterns" of algebraic relationships. These entities may be studied, characterized, and finally implemented and manipulated mechanically without concern for the particular values that are finally passed through the mill of the calculating machine. This is an example of the "abstraction and manipulation of form" first described by Aristotle and later by Leibniz.

The goal of creating a formal language for thought also appears in the work of George Boole (1847, 1854), another nineteenth-century mathematician whose work must be included in any discussion of the roots of artificial intelligence. Although he made contributions to a number of areas of mathematics, his best-known work was in the mathematical formalization of the laws of logic, an accomplishment that forms the very heart of modern computer science.

Although Boole's role in the creation of Boolean algebra and the design of logic circuitry is well known, Boole's own goals in developing his system seem closer to those of many contemporary AI researchers. Boole (1854), in the first chapter of *An Investigation of the Laws of Thought, on which are founded the Mathematical Theories of Logic and Probabilities*, described his goals as:

> … to investigate the fundamental laws of those operations of the mind by which reasoning is performed: to give expression to them in the symbolical language of a Calculus, and upon this foundation to establish the science of logic and instruct its method; … and finally to collect from the various elements of truth brought to view in the course of these inquiries some probable intimations concerning the nature and constitution of the human mind.

The importance of Boole's accomplishment is in the extraordinary power and simplicity of the system he devised: three operations, "AND," denoted by $*$ or $\wedge$; "OR" denoted by $+$ or $\vee$; and "NOT," denoted by $\neg$ or not, formed the heart of his logical calculus. These operations have remained the basis for all subsequent developments in formal logic, including the hardware design of modern computers.

While keeping the meaning of these symbols nearly identical to the corresponding algebraic operations, Boole noted "the Symbols of logic are further subject to a special law, to which the symbols of quantity, as such, are not subject." This law states that for any X, an element in the algebra, $X * X = X$, or that once something is known to be true, repetition cannot augment that knowledge. This led to the characteristic restriction of Boolean values to the only two numbers that can satisfy this equation: 1 and 0. The standard definitions of Boolean multiplication and addition follow from this insight.

Boole's system not only provided the basis for binary arithmetic but also demonstrated that an extremely simple formal system was adequate to capture the full power of logic. This assumption, and the system Boole developed to demonstrate it, forms the basis of all modern efforts to formalize logic, from Russell and Whitehead's *Principia Mathematica* (1950), through the work of Turing and Gödel, up to modern automated reasoning systems.

Gottlob Frege, in his *Foundations of Arithmetic* (Frege 1879, 1884), created a mathematical specification language for describing the basis of arithmetic in a clear and precise fashion. With this language, Frege formalized many of the issues first addressed by Aristotle's *Logic*. Frege's language, now called the *first-order predicate calculus*, offers a tool for describing the propositions and truth-value assignments that make up the elements of mathematical reasoning and describes the axiomatic basis of "meaning" for these expressions.

The predicate calculus, which includes predicate symbols, a theory of functions, and quantified variables, was intended to be a language for describing the foundations of mathematics. It also plays an important role in creating a theory of representation for AI, as seen in Sect. 1.3. The first-order predicate calculus offers the tools necessary for automating reasoning: a language for expressions, a theory for assumptions related to the meaning of expressions, and a logically sound calculus for inferring new true expressions. It also creates a language for expressing the knowledge and reasoning of modern expert systems, as we see in Sect. 4.1.

Alfred North Whitehead and Bertrand Russell's (1950) research is particularly important to the foundations of AI, in that their stated goal was to derive the whole of mathematics through formal operations on a collection of axioms. Although many mathematical systems have been constructed from basic axioms, what is interesting is Russell and Whitehead's commitment to mathematics as a purely formal system. This meant that axioms and theorems would be treated as strings of characters: proofs would proceed solely through the application of well-defined rules for manipulating these strings. There would be no reliance on intuition or the possible "meaning" of theorems as a basis for proofs.

What "meaning" the theorems and axioms of the system might have in relation to some AI application domain would be independent of their logical derivations. This treatment of mathematical reasoning in purely formal, and hence mechanical terms, provided an essential basis for its automation on physical computers. The logical syntax and formal rules of inference developed by Russell and Whitehead are still a basis for automatic theorem-proving systems as well as for the theoretical foundations of artificial intelligence. Automated reasoning, of course, is the answer to Leibniz's "mathematical calculus" described in Sect. 2.4.

Alfred Tarski (1944, 1956) is another mathematician whose work is essential to the foundations of AI. Tarski created a *theory of reference*, wherein the *well-formed formulae* of Frege or Russell and Whitehead can be said to refer, in a precise fashion, to a physical world. This insight underlies most theories of formal semantics. In his paper, *The Semantic Conception of Truth and the Foundation of Semantics*, Tarski describes his theory of reference and truth–value relationships. Modern computer scientists have related this theory to programming languages and other specifications for computing.

The formalization of science and mathematics in the eighteenth-, nineteenth-, and early twentieth centuries created the intellectual prerequisite for the study of artificial intelligence. It was not until the mid-twentieth century, however, and the introduction of the digital computer that AI became a viable scientific discipline. By the end of the 1940s, electronic digital computers had demonstrated their potential to provide the memory and processing power required to build intelligent programs. It was then possible to implement formal reasoning systems on a computer and empirically test their sufficiency for exhibiting intelligence. An essential component of the science of artificial intelligence is this commitment to computers for creating, testing, and revising "intelligent" programs.

Digital computers are not merely a vehicle for testing theories of intelligence. Their architecture also suggests a specific paradigm for such theories: intelligence is a form of information processing. The notion of search as a problem-solving methodology, for example, owes more to the sequential nature of computer operation than it does to any biological model of intelligence. Most AI programs represent knowledge in some formal language that is then manipulated by algorithms, honoring the separation of data and program fundamental to the von Neumann style of computing.

Formal logic has emerged as an important representational technique for AI research, just as graph theory plays an indispensable role in the analysis of problem spaces as well as provides a basis for semantic networks and similar models of semantic meaning. These tools and formalisms are discussed in detail in Chaps. 4 and 5; we mention them here to emphasize the symbiotic relationship between the digital computer and the mathematical underpinnings of artificial intelligence.

We often forget that the tools we create for our own purposes tend to shape our conception of the world through their structure and limitations. This interaction is an essential aspect of the evolution of human knowledge: A tool, and programs are only tools, is developed to solve a particular problem. As it is used and refined, the tool itself suggests other applications, leading to new questions and, ultimately, to the development of new tools.

2.10   The Turing Test and the Birth of AI

In 1950, the British mathematician Alan Turing published *Computing Machinery and Intelligence,* one of the earliest papers to address the question of whether "intelligence" might be possible using the technology of the digital computer. Turing's ideas remain timely in both their promise for the successes of what would become the AI research community and in his assessment of the arguments against the possibility of creating an intelligent computing mechanism.

Turing, known mainly for his design of the universal computing machine and his contributions to the theory of computability, Sect. 1.2, considered the question of whether or not a machine could actually be made to think. Turing noted that there were fundamental ambiguities in the question itself: What is thinking? What is a machine? Since these concerns precluded any rational answer, Turing proposed that the question of "machine intelligence" be replaced by a better-defined empirical test.

The *Turing test* measures the performance of an allegedly intelligent machine against that of a human being, arguably our best and only standard for intelligent behavior. The test, which Turing called the *imitation game*, places the machine and a human counterpart in rooms apart from a second human being, referred to as the *interrogator*, see Fig. 2.1. The interrogator is not able to see or speak directly to either of them, does not know which entity is actually the machine and may communicate with them solely by the use of a text-based device such as a terminal. The interrogator is asked to distinguish the computer from the human solely based on their answers to questions asked using this device. If the interrogator cannot distinguish the machine from the human, then, Turing argues, the machine must be assumed to be intelligent.

By isolating the interrogator from both the machine and the other human participant, the test ensures that the interrogator will not be biased by the appearance of the machine or any mechanical property of its voice. The interrogator is free, however, to ask any question, no matter how devious or indirect, in an effort to uncover the computer's identity. For example, the interrogator may ask both subjects to perform a rather involved arithmetic calculation, assuming that the computer will be more likely to get it correct than the human. To counter this strategy, the computer will need to know when it should fail to get a correct answer to such problems in order to seem more like a human. To discover the human's identity, the interrogator may ask for a response to a poem; this strategy will require that the computer have knowledge concerning the emotional makeup of human beings.

Fig. 2.1 A form of the Turing test, where the interrogator asks questions and then is asked to determine whether a computer or human answered

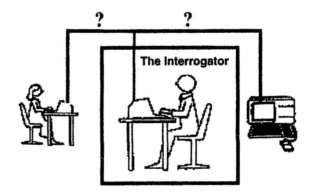

The important features of Turing's test are:

1. It attempts to give an objective notion of intelligence, i.e., the behavior of a known intelligent entity in response to a particular set of questions. This provides a standard for determining intelligence that avoids the inevitable debates over its "true" nature.
2. It prevents us from being sidetracked by confusing and currently unanswerable questions such as whether or not the computer uses the appropriate internal processes or whether or not the machine is actually conscious of its actions.
3. It eliminates any bias in favor of living organisms by forcing the interrogator to focus solely on the content of the answers to questions.

Because of these advantages, the Turing test provides a basis for many of the schemes actually used to evaluate modern AI programs. A program that has potentially achieved intelligence in some area of expertise may be evaluated by comparing its performance on a given set of problems to that of a human expert. This evaluation technique is just a variation of the Turing test: A group of humans are asked to blindly compare the performance of a computer and a human being on a particular set of problems. This methodology has become an essential tool in both the development and the verification of modern expert systems (Luger 2009a).

The Turing test, despite its intuitive appeal, is vulnerable to a number of justifiable criticisms. One of the most important of these is aimed at its bias toward purely symbolic problem-solving tasks. It does not test abilities requiring perceptual skill or manual dexterity, even though these are important components of human intelligence.

From another viewpoint, it is sometimes suggested that the Turing test needlessly constrains machine intelligence to fit a human mold. Perhaps machine intelligence is simply different from human intelligence and trying to evaluate it in human terms is a fundamental mistake. Do we really wish a machine would do mathematics as slowly and inaccurately as a human? Shouldn't an intelligent machine capitalize on its own assets, such as a large, fast, reliable memory, rather than trying to emulate human cognition? We discuss these issues again in Sect. 9.5.

A number of AI practitioners see responding to the full challenge of Turing's test as a mistake and a major distraction to the more important work at hand: developing general theories to explain the mechanisms of intelligence in humans and machines and applying those theories to the development of tools to solve specific, practical problems. Although agreeing with these concerns, we still see Turing's test as an important component in the verification and validation of modern AI software.

Turing also addressed the very feasibility of constructing an intelligent program on a digital computer. By thinking in terms of a specific model of computation, an electronic discrete state computing machine, he made some well-founded conjectures concerning the storage capacity, program complexity, and basic design philosophy required for such a system. Finally, he addressed a number of moral, philosophical, and scientific objections to the possibility of constructing such a program. The reader is referred to Turing's (1950) article for a perceptive and still relevant summary of the debate over the possibility of intelligent machines.

Two of the objections cited by Turing are worth considering further. *Lady Lovelace's Objection*, first stated by Ada Lovelace, argues that computers can only do as they are told and consequently cannot perform original, hence, intelligent actions. This objection has become a reassuring if somewhat dubious part of contemporary technological folklore. Expert systems, presented in Sect. 4.1, especially in the area of diagnostic reasoning, have reached conclusions unanticipated by their designers. A number of researchers feel that human creativity can be expressed in a computer program as we see in detail in Part II.

The second objection, the *Argument from Informality of Behavior*, asserts the impossibility of creating a set of rules that will tell an individual exactly what to do under every possible set of circumstances. Certainly, the flexibility that enables a biological intelligence to respond to an almost infinite range of situations in a reasonable if not necessarily optimal fashion is a hallmark of intelligent behavior.

Although it is true that the control structures used in most traditional computer programs do not demonstrate great flexibility or originality, it is not true that all programs must be written in this fashion. Much of the work in modern AI has been to develop programming languages, representations, and tools such as production systems, object-based models, neural network representations, and mechanisms for deep learning, all discussed later in the book, that attempt to overcome this deficiency.

Many modern AI programs consist of a collection of modular components or rules of behavior that do not execute in a rigid order but rather are invoked as needed in response to a particular problem instance. Pattern matchers allow general rules to apply over a range of instances. These systems have an extreme flexibility that enables relatively small programs to exhibit a vast range of possible behaviors in response to differing problems and situations.

Whether these systems can ultimately be made to exhibit the flexibility shown by a living organism is still the subject of much debate. Herbert Simon, Nobel laureate in economics and ACM Turing award recipient, argues that much of the originality and variability of behavior shown by living creatures is due to the richness of their environment rather than in the complexity of their own internal programs.

In *The Sciences of the Artificial*, Simon (1981) describes an ant progressing circuitously along an uneven and cluttered stretch of ground. Although the ant's path seems quite complex, Simon argues that the ant's goal is very simple: to return to its colony as quickly as possible. Simon claims that the twists and turns in the ant's path are caused by the obstacles it encounters on its way. Simon concludes that

> An ant, viewed as a behaving system, is quite simple. The apparent complexity of its behavior over time is largely a reflection of the complexity of the environment in which it finds itself.

This idea, if ultimately proven to apply to organisms of higher intelligence as well as to such simple creatures as insects, constitutes a powerful argument that such systems are relatively simple and, consequently, comprehensible. If one applies this idea to humans, it becomes a strong argument for the importance of culture in the forming of intelligence. Rather than growing in darkness and isolation, intelligence depends on interactions within a suitably rich environment.

2.11   In Summary

Early Greek philosophical positions and the emergence of methods for scientific enquiry portend well for later more sophisticated approaches to scientific reasoning. The skeptic tradition is important for infusing the thinking world with systematic doubt: what one perceives is not always what is real. Truth is an elusive goal. The roots of empiricism, rationalism, and pragmatism provide epistemic support for much of our modern work in artificial intelligence.

Further, although previous centuries saw the emergence and formalization of philosophy, science, and mathematics, it was not until the creation of the computer that artificial intelligence became a viable scientific discipline. By the late 1940s, electronic digital computers had demonstrated their potential to provide the memory and processing power required for building intelligent programs. It was now possible to implement formal reasoning systems and to test empirically their sufficiency for progressively approximating intelligence.

Further Thoughts and Readings Most of the philosophic tradition supporting work in artificial intelligence is very accessible. To read important contributions consider (see the Bibliography for full reference details):

> Plato's *Dialogues* (1968 translation), especially the *Republic* (2008 translation), and the *Apology* of Socrates.
> Descartes' *Meditations* (1680).
> Hume's writing (1739/1978, 1748/1975).
> Hobbes' *Leviathan* (1651).
> Spinoza's *Ethics* (1677).
> Kant's *Critique of Pure Reason* (1781/1964).
> The writings of James (1981), Dewey (1916), and Peirce (1931–1958). Peirce's reference is to a posthumously published collection of his writings.
> Alan Turing's (1950) paper *Computing Machinery and Intelligence*.

I enjoyed reading Anthony Gotlieb's summaries of western philosophical traditions, and some of his insights have found their way into this chapter:

> *The Dream of Reason: A History of Western Philosophy from the Greeks to the Renaissance* (2000).
> *The Dream of Enlightenment: The Rise of Modern Philosophy* (2016).

I am indebted to Prof. Russell Goodman and Drs. Bill Stubblefield and Carl Stern for their assistance in the creation of this chapter. Many of these ideas were presented in (Luger 1995) *Cognitive Science: The Science of Intelligent Systems*.

Chapter 3
Modern AI and How We Got Here

We propose that a 2 month, 10 man (sic) study of artificial intelligence be carried out during the summer of 1956 at Dartmouth College in Hanover, New Hampshire. The study is to proceed on the basis of the conjecture that every aspect of learning or any other feature of intelligence can in principle be so precisely described that a machine can be made to simulate it. An attempt will be made to find how to make machines use language, form abstractions and concepts, solve kinds of problems now reserved for humans, and improve themselves. We think that a significant advance can be made in one or more of these problems if a carefully selected group of scientists work on it together for a summer.
August 31, 1955
J. MCCARTHY, Dartmouth College
M. L. MINSKY, Harvard University
N. ROCHESTER, I.B.M. Corporation
C.E. SHANNON, Bell Telephone Laboratories

Proposal for the 1956 Dartmouth Summer research project on artificial intelligence. (url 3.1)

Contents

© Springer Nature Switzerland AG 2021
G. F. Luger, *Knowing our World*, https://doi.org/10.1007/978-3-030-71873-2_3

In Chap. 2, we gave a brief historical perspective on philosophical, mathematical, and engineering issues that led to the creation of the digital computer, the birth of artificial intelligence, and the promise for a modern epistemology. We concluded Chap. 2 with Alan Turing's test for determining when a computer program might be considered intelligent. Because of this test and his earlier foundational work in the science of computing, Alan Turing is seen as *the father of artificial intelligence*. In this chapter, we discuss AI's first workshop at Dartmouth College in the summer of 1956, summarize several early AI research projects, and describe the origins of the Cognitive Science discipline. We begin this chapter with several recent successes of modern AI.

3.1 Three Success Stories in Recent AI

Several recent projects have added greatly to the ethos of the artificial intelligence enterprise. It is deceptive, however, to circumscribe artificial intelligence with these three well-known stories. AI is much bigger and more pervasive than these projects might suggest. The notoriety of IBM's and Google's programs is also deceptive because extensive exposure and advertising alone do not measure their scientific validity. Nonetheless, these results are both impressive and important.

3.1.1 Deep Blue at IBM (Hsu 2002; Levy and Newborn 1991; url 3.2)

IBM developed *Deep Blue*, a chess-playing program, in the late 1980s and early 1990s. Deep Blue is the first computer chess program that won a game, in February 1996, playing against a world grandmaster champion, Garry Kasparov. In May 1997, Deep Blue completed a full chess match, also against Kasparov, winning 3.5 to 2.5. These games were played under the constraints of normal professional chess competitions.

Research in game-playing technology had been part of AI from the beginning including Arthur Samuel's 1959 checker playing program described further in Sect. 3.2.3. IBM supported Samuel's early work as well as early chess research by Hans Berliner. Carnegie Institute of Technology, now Carnegie Mellon University, was also an early supporter of computer game playing and Berliner went to CMU to complete his PhD researching and building chess programs. After completing his degree in 1974, he joined the CMU faculty and continued his work on computer gaming. In 1979, his Backgammon program, *BFG*, was the first computer program to beat a reigning world champion.

At Carnegie, Berliner led the development of the chess-playing program, *HiTech*. In the early 1980s, Feng-hsiung Hsu, also at Carnegie, developed the chess programs *ChipTest* and *Deep Thought*. These programs could explore nearly half a billion chess positions for each move in tournament play. When IBM decided to develop the Deep Blue program, they hired many of the chess researchers working at Carnegie, including Hsu's research group and Berliner's student, Murray Campbell.

At the core of Deep Blue is a board evaluation function. This procedure measures the "goodness" of any possible chess position. Board evaluation considers four measures, first, the pieces each player has, for example, a pawn =1, a rook = 5, queen = 9, etc. Second, it considers a player's position, such as how many locations each piece can safely attack. Third, it considers the safety of the king, and finally, it has a measure for a player's overall control of the board.

Deep Blue's parallel search algorithm can generate up to 200,000,000 board positions a second. IBM researchers developed a system called *selective extensions* for considering board situations. This allows the computer to selectively choose "promising" board positions for a deeper search. Because the exhaustive search of chess positions is computationally intractable, see Sect. 1.3, selective extensions allow the computer to search deeper into the space of possible good moves.

Although Deep Blue does not search exhaustively, using a 32-node IBM high-performance computer with multiple processors, it pursues multiple move possibilities at the same time. Each of the 32 nodes contains eight dedicated chess evaluators, for a total of 256 processors. The net result is a highly parallel system able to calculate 60 billion possible moves within 3 min, the time allotted for each move in traditional chess. Other hardware/software details of the Deep Blue chess-playing program are in the literature (Hsu 2002, Levy and Newborn 1991, url 3.2). We present game graphs and intelligent search algorithms in Sect. 4.1.

3.1.2   IBM's Watson (Baker 2011, Ferrucci et al. 2010, 2013, url 3.3)

AI researchers have focused on computer-based question answering since the mid-1960s. Very early programs, such as *Eliza* (Weizenbaum 1966), responded to questions by matching words from the question to preprogrammed responses. Semantic networks, described in more detail in Sect. 5.1, were often used as data structures to capture meaning relationships. Researchers could ask this semantic medium to answer questions posed in English such as "What color is a snowman?" Later, Schank and Abelson (1977) created a representation called *scripts* to capture semantic meaning in archetypical situations such as a child's birthday party or eating in a restaurant, as described further in Sect. 5.1.2.

With *Watson*, named after IBM's first president Thomas J. Watson, the question-answering challenge was reversed: Watson was given an answer and asked to produce the appropriate question requiring that answer. Watson was designed to be a contestant of the televised quiz show, *Jeopardy!*, where an answer for a question is presented in English and three competitors try to be the first to give the correct question supporting that answer. At IBM, David Ferrucci was the principal investigator of the Watson project. The idea was to let Watson have access to collected stored information for its search. Watson did not have a direct link to the internet during its competitions but did have access to over 200 million pages of structured and unstructured data, including all of Wikipedia.

IBM claims that "more than 100 different techniques are used to analyze natural language, identify sources, find and generate hypotheses, find and score evidence, and merge and rank hypotheses" to produce its response to each set of clues. In testing, Watson consistently outperformed its human competition but had problems with questions where the clues contained very few words. In 2011, Watson competed against two former Jeopardy! winners and beat them both to claim a one-million-dollar prize.

In 2013, IBM turned Watson to commercial applications, including making treatment decisions for lung cancer therapies. In succeeding years, the Watson technology has been applied to many other government, commercial, and industrial venues, where human language-based question answering is appropriate.

3.1.3 Google and AlphaGo (Silver et al. 2017, url 3.4)

Go, invented about 2500 years ago in China, is a two-person board game played on a 19 × 19 grid. Each player has a set of *stones*. Stones are usually black or white and placed, one per turn, on the intersecting lines of the grid. The goal in the game is to encircle the other player's stones and by so doing capture that territory. The Go winner is the player that controls most of the board when the game is ended.

The complexity of Go is far greater than that of chess, with a larger board and many more possible choices for each player's turn to place a stone. This complexity constrained the use of traditional AI game-playing technologies, including tree search, alpha–beta pruning, and multiple heuristics, topics to be introduced in Sect. 4.1. Because of complexity issues, even after the success of IBM's Deep Blue, it was thought that a computer Go program would never defeat top human players.

AlphaGo is a computer program developed by Google's DeepMind group in London. The project was set up in 2014. The task was to see if a multilayered neural network, a technique called deep learning, to be described in Sect. 5.3, could learn to play Go. When playing against humans, AlphaGo used *value networks* to evaluate board positions and *policy networks* to choose next moves. Value and policy networks are instances of multilayer deep learning networks with *supervised training*. AlphaGo used *reinforcement learning*, described further in Sect. 5.3, when playing against a version of itself.

In October 2015, AlphaGo became the first computer program to beat a top-ranked human player without any handicap and on a full 19 × 19 board. In March 2016, it beat Lee Sedol, a *9 dan* (highest ranked) human Go player, 4 to 1 in a Go competition. In 2017, AlphaGo beat the world number one Go player Ke Jie in a three-game match. As a result of its successes, AlphaGo was itself awarded the 9 dan ranking by both the Korea Baduk and the Chinese Weiqi associations. After the match with Ke Jie, AlphaGo was retired and Google's DeepMind research group continued research in other AI problem domains.

IBM's chess-playing research was discontinued shortly after Deep Blue's successes and more recent research in computer game playing has moved to Google. In Sect. 5.3 on neural networks and deep learning, we present further detail describing Google's game-playing programs and how they have surpassed the DeepMind effort. Google's AlphaZero program uses deep learning methodology, coupled with reinforcement learning, to play chess, go, and other games, given only the rules for each game (Silver et al. 2018).

Research in computers' understanding and use of human language, called natural language processing, or *NLP*, has had an important history in AI. As mentioned in Sect. 3.1.2, this began with simple word matching in questions to produce preprogrammed answers. Watson demonstrated a major advance in NLP with question–answer relationships determined from extensive search through databases and linked web pages. But these early approaches did not address the notion of the user's *intent* in asking a question. The answer to "Do you have a watch?" is not the usual "yes" but to give the current time of day. We show examples of modern NLP web bots able to address why a user asked a question in Sects. 5.3 and 8.3.

Finally, although these three research projects received much notoriety, there are hundreds of other successes that the AI community has produced. Among these are improved health care delivery, self-driving vehicles, control of deep space travel, and robot technologies that can search the solar system for extraterrestrial life and guide neurosurgeons in complex surgery. Many of these topics will be seen in subsequent chapters.

We next go back to the middle of the last century to review the origins of the modern AI enterprise.

3.2 Very Early AI and the 1956 Dartmouth Summer Research Project

Alan Turing, in lectures at Manchester University in 1946 (unpublished) and for the London Mathematical Society in 1947 (Woodger 1986), laid out the foundations for implementing intelligence on a digital computer. This was even prior to his 1950 proposal of the Turing Test, Sect. 2.10, for determining whether a computer's actions could be seen as intelligent. The first modern workshop/conference for AI practitioners was held at Dartmouth College in the summer of 1956. The introduction for the proposal to fund this workshop was presented as the introductory quotation for this chapter. This workshop, where the name *artificial intelligence,* suggested earlier by John McCarthy, was adopted brought together many of the then active researchers focused on the integration of computation and intelligence.

By the mid-1950s, however, there were already a number of research groups building computer programs that captured aspects of human intelligence and skill. We briefly describe three of these and then present the list of topics addressed by the 1956 Dartmouth summer workshop.

3.2.1 The Logic Theorist (Newell and Simon 1956; Newell et al. 1958)

In 1955, Allen Newell, J.C. Shaw, and Herbert Simon at Carnegie Institute of Technology created the *Logic Theorist*, a program designed to solve problems in propositional logic. Propositional, or variable-free logic, was first proposed by the Stoics in the third-century BCE and reinvented by Abelard in the twelfth century. It was finally formalized by Leibniz, Boole, and Frege as described in Sect. 2.9.

A major goal of the Newell, Shaw, and Simon effort was to solve the problems that Albert North Whitehead and Bertrand Russell had proved in their major work, the Principia Mathematica (1950). The logic Theorist eventually was able to solve about 75% of these problems.

An interesting component of the Logic Theorist project was that the researchers examined non-mathematically skilled subjects to see how these naive humans might go about solving problems in logic. Components of the strategies the humans used, for example, "difference reduction" and "means-ends analysis," were built into the Logic Theorist's search algorithms. Recreating search strategies of humans to run on a computer was an early example of work in Cognitive Science, to be seen in Sect. 3.5.

3.2.2 Geometry Theorem Proving (Gelernter 1959; Gelernter and Rochester 1958)

In 1954, Herbert Gelernter and Nathaniel Rochester established a research program at IBM focused on the issues of intelligent behavior and computer learning. One of the products of this research was a computer program that was able to prove theorems in plane geometry at the secondary school level. An important component of Gelernter's work was to establish appropriate heuristics to cutoff possible next moves by the computer that would likely not be profitable. One of the heuristics implemented in their program was George Polya's suggestion for solving problems by working backward from the problem's possible solution (Polya 1945).

3.2.3   A Program that Plays Checkers (Samuel 1959)

The first program to play checkers was written by Christopher Strachey, the British computer scientist and pioneer in computer language design, in 1950–1951 for the Ferranti Mark 1 computer at the University of Manchester (url 3.5). In 1952, Arthur Samuel, while working at IBM, designed a checker program that could search from the current board position several levels deep in the space to make next move recommendations. Eventually, a *mini-max* algorithm (von Neumann 1928; described by Luger 2009a, Sect. 4.4) was added to give the program the best opportunity to do the worst damage to its opponent.

In 1955, Samuel added an early form of reinforcement learning, Sect. 5.3, to his checker-playing program, and the program was demonstrated on television in 1956. Learning was accomplished by adding a set of adjustable "weighting" parameters to the components of his position evaluation procedure. When checker moves, once selected, turned out to be good for improving the play, these parameters would be rewarded. Samuel and his colleagues played many games against the computer and also let the program play against itself. Samuel commented that letting the program play a weak human competitor damaged the quality of the computer's play!

3.2.4   The Dartmouth Summer Workshop in 1956

There were a number of other early research programs in domains that would later be considered part of artificial intelligence, including a chess-playing program built by J. Kister and colleagues in 1956 at Los Alamos National Laboratories. Many of these early researchers were on the list of people called to attend the Dartmouth Summer Workshop in 1956. The topics proposed for discussion at this summer workshop, as quoted from the original proposal for that workshop, url 3.1, were:

1. Automatic Computers

    If a machine can do a job, then an automatic calculator can be programmed to simulate the machine. The speeds and memory capacities of present computers may be insufficient to simulate many of the higher functions of the human brain, but the major obstacle is not lack of machine capacity, but our inability to write programs taking full advantage of what we have.

2. How Can a Computer be Programmed to Use a Language

    It may be speculated that a large part of human thought consists of manipulating words according to rules of reasoning and rules of conjecture. From this point of view, forming a generalization consists of admitting a new word and some rules whereby sentences containing it imply and are implied by others. This idea has never been very precisely formulated nor have examples been worked out.

3. Neuron Nets

How can a set of (hypothetical) neurons be arranged so as to form concepts. Considerable theoretical and experimental works have been done on this problem by Uttley, Rashevsky, and his group; by Farley and Clark; by Pitts and McCulloch; and by Minsky, Rochester, Holland, and others. Partial results have been obtained but the problem needs more theoretical work.

4. Theory of the Size of a Calculation

If we are given a well-defined problem, i.e., one for which it is possible to test mechanically whether or not a proposed answer is a valid answer, one way of solving it is to try all possible answers. This method is inefficient, and to exclude it, one must have some criterion for the efficiency of a calculation. Some consideration will show that to get a measure of the efficiency of a calculation, it is necessary to have on hand a method of measuring the complexity of calculating devices which in turn can be done if one has a theory of the complexity of functions. Some partial results addressing this problem have been obtained by Shannon and also by McCarthy.

5. Self-improvement

Probably a truly intelligent machine will carry out activities that may best be described as self-improvement. Some schemes for doing this have been proposed and are worth further study. It seems likely that this question can be studied abstractly as well.

6. Abstractions

A number of types of "abstraction" can be distinctly defined and several others less distinctly. A direct attempt to classify these and to describe machine methods of forming abstractions from sensory and other data would seem worthwhile.

7. Randomness and Creativity

A fairly attractive and yet clearly incomplete conjecture is that the difference between creative thinking and unimaginative competent thinking lies in the injection of ... some randomness. The randomness must be guided by intuition to be efficient. In other words, the educated guess or the hunch includes controlled randomness in otherwise orderly thinking.

Many of the topics proposed for this first summer workshop, including complexity theory, methodologies for abstraction, computer language design, improving hardware/software speed, and machine learning, make up the focus of modern computer science. In fact, many of the defining characteristics of computer science, as we know it today, have their roots in the research methodologies that evolved from work in artificial intelligence.

Considering point 2 above, building high-level programming languages, a powerful new computational tool, the Lisp language, emerged at about this time. Lisp (the name stands for LISt Processor) was built under the direction of John McCarthy, one of the original proposers of the Dartmouth workshop. Lisp addressed several of the topics of the workshop, supporting data abstraction and the ability to create relationships that could themselves be manipulated by other structures of the language. Lisp gave artificial intelligence a highly expressive language, rich in its ability to capture abstractions, as well as a language that could evaluate (interpret) other expressions written in the Lisp language.

The availability of the Lisp programming language did shape much of the early development of AI, including use of the predicate calculus and semantic networks as representational media. It also supported building search algorithms to explore the efficacy of different logic or inheritance alternatives. The Prolog language developed in the mid-1970s, (the name stands for PROgramming in LOGic) was based on the first-order predicate logic, also offered AI developers a powerful computational tool.

Several of the topics for the Dartmouth workshop considered artificial intelligence in terms of human thinking and problem-solving, especially point 3, research on Neuron Nets. In fact, the expression "Neuron Nets" itself reflects the results of mid-1940s research at MIT by W. S. McCulloch and W. Pitts (1943) showing how the human neuronal system could compute *and* and *or* as well as other propositional calculus relationships. D. O. Hebb (1949), also at MIT, demonstrated how human neurons could "learn" through conditioning, i.e., repeated use of neuronal pathways.

There are now many other approaches, besides Hebb's, to computer "self-improvement" or learning, and they are important components of modern AI. These include supervised and unsupervised classification using neural networks. Deep learning, seen in Google's AlphaGo program of Sect. 3.1.3, uses multiple hidden layers in neural networks to find abstract patterns and relationships. See Sect. 5.2 for further detail.

The appreciation of "Randomness and Creativity" also has made its mark on modern artificial intelligence. We see this especially in the areas of genetic algorithms and artificial life, where random factors are often added to search exploration strategies in an attempt to expand the consideration of possible solutions; see Sects. 6.2 and 6.3 for further detail. It is still conjectured that creativity might be the result of injecting some randomness into so-called "normal" thinking.

In the mid-1940s, Max Black (1946) proposed a problem that required "Randomness and Creativity" for finding a solution. This problem also posed a serious challenge to AI's traditional search-based methods. The problem, often called *the mutilated chessboard*, is described in Fig. 3.1.

Suppose a standard 8 × 8 chessboard has its two diametrically opposite corners removed; in Fig. 3.1 the upper left and lower right corners are removed, leaving 62 squares for the board. Suppose a domino will cover exactly two squares of that chessboard. Is it possible to place 31 dominoes on the chessboard so that all 62 squares of the board are covered?

We might attempt to solve this problem by trying all possible placements of dominos on the board. This approach is an obvious search-based attempt, a natural consequence of representing the board as a set of black and white squares. The complexity of such a search is enormous, even when we discontinue partial solutions that leave single squares isolated. We might also try solving the problem for a smaller board, say a 3 × 3 or 4 × 4, and see what happens.

A more sophisticated solution, relying on a more complex representational scheme, notes that every placement of a domino must cover both a black and a white square. This truncated board has 32 black squares but only 30 white squares; thus, the desired placement is not going to be possible.

This example raises a serious question for computer-based reasoning systems: Do we have representations that allow problem solvers to access knowledge with appropriate degrees of flexibility and creativity? How can a particular representation automatically change its structure when it fails or as more information is learned about the problem? This topic offers a continuing challenge for AI.

We next consider possible definitions for artificial intelligence.

3.3   Artificial Intelligence: Attempted Definitions

The word *artificial* is derived from two Latin words: first the noun, *ars/artis* means "skilled effort," such as that of the artist or artisan, and second, the verb *facere* "to make." The literal meaning, then, of artificial intelligence is that something, namely, intelligence, is made by skilled effort.

It is appropriate to make the first definition of Artificial Intelligence to be that described near the end of the Dartmouth summer workshop proposal (url 3.1):

> For the present purpose the artificial intelligence problem is taken to be that of making a machine behave in ways that would be called intelligent if a human were so behaving.

This definition could be seen as directly related to Turing's test, Sect. 2.10. If observers are not able to determine whether they are interacting with a human or with a computer, the software on the computer must be seen as intelligent. However, it is important to understand how the workshop attendees thought to actualize their definition of AI as computer programs. To appreciate this, we quote another segment of the workshop proposal, cited at the beginning of this Chapter (url3.1). Here the claim is that the mechanisms of intelligence can be sufficiently understood to be automated:

Fig. 3.1 The mutilated chessboard problem where the top left and lower right corner squares of the chessboard are removed. One domino, the grayed area upper right, covers exactly two adjacent squares on the board. The task is to cover the remaining 62 squares with 31 dominoes

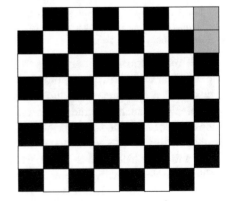

The (workshop) study is to proceed on the basis of the conjecture that every aspect of learning or any other feature of intelligence can in principle be so precisely described that a
machine can be made to simulate it.

This definition still suffers from the fact that human intelligence itself is not very
well defined or understood. Most of us are certain that we know intelligent behavior
when we see it. It remains doubtful, however, that we could come close to defining
intelligence in specific enough detail to help in designing an intelligent computer
program. How could our detailed solution algorithm still capture the vitality and
complexity of the human mind?

And thus, the task of *defining* the full field of artificial intelligence becomes one
of defining intelligence itself: is intelligence a single faculty, or is it just a name for
a collection of distinct but interrelated abilities, Minsky's (1985) *Society of Mind*?
To what extent can intelligence be learned as opposed to it just being a fixed disposition? Exactly what does happen when learning occurs? What is creativity? What is
intuition? Can intelligence be inferred from observable behavior, or does it require
evidence of a particular internal mechanism? How is knowledge represented in the
nerve tissue of a living being, and what lessons does this have for the design of intelligent machines? What is self-awareness and what role does awareness play in
human or machine intelligence?

As a result of the daunting task of building a general intelligence, AI researchers
often assume the roles of engineers fashioning particular intelligent artifacts. These
programs come in the form of diagnostic, prognostic, or visualization tools that
enable their human users to perform complex tasks. Examples of this include hidden Markov and deep learning models for language understanding, automated reasoning systems for proving new theorems in mathematics, dynamic Bayesian
networks for tracking signals across cortical networks, and visualization of patterns
of gene expression data. Many of these technologies are considered in later chapters.

Furthermore, is it necessary to pattern an intelligent computer program after
what is known about human intelligence or is a strict "engineering" approach to the
problem sufficient? Is it even possible to achieve general intelligence on a computer,
or does an intelligent entity require the richness of sensation and experience that
might be found only in a biological existence, as critics have suggested (Dreyfus
1972, 1992)?

These are unanswered questions, and all of them have helped to shape the problems and solution methodologies that constitute the core of modern AI. In fact, part
of the appeal of artificial intelligence is that it offers a unique and powerful tool for
exploring exactly these questions. AI offers a medium and a testbed for theories of
intelligence: Such theories may be stated in the language of computer programs and
consequently tested and verified through the execution of these programs on an
actual computer. We continue this discussion in Sect. 3.4, The Birth of Cognitive
Science.

Our initial definitions of artificial intelligence fall short of unambiguously defining the field. If anything, it has only led to further questions and the paradoxical
notion of a field of study whose major goals include its own definition. But this

difficulty in arriving at a precise definition of AI is entirely appropriate. Artificial intelligence is still a young discipline, and its structure, concerns, and methods are less clearly defined than those of more mature sciences such as physics.

In more recent years, artificial intelligence is often seen and taught as a component of the discipline of computer science. From this perspective, a generic definition of AI might be: *Artificial intelligence is defined as that branch of computer science that is concerned with the automation of intelligent behavior.* This definition is appropriate in that it emphasizes that AI is currently a part of the study of computer science and, as such, must be based on sound theoretical and applied principles of that field. These principles include the data structures used in knowledge representation, the algorithms needed to apply that knowledge, and the languages and programming techniques used in their implementation. Artificial intelligence has always been more concerned with expanding the capabilities of computer science than with defining its limits. Keeping this exploration grounded in sound theoretical principles is one of the challenges facing AI researchers.

Because of its scope and ambition, artificial intelligence defies any simple definition. For the time being, we will simply say it is *the collection of problems and methodologies studied by artificial intelligence researchers.* This definition may seem silly and meaningless, but it makes an important point that artificial intelligence, like every science, is a human and evolving endeavor, and perhaps is best understood in that context.

3.4 AI: Early Years

In this section, we present different "philosophies" of problem-solving taken by the AI community in its earliest years. We briefly describe two: first, the divide between the so-called "neat" and "scruffy" approaches to AI. Second, we ask whether the AI enterprise should be to create programs that emulate human intelligence or, ignoring how humans solve problems, to simply use good engineering practice to obtain "intelligent" results. There might also be a middle alternative that uses successful human approaches to solving problems to suggest related engineering decisions. Section 3.5, The Birth of Cognitive Science, introduces the use of AI technologies to better understand human skilled behavior.

3.4.1 The Neats and Scruffies

Describing groups of AI program designers as *neats* or *scruffies* was an interesting part of the early AI world view. The neats were program builders that often crafted their products with mathematics-based languages and representational tools, such as the first-order predicate calculus. Although the Prolog programming language was ideally suited to this task, it is straightforward to make logic structures in other languages, especially Lisp, and in the early days, Lisp was the language of choice.

In these early decades of AI work, an important component of the neats' approach was the *logicist* worldview. From this perspective, any program, including those intended to capture commonsense reasoning, could be built with mathematics-based representations and reasoning (McCarthy 1968; McCarthy and Hayes 1969). The logicist view was correct in this claim, given the Church-Turing thesis, Sect. 1.2, which suggests that a logic-based language does not offer any limit on what that language can compute.

The neats used logic-based schemes, including if-then rules, to represent knowledge in specific domains. They also used the reasoning methods of logic, including *modus ponens* and *resolution*, the reasoning engine of the Prolog language, within the program itself. In several applications, e.g., the STRIPS *planner* for scheduling the moves of a robot (Fikes and Nilsson 1971) and the *MECHO* solver for addressing problems in applied mathematics (Bundy et al. 1979; Bundy 1983), the program's control scheme was implemented using rules of logic. Early AI textbooks representing the neats' worldview include those of Nils Nilsson (1971, 1980).

The scruffies felt that mathematics-based programming and design tools were not a prerequisite for building intelligent programs. Their philosophy was to "just build it," and the result, a program that performs actions that normal people would call intelligent, will speak for itself. Quality software design techniques were used, however, as no serious AI programmer has ever believed that a big messy and unstructured program could be successful, extendable, maintainable, or necessarily reflect intelligence.

The hallmark of the scruffy group was that good programs were built using disciplined engineering practice, and that mathematics-based software tools were not required to create successful AI programs. An early AI textbook representing the scruffy worldview is that of Patrick Henry Winston (1977). An interesting conjecture is that the scruffy approach to solution building emerged from the even earlier *hacker* zeitgeist that was so important in developing the 1950s and 1960s programming technology at MIT and elsewhere (Levy 2010). In those days, the hackers were the good guys!

3.4.2   AI: Based on "Emulating Humans" or "Just Good Engineering?"

Another question, orthogonal to the early neat/scruffy worldviews, is whether AI program designers should strive for "human emulation," that is, being aware of and consciously imitating how humans address problem-solving tasks, or whether they should adopt a skilled engineering perspective. Should the AI practitioner, neat or scruffy, rely on understanding human information processing or could she simply use sound software practice to produce intelligent solutions to problems? For example, to get a computer to "understand" human language is it best to use psycho-linguistic knowledge? Is a clever parser all that is needed? How about a probabilistic match on a large database, or *corpus*, of human language fragments? What about some of the newer language models created using deep learning? The AI community remains divided on these issues.

In many situations, the issue of creating human-type intelligence rarely comes up, for example, in developing proofs for theorems in mathematics (Wos 1988, 1995) or building control systems for robotic arms or deep-space vehicles (Williams and Nayak 1996, 1997). Even in these areas, however, human-generated common-sense heuristics including striving for simplicity, breaking a problem into sub-problems, reducing structures to canonical forms, and analogy-based reasoning are often important components of success.

IBM's Deep Blue chess-playing program, discussed in Sect. 3.1, is an example of good engineering in that it searched a huge array of chessboard positions far faster than a human grandmaster ever could (200 million board positions each second). Deep Blue's designers have commented, however, that when the exhaustive chess-search space is considered, a space so large that it never could be fully searched, it was critical to draw from the decision-making expertise of the human grandmaster to guide the search (Hsu 2002; Levy and Newborn 1991).

Expert system technology, described in detail in Sect. 4.1, offers an intermediate position between the engineering and the human emulation approaches to AI. In these programs, the human *knowledge engineer* usually gathers knowledge from the human *domain expert* through interviews, focus groups, or other methods. The computational processes then used to run the expert system employ decision tree technology, a production system, or some other algorithmic control strategy. When expert systems are thought to be sufficiently engineered and ready for human use, the transparency of their reasoning and the quality and justifications for their answers are often compared to those of human experts solving problems in similar situations. An example of this was MYCIN (Buchanan and Shortliffe 1984), the expert system developed at Stanford to diagnose symptoms of meningitis. MYCIN was evaluated with a form of the Turing test.

A large fraction of the AI research community, however, remains committed to understanding how humans process information while problem-solving. They feel that this knowledge is also important in good human–computer interface design, creating solutions that are transparent and understandable. Further, they feel that many of the artificial intelligence representational techniques could be used to shed understanding on the cognitive processes that humans used in problem-solving. This philosophy was the enabling force behind the creation, in the late 1970s, of the *cognitive science* community described in Sect. 3.5.

But long before the founding of the cognitive science consortium, human emulation was an important component of AI research. We noted this previously with Alan Turing's lectures at the University of Manchester and for the London Mathematical Society (Woodger 1986) in the late 1940s. A further example of human emulation, mentioned in Sect. 3.2.1, was the *Logic Theorist* research of Newell, Shaw, and Simon (1958), who analyzed human subjects solving logic problems. The models derived from this analysis, e.g., *GPS* and including *means-ends analysis*, became important tools for information-processing psychologists, also described in Sect. 3.5.

Research groups focused on understanding how humans solve problems were aware of the differences between the computer and the human memory systems. Although computers are able to store great quantities of information, usually located with various memory access algorithms, humans "associated" fewer concepts in their memories but often in a very "useful" fashion for retrieval. For example, Collins and Quillian (1969) created a set of reaction-time studies in an attempt to determine how information was associated with human memory.

Collins and Quillian asked human subjects a series of questions such as whether a canary can sing, can fly, or has skin. They then used the subjects' response times in answering each question to conjecture how this information might be associated in human memory. This research was the beginning of the *semantic network* tradition in AI and led to many successful programs for understanding human language (Quillian 1967; Shapiro 1971; Wilks 1972) and other aspects of human performance (Anderson and Bower 1973; Norman et al. 1975). Section 5.1 has further discussion of these association-based representations.

Schank (1982) and his research group at Yale University (Schank and Colby 1973; Schank and Abelson 1977) attempted to systematize semantic networks into a language called *conceptual dependencies* that they used for understanding stories, interpreting language-based concepts, and supporting computer translation between languages. Schank's language of concepts and relationships was an attempt to capture the semantic meaning that supported human language expressions.

The object-oriented design and programming languages are perhaps the final embodiment of the semantic network and association-based AI representations. The first of these languages was Smalltalk, built at Xerox PARC in the early 1970s, a language designed for teaching children to program. These early languages with inheritance relationships and program procedures embedded in "objects" led to subsequent generations of object-oriented languages.

Logo, created by Seymour Papert at MIT (1980), was another early computer language. Logo was intended to assist children learning mathematical concepts. In a real-time interactive environment, a robotic "turtle" would draw patterns as it moved around on the floor. These patterns could be geometric objects including circles, squares, or "stair steps." Logo also made it possible to create patterns such as trees that used recursive procedures, where a program is built that refers back to itself, and in the process constructs multiple patterns with similar structure.

The intuition supporting the Logo learning process was that the programmers, usually children, could begin to understand mathematical concepts and structures as they built and then revised their programs to reflect those structures. For example, if the turtle did not draw an intended pattern, then the child had not defined the pattern properly in his/her program. This approach to building programs is an early example of the iterative refinement methodology, where programmers come to understand their world by continuing to reshape their programs until the result is good enough for all the pragmatic purposes its designer had intended, with the Logo program, when the turtle drew the desired pattern.

To discover useful algorithms for solving algebra "word problems," Carnegie Mellon University conducted research into how middle and high school students performed this task. Hayes and Simon (1974), Simon (1975), and Simon and Hayes (1976) tested whether algebra students could properly classify sets of word problems into appropriate groups. They found that students did successfully group problems, e.g., "distance, rate, time," or "work" problems. The students had also learned different problem-solving techniques (algorithms) to cope with each specific type of problem.

In the early 1970s, research at the University of Pennsylvania by Goldin and Luger (1975) asked how the *structure* of a problem or puzzle could affect human problem-solving performance. Problem structure was represented by a problem's state-space graph, an AI model for problem analysis described in Sect. 4.1. The four-ring *Tower of Hanoi* problem, for example, had a state space that reflected the problem's subproblem breakdown as well as its symmetry structure. It was found, through carefully tracking naive subjects trying to learn the Tower of Hanoi puzzle, that their learning behavior did reflect that problem's structure.

For example, in the four-ring Tower of Hanoi problem, there are three three-ring subproblems. Once the subject learned how to solve one of these three-ring subproblems, she was usually able to apply this learning to any other three-ring subproblems she encountered. Similar results came with problem symmetries. Once a substructure of the problem was learned, the results were applied to other symmetric situations found in the problem. Continuing this approach, researchers in the AI Department at the University of Edinburgh (Luger 1978; Luger and Bauer 1978) tested for transfer learning in similarly structured problems. It was found that naive subjects learned to solve new problems faster if these problems had a structure similar to problems they had already learned. Interestingly, subjects were often unaware of the similar structures of these testing tasks. Transfer effects in related problems were also studied at CMU (Simon and Hayes 1976).

The projects and researchers just mentioned were among the group that came together to become the cognitive science community. Cognitive science did not simply emerge from human emulation projects in the AI community but rather joined with components of the already existing *cognitive psychology* and *information processing psychology* communities.

3.5   The Birth of Cognitive Science

Cognitive psychology offered an important reaction to the early twentieth-century behaviorist tradition in psychology. Behaviorism suggested that the human response system could be fully understood by describing external responses to specific stimuli. Cognitive psychologists contended that the human system actually processed information when operating in the world, rather than simply responded to stimuli.

Information processing psychology became an important component of the cognitive psychologists' worldview, as it gave a language and medium for understanding information processing in humans.

In the mid-nineteenth century, Broca's and Wernicke's identification of components of the cortex responsible for language comprehension and production had suggested the importance of cortical analysis as a component of understanding human intelligence. Plato, Descartes, and other earlier philosophers, as discussed in Chap. 2, had already seen the brain as the enabler of complex reasoning schemes. The modern cognitive revolution began in the 1930s with researchers including Bartlett (1932), Piaget (1954) and others in Europe, and Bruner, Goodnow, and Austin (1956), Miller, Galanter, and Pribram (1960), and others in America. These researchers ushered in the modern revolution in psychology.

In the late 1950s, Noam Chomsky (1959) reviewed B.F. Skinner's book *Verbal Behavior* (1957), which at that time dominated the field of psychology. While behaviorists focused on functional relations between stimulus and response, without the need for "internal" processes, Chomsky's "cognitive" argument was that a theory such as his generative grammar with ordered internal representations was needed to explain human language.

With the arrival of the digital computer in the 1950s, many of the constructs needed to enable computation, such as control processes, buffers, registers, and memory devices, were explored as potential "models" for the intermediate structures for decision-making in human information processing. This approach of using well-understood concepts and tools from early computation to elucidate aspects of human problem-solving performance was called *Information Processing Psychology* (Miller et al. 1960; Miller 2003; Proctor and Vu 2006).

It is only natural that information-processing models of human performance would expand with the representational media and algorithms proffered by the artificial intelligence community. Research at Carnegie Institute, for example, used production rule systems and problem behavior graphs to represent the search strategies of expert chess players (Newell and Simon 1972). Using these representations, they could identify strategies such as *iterative deepening* and saw this approach as a method supporting the use of limited memory as part of intelligent search.

The British psychologist and philosopher, Christopher Longuet-Higgins, first used the term *cognitive science* in 1973. He used the term in discussing the Lighthill report on the then-current credibility of AI research in Britain. In the late 1970s, the journal *Cognitive Science* and the *Society for Cognitive Science* were created. The first meeting of the Cognitive Science Society was in 1979 at the University of California, San Diego.

We next mention several early research projects within the cognitive science community, projects that also relate to the major themes of later chapters: First, the symbol-based research at Carnegie Mellon University; second, the parallel distributed processing, or neural networks, research that came to a renewed importance in the mid-1980s at the University of California, San Diego, and finally, several cognitive science projects supporting a constructivist epistemology.

Although early work at Carnegie Institute was an important contribution to information processing psychology, the later research at Carnegie Mellon University, led by Newell, Simon, and their colleagues and students vastly extended our knowledge of how humans solved problems. The CMU research group conducted experiments involving master chess players and experts who solved other types of manipulation problems and puzzles. Their research produced two notable results: first, a book entitled *Human Problem Solving* (1972), and second, the *Association of Computing Machinery's* (ACM's) 1976 Turing Award given to Allen Newell and Herbert Simon.

In accepting the Turing Award, Newell and Simon wrote a seminal paper called "Computer Science as Empirical Inquiry: Symbols and Search" (1976). In this and other papers, they claimed:

The necessary and sufficient condition for a physical system to exhibit general intelligent action is that it be a physical symbol system.

Sufficient means that intelligence can be achieved by any appropriately organized physical symbol system.

Necessary means that any agent that exhibits general intelligence must be an instance of a physical symbol system. The necessity of the physical symbol system hypothesis requires that the intelligent agent, whether human, space alien, or computer, achieve intelligence through the physical implementation of operations on symbol structures.

General intelligent action means the same scope of action seen in human action. Within physical limits, the system exhibits behavior appropriate to its ends and adaptive to the demands of its environment.

This conjecture became known as the *physical symbol system* hypothesis. The software architecture developed at CMU and elsewhere that embodied this hypothesis was based on the *production system*, an interpretation of the Post rule system seen in Sect. 1.2. In the 1990s, Newell (1990) and his colleagues extended the production system so that with reinforcement learning it could automatically create new rules and add them to production memory. This project is called *SOAR*, the State, Operator, And Result, architecture. At that time, the Newell and Simon research group was the leading proponent in the cognitive science community for using the physical symbol system technology. This symbol system approach to AI is described further in Chap. 4.

Many philosophers, psychologists, and AI researchers have proposed arguments to support or refute the physical symbol system hypothesis. Its boldest claim is the "necessary and sufficient" argument. Although the "necessary" component of the argument is often considered not provable, the "sufficient" component has been supported by much of the research effort of the cognitive science community, where the requirement of having computational models to support conjectures related to human intelligent activity is paramount.

Besides the physical symbol system approach to understanding human behavior, connectionist networks also came to maturity as a supporting technology for the cognitive science enterprise. Work on "Neuron Nets" had flourished in the late 1940s and 1950s and perhaps the product most indicative of its success was the *perceptron*, built at the Cornell Aeronautical Laboratory by Frank Rosenblatt

(1958). The original Perceptron was a 20 × 20 array of photocells that could be trained (using supervised learning, see Sect. 5.2) to recognize images. Interestingly, Rosenblatt's 1958 results were published in the journal *Psychology Review*.

Although the Perceptron originally showed promise, it was soon proven to have limitations solving certain classes of problems. The book *Perceptrons* written by Marvin Minsky and Seymour Papert (1969) demonstrated fundamental limitations of the Perceptron technology, including being unable to solve the *exclusive-or* problem. (In Sect. 5.2, we present a solution to the exclusive-or problem using a perceptron network with one hidden layer). The result of the perceptron book, as well as other political decisions in AI funding made at that time, put neural network research into background mode for the next several decades.

The physics, mathematics, and other communities, however, continued to research various types of connectionist systems, including competitive, reinforcement, and attractor networks, even while these were out of favor in the AI community. In the late 1980s, connectionist research again became mainstream with the creation of the *Boltzmann* machine and *backpropagation* (Hecht-Nielsen 1989, 1990). These algorithms demonstrated how the weights of nodes in a multilayer network could be appropriately conditioned, based on the expected output of the network.

Possibly the most important research heralding the revival of connectionism was that of David Rumelhart and James McClelland. In 1986, they, along with their research group, wrote a two-volume set of books called *Parallel Distributed Processing: Explorations in the Microstructure of Cognition*. This research demonstrated the utility of neural networks for solving cognitive tasks, including several in the area of human language analysis. Parallel distributed processing (PDP) models of many aspects of human perception, including vision and speech, led more recently to the analysis of very large data sets, using *deep learning,* i.e., neural networks with multiple hidden layers. We present connectionist networks and deep learning approaches to AI in Chap. 5.

In the mid-twentieth century, Jean Piaget and his colleagues at the University of Geneva described a fundamentally new understanding of how children, actively experimenting within their environment, came to understand and know their world. Piaget called this staged developmental learning *genetic epistemology*. (I was fortunate to attend one of Piaget's lectures in the early 1970s at Temple University in Philadelphia and later presented my own PhD research (Luger and Goldin 1973) at Piaget's institute, the *Center for Genetic Epistemology*, in Geneva in 1975).

Piaget's insights inspired a flood of research from both the cognitive psychology and the cognitive science communities. T.G.R. Bower at Harvard University, and later a Professor of Psychology at the University of Edinburgh, studied children in their earliest stages of development. An important development stage empirically tested by Bower (1977) was called *object permanence*. Children just months old can lose interest in an object when it goes out of sight as though it no longer exists. Months later, when the child actively looks for an object that she has lost sight of, she has reached the stage of object permanence. At the University of Edinburgh,

Luger (1981), Luger et al. (1983) created sets of production rules that simulated a child's actions at each stage of her development in achieving object permanence.

Other cognitive science research in the AI Department of the University of Edinburgh in the mid 1970s included a production system-based analysis of children performing *seriation tasks*. A seriation task is asking the child, when presented with a set of blocks, to order them by size (Young 1976). (More recently McGonigle and his colleagues (2002) in the Psychology Department at the University of Edinburgh trained primates to seriate objects!). Young and O'Shea (1981) used sets of production rules to analyze the errors children made when learning to subtract.

During the late 1970s and early 1980s, there was a considerable effort at Carnegie Mellon University by Allen Newell, Herbert A. Simon, and their colleagues to model Piagetian developmental learning skills in children. The production system was the modeling system of choice. Individual production rules could embody particular skills while groups of skills could be wrapped into new rules.

At CMU Wallace, Klahr, and Bluff (1987) created a production system-based model of children's cognitive development called BAIRN. BAIRN organizes knowledge into structures called *nodes*. Each node is made up of a set of productions. A node is schema-like in that, when triggered, it produces specific actions. Their program was able to account for many aspects of children's developmental stages in the conservation of number, or how different groupings of objects does not change the number of objects. Klahr, Langley, and Neches (1987) collected papers on a number of CMU research projects, including BAIRN, in *Production System Models of Learning and Development*. Chapter 1 of this collection offers motivation for using production rules to model developmental learning.

At MIT, Gary Drescher (1991) created an artificial cognitive system able to demonstrate Piaget's object permanence. In his book, *Made Up Minds: A Constructivist Approach to Artificial Intelligence*, Drescher addresses two fundamental issues: how a child can interpret experiences well enough to learn from them, and how a child can form concepts from learned experiences. Drescher implements a *schema mechanism* that receives information from a body that it controls. From this interaction with its world, the mechanism discovers regularities and, based on these, constructs new concepts. This constructivist engine uses knowledge it acquires to guide future action that results in acquiring further knowledge.

In the late 1970s, Alan Bundy and his research group (Bundy et al. 1979; Bundy 1983), at the Artificial Intelligence Department of the University of Edinburgh, created a program called MECHO, for MECHanics Oracle. MECHO was designed to solve applied mathematics problems including "pulley" or "blocks sliding on inclined planes" problems. To build this problem-solver, the researchers asked British university students who had completed the applied mathematics course to solve particular problems. The research demonstrated (Luger 1981) that when a problem was proposed, the human solver would utilize already learned knowledge and assumptions about that type of problem.

This prior knowledge acquired in mathematics classes included: *if no coefficient of friction was mentioned in the problem statement, that system was assumed to be frictionless* and *if no other angle was given for a hanging object, it would hang vertically.* The successful human solver also had learned equations appropriate for different problem situations. The research group called this *a priori* knowledge, and the successful students used *"schemas,"* a term used by the British psychologist Bartlett (1932) in his research on human understanding of story narratives. The term schema, representing the collected expectations for known situations, also refers back to Kant as mentioned in Sect. 2.7. Building Prolog representations to capture the schema knowledge of the skilled human was an important component of the success of the MECHO project (Bundy 1983; Luger 1981).

Section 3.5 described the origins and early research projects of the cognitive science community. Their goal was to demonstrate the sufficiency of computational models to characterize the activity of the human cognitive system. The journal of the Cognitive Science Society and the proceedings of their annual conferences reflect the growth and maturity of the modern cognitive scienc project. In the final section of this chapter, we introduce four current artificial intelligence research themes: the underlying technologies that have been used to create successful AI results. These themes are demonstrated in more detail in Chaps. 4–6, and 8.

3.6 General Themes in AI Practice: The Symbolic, Connectionist, Genetic/Emergent, and Stochastic

In the previous section, we described the cognitive scientist as an active research participant in the task of understanding human information processing. In this final section, we step back to the original AI enterprise and summarize continuing research according to four themes: the *symbolic*, the *subsymbolic* or *connectionist*, the *genetic* or *emergent*, and the *stochastic* technologies. Each of these approaches to AI has had its important flourishing periods, and we introduce them briefly. In Chaps. 4–6, and 8, we consider each in more detail. We also discuss their supporting epistemic assumptions, often responsible for their successes and failures.

"Neuron Nets" were an early and important concern of AI research. But as a result of the *Perceptrons* book (Minsky and Papert 1969) and the politics of early funding, the symbolic approach to AI became the predominant research theme from the 1960s through much of the 1980s. Symbol-based AI is often considered first-generation AI and sometimes called *GOFAI* or *good old-fashioned AI* (Haugeland 1985).

Symbol-based AI, as we have seen in several examples already, requires that explicit symbols and sets of symbols reflect the world of things and relationships within the problem domain. Several forms of representation are available, especially the predicate and the propositional calculi as well as association-based representations including semantic networks. The AI practitioner Brian Cantwell Smith (1985) offered a characterization of the symbolic approach referred to as the *knowledge representation hypothesis*:

> Any mechanically embodied intelligent process will be comprised of structural ingredients that (a) we as external observers naturally take to represent a propositional account of the knowledge that the overall process exhibits, and (b) independent of such external semantical attribution, play a formal role in engendering the behavior that manifests that knowledge.

Examples of the symbol-based approach to AI include many game-playing programs including chess and checkers; expert systems, where knowledge is encoded in explicit rule relationships; and control systems for robotics and directing craft for exploring deep space. The explicit-symbol system approach has been highly successful, although its critics point out, and as we will see further in Chap. 4, the resulting programs can be inflexible. For example, how can an explicit symbol system adjust when the problem situation changes over time and is no longer exactly as encoded in the original program? Or how can such a system compute useful results from incomplete or imprecise information?

The second approach to developing AI technology, the connectionist or subsymbolic, began with conjectures in the late 1940s by Warren McCulloch, a neuroscientist, Walter Pitts, a logician, and Donald Hebb, a psychologist. The basis for neural network computing is the artificial neuron, an example of which may be seen in Fig. 3.2. The artificial neuron consists of *Input signals x_i* and often a *bias* that comes from the environment or other neurons. There is also a *set of weights*, w_i. that enhance or weaken the strengths of the input values. Each neuron also has an *activation level*, $\Sigma w_i x_i$, the value of net: the summed strengths of the input times weight measures. Finally, there is a *threshold function f* that computes the neuron's output by determining whether the neuron's activation level is above or below a predetermined threshold.

In addition to the properties of individual neurons, a neural network is also characterized by global properties including the *topology* of the network, that is, the pattern of connections between the individual neurons and the layers of neurons. A further property is the *learning algorithm*, several of which are described in more detail in Chap. 5. Finally, there is the *encoding scheme* supporting the interpretation of both problem data by the network and the output results from the network processing. The encoding determines how an application situation is presented to the nodes of the network as well as how the results from the network are interpreted back into the application domain.

There are two primary approaches to neural network learning: *supervised* and *unsupervised*. In supervised learning, during the training period for the network, an oracle analyzes each output value of the network, given the input data. The oracle then either strengthens the weights that supported the correct output or weakens the weights supporting incorrect results. The most common approach, as seen in the *backpropagation algorithm* of Sect. 5.2.2, is to ignore correct results and to weaken the weights supporting incorrect results.

In unsupervised learning, there is no feedback to the input weights w_i, given the output values. In fact, some algorithms do not require weights at all. Output values are calculated by the structure of the data itself interacting with the network or combine with other outputs as they self-organize into useful clusters. This approach can be seen with some classifier systems.

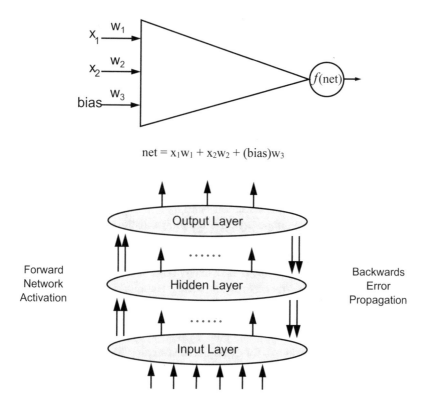

$$net = x_1w_1 + x_2w_2 + (bias)w_3$$

Fig. 3.2 (Above). A single artificial neuron whose input values, multiplied by trained weights, produce a value, net. Using some function, f(net) produces an output value that may, in turn, be an input for other neurons. (Below) A supervised learning network where input values move forward through the nodes of the network. During training, the network weights are differentially "punished" for incorrect responses to input values as is discussed in more detail in Sect. 5.2.

With the advent of very high-performance computing and parallel algorithms for computing neural network architectures, it has now become common to have networks with multiple internal layers and complete networks passing data off to other networks. This approach, sometimes referred to as *deep learning,* has brought an entirely new dimension to the power and possibilities of connectionist computing. This is the type of computation that made the AlphaGo success possible, as seen in Sect. 3.1.3. Further examples of the connectionist and deep learning approaches are presented in Chap. 5.

A third theme of current artificial intelligence problem-solving is the genetic and emergent approach. John Holland of the University of Michigan, a primary designer of *genetic algorithms*, was an influential attendee of the 1956 Dartmouth summer workshop. Holland's algorithms are a natural extension of the "Randomness and Creativity" goal of that workshop. Genetic algorithms, seen in more detail in Chap. 6, use operators such as *mutation, inversion,* and *crossover* to produce potential solutions for problems. Using a *fitness function,* once possible solutions are generated, the best of these are selected and used to create the next generation of possible solutions.

The history of evolutionary programming actually goes back to the creation of computers. In 1949, John von Neumann asked what levels of organizational complexity were necessary for self-replication. John von Neumann's goal according to Burks (1971) was:

> ... not trying to simulate the self-reproduction of a natural system at the level of genetics or biochemistry. He wished to abstract from the natural self-reproduction problem its logical form.

Chapter 6 goes further into the genetic and emergent approaches to AI. We demonstrate several simple problems solved by genetic algorithms, consider genetic programming, and see examples from *artificial life*, or *a-life*, research.

The final theme for contemporary AI is the probabilistic, often referred to as the stochastic, approach to model building. In the mid-eighteenth century, a Church of England clergyman, Thomas Bayes (1763), proposed a formula for relating information already learned, the *prior*, to data newly observed, the *posterior*. As we see in detail in Chap. 8, Bayes' theorem can be seen as a computational implementation of Kant's schemata. Because of complexity issues, the computation of full Bayesian relationships can be prohibitive in many situations, where there are multiple hypotheses and large amounts of supporting data. Nonetheless, Bayes' theorem was used in several early expert systems, for example, in searching for mineral deposits and in diagnostic systems for internal medicine.

Judea Pearl's 1988 book, *Probabilistic Reasoning in Intelligent Systems: Networks of Plausible Inference*, introduced the *Bayesian belief network*, or *BBN*, technology. The BBN is a reasoning graph with the assumptions that the network is directed, reflecting causal relationships, and acyclic, with no loops, i.e., no nodes with links back to themselves. With the creation of the BBN, several computationally efficient algorithms became available for reasoning. To describe events over time, *dynamic Bayesian networks*, or *DBNs*, offer a representation able to characterize how complex systems can be modeled and understood as they change. Pearl (2000) also wrote *Causality: Models, Reasoning, and Inference*, in which his *do-calculus* offered a mathematical framework for building models in which this network-based representation supported reasoning about possible causal relationships or "what if" scenarios. For his research in probabilistic reasoning, Judea Pearl received the Association for Computing Machinery's Turing Award in 2011.

The stochastic approach is used extensively in machine learning and robotics. It is especially important for human language processing, leading to important results in computer-based speech and written language understanding. In Chaps. 8 and 9, we present both Bayes theorem and Bayesian belief networks. Finally, in Chap. 9, we demonstrate how these stochastic representations and reasoning schemes are sufficient to capture critical components of human perception and reasoning.

3.7 In Summary

It is difficult to fully define the artificial intelligence project. The general goal that AI strives toward might be described as the task of shedding light on the nature and use of human intelligence by creating artifacts and processes that reflect that intelligence. It seems futile, and perhaps wrongheaded, to limit what might be called AI.

Artificial intelligence's products are increasingly part of the human landscape. One important, if often overlooked, contribution is to modern computer science. As we have seen, many of the insights and goals of the Dartmouth workshop of 1956, as they have evolved and continue to generate new technology, are now studied as core components of modern computing. In recognition of this, two of the 1956 Dartmouth Summer Workshop contributors, Marvin Minsky in 1969 and John McCarthy in 1971, were awarded the prestigious ACM Turing Award. Finally, the emergence of research in cognitive science can be seen as an important outgrowth of research in cognitive psychology supported by the methods, tools, and models developed by the AI community.

Part II presents further detail and examples of modern AI. In Chap. 4, we consider the symbol-based approach to artificial intelligence. We see in symbol-based systems an implicit rationalist perspective that helps explain the strengths and limitations of this first-generation approach to AI. In Chap. 5, we present neural, or connectionist networks. In Chap. 6, we describe genetic algorithms, genetic programming, and artificial life.

Further Thoughts and Readings There are a number of articles, with full publication details found in the Bibliography, that further describe the three successful AI research projects mentioned at the beginning of the chapter. These include:

Hsu, Feng-hsiung (2002): "Behind Deep Blue: Building the Computer that Defeated the World Chess Champion."
Ferrucci, D., et al. (2010): "Building Watson: An Overview of the DeepQA Project."
Silver, D. S., et al. (2017): "Mastering the Game of Go without Human Knowledge."

The original proposal for the Dartmouth 1956 Summer Workshop is here: url 3.1. Two books containing early research papers from the AI community:

Feigenbaum, E. and Feldman, J. editors, (1963): *Computers and Thought.*
Luger, G., editor, (1995): *Computation and Intelligence: Collected Readings.*

The 1975 Turing Award address by Newell and Simon:

Newell, A. and Simon, H.A. (1976): "Computer Science as Empirical Inquiry: Symbols and Search."

This two-volume series began the major breakthrough in neural net research in the late1980s:

Rumelhart, D.E., McClelland, J.L., and The PDP Research Group (1986a). *Parallel Distributed Processing.*

Three books demonstrating Piaget's developmental stages and the cognitive science community's response:

Piaget, J. (1970): *Structuralism.*
Klahr, D., Langley, P., and Neches, R, editors, (1987): *Production System Models of Learning and Development.*
Drescher, G.L., (1991): *Made-Up Minds: A Constructivist Approach to Artificial Intelligence*

Finally, further references for the histories of AI and Cognitive Science are:

McCorduck, P. (2004): *Machines Who Think.*
Boden, M. (2006): *Mind as Machine: A History of Cognitive Science.*

The figures of this chapter were created for my own teaching requirements at the University of New Mexico (UNM). Several were used in my AI and Cognitive Science books.

Part II
Modern AI: Structures and Strategies for Complex Problem-Solving

Part II, Chapters 4, 5, and 6, introduces three of the four main paradigms supporting research and development in the artificial intelligence community over the past 60-plus years: the symbol-based, the neural network or connectionist, and the genetic or emergent. In each of these chapters, we present introductory-level examples and describe their applications. These sample programs are included to demonstrate the different representational approaches to AI. We also describe several of the more recent research and advanced projects in these areas. We end each chapter by critiquing the strengths and the limitations of that paradigm.

Chapter 4
Symbol-Based AI and Its Rationalist Presuppositions

Two roads diverged in a yellow wood
And sorry I could not travel both
And be one traveler, long I stood
And looked down one as far as I could
To where it bent in the undergrowth;
Then took the other...
     —ROBERT FROST, *"The Road Not Taken"*

I been searchin'...Searchin' ... Oh yeah,
Searchin' every which-a-way...
     —LIEBER AND STOLLER

Contents

In the next three chapters, Part II, we describe a number of approaches specific to AI problem-solving and consider how they reflect the rationalist, empiricist, and pragmatic philosophical positions. In this chapter, we consider artificial intelligence tools and techniques that can be critiqued from a rationalist perspective.

© Springer Nature Switzerland AG 2021
G. F. Luger, *Knowing our World*, https://doi.org/10.1007/978-3-030-71873-2_4

4.1 The Rationalist Worldview: State-Space Search

A *rationalist* worldview can be described as a philosophical position where, in the acquisition and justification of knowledge, there is a bias toward utilization of unaided reason over sense experience (Blackburn 2008). Rene Descartes, as mentioned in Chap. 2, was arguably the most influential rationalist philosopher after Plato, and one of the first thinkers to propose a near axiomatic foundation for his worldview. Leibniz, as also noted, was committed to a similar perspective.

Descartes' mind/body dualism was an excellent basis for his later creation of logic systems, including an *analytic geometry*, where mathematical relationships could provide the constraints for describing the physical world. It was a natural further step for Newton to model the orbits of planets in the language of elliptical relationships determined by distances, masses, and velocities. Descartes' clear and distinct ideas themselves became the *sine qua non* for understanding and describing "the real." His physical, *res extensa*, and nonphysical, *res cogitans*, dualism supports the body/soul or mind/matter biases of much of modern life, literature, and religion. (How else can *the spirit is willing, but the flesh is weak* be understood?)

Most early work in artificial intelligence can be described as a search through the "states" of a problem using well-defined rules to change states. This approach is sometimes referred to as *GOFAI*, or *good old-fashioned AI*. State-space search in AI began in the 1940s and 1950s and continues to the present. Its most important years were between 1955 and the release of the *Parallel Distributed Processing* volumes of McClelland & Rumelhart in 1986. State-space work in AI still remains very successful, e.g., IBM's Deep Blue, Sect. 3.1.1, and with other examples we see later in this chapter.

4.1.1 Graph Theory: The Origins of the State Space

At the core of state-space search is graph theory: the ability to represent problem situations and solutions as paths through the states of a graph. To make these ideas clearer, we consider graph theory and its use in representing problems.

A graph consists of a set of *nodes* and a set of *arcs* or *links* connecting pairs of these nodes. In the state-space model of problem-solving, the nodes of a graph are taken to represent discrete *states* in a problem-solving process, such as the results of applying logic rules or a player's legal moves on a game board. The arcs of the graph represent the transitions between states. In expert systems, states describe the knowledge of a problem situation at some stage of a reasoning process. Expert knowledge, often in the form of *if ... then* rules, supports the generation of new information and the act of applying that rule is represented as an arc between states of knowledge about the problem, as we see in Sect. 4.1.3.

Graph theory is often the best tool for reasoning about objects or situations and their relationships with each other. As first noted in Sect. 2.9, in the early eighteenth century the Swiss mathematician Leonhard Euler created graph theory in his effort to address the *Bridges of Königsberg* problem. The city of Königsberg occupied both banks and two islands of the Pregel river. Seven bridges connected the islands and the two riverbanks of the city, as shown in Fig. 4.1.

The bridges of Königsberg problem asks if it is possible to walk through all parts of the city while crossing each bridge exactly once. Although the residents had failed to find such a walk and doubted that it was possible, no one was able to prove its impossibility. Devising an early form of *graph theory*, Euler created an alternative representation for the physical map, presented in Fig. 4.2. The riverbanks (rb1 and rb2) and islands (i1 and i2) are described by the nodes of a graph; the seven bridges are represented by labeled arcs between the nodes (b1, b2, …, b7). The graph representation preserves the essential structure of the city and its bridges while ignoring extraneous features such as bridge lengths, city distances, and the order of bridges in the walk.

In showing that the walk was impossible, Euler focused on the *degree* of the nodes of the graph, observing that a node could have either an *even* or *odd* degree. An *even* degree node had an even number of arcs joining it to neighboring nodes, while an *odd* degree node had an odd number. With the exception of the beginning and ending nodes of the walk, the journey would have to leave each node exactly as many times as it entered that node. Thus, nodes of odd degree could be used only as the beginning or ending of the walk because these nodes could be crossed only a certain number of times before they proved to be a dead end, where the traveler could not exit the node without using a previously traveled arc.

Euler noted that unless a graph contained either zero or two nodes of odd degree, the walk was impossible. If there were two odd-degree nodes, the walk could start at the first and end at the second; if there were no nodes of odd degree, the walk could begin and end at the same node. The walk is not possible for graphs with more

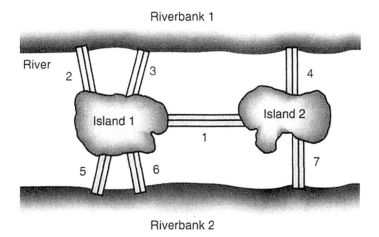

Fig. 4.1 The City of Königsberg with its seven bridges on the Pregel river

Fig. 4.2 A graph
representing the city of
Königsberg and its seven
bridges

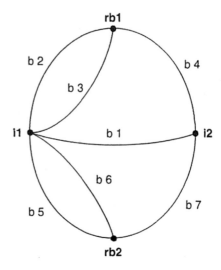

than two nodes of odd degree, as is the case with the city of Königsberg, where all
the nodes are odd. This problem is now called finding an *Euler path* through a
graph. A related problem, called finding an *Euler circuit*, requires the Euler path to
begin and end at the same location.

To summarize, a *graph* is a set of *nodes* or *states* and a set of *arcs* that connect
the nodes. A *labeled* graph has one or more descriptors (labels) attached to each
node that distinguish that node from any other node in the graph. A graph is *directed*
if arcs have an associated direction, as in selecting a move to change the state of a
game. The arcs in a directed graph are usually drawn with arrowheads to indicate
the direction of movement. Arcs that can be crossed in either direction may have
two arrowheads attached but more often have no direction indicators at all. Figure 4.2
is an example of a labeled graph where arcs can be crossed in either direction. A
path in a graph links a sequence of nodes through their connecting arcs. The path is
described by the list of the nodes in the order they occur in the path.

4.1.2   Searching the State Space

In a *state-space graph*, the node descriptors identify states in the problem-solving
process. We saw the state space of the tic-tac-toe problem in Fig. 1.7. Once the state-
space graph for a problem is created, the question arises of how to search that space
looking for possible solutions. There are a number of ways to search and we next
describe three. For full detail on these graph search strategies, see Luger (2009b,
Sect. 3.2.3).

The first search, called *left-to-right backtrack,* selects the first option, the left-
most state leaving the top state, A, of the graph; see Fig. 4.3. This left-most option
is B. Continuing, the search selects the left-most option from B, namely, E. Only

after a dead end, state H in Fig. 4.3 with no new states to visit, does the search go back to the most recently visited state and looks for its left-most alternative; in this example, state I. Since I is also a dead end, the search backtracks until it finds state F and proceeds from there. This procedure, going as deep as possible and then backing up when a dead end is encountered, will eventually, depending on complexity issues and keeping track of the already visited states, search the entire graph. In Fig. 4.3, the numbers next to each state indicate the order in which that state is visited.

The second search, *left-to-right depth-first search*, is similar to backtrack except that two lists of states are used to organize the search. The Open list records all the possible next states, with the left-most state on the list considered next. The Closed list contains states already visited. Depth-first search, see Fig. 4.4, considers all the possible next states from the start state A and places them in order, B C D, on the Open list. Depth-first search then selects the left-most state, B, and leaves the non-selected states C and D on Open. Continuing, depth-first takes the left-most of state B's options, in this case only, F, and puts the remaining states on the left end of Open: E F C D. The search continues, and after five iterations of depth-first search, Fig. 4.4 shows the Open and Closed lists.

The third strategy, called *breadth-first search*, Fig. 4.5, again uses the Open and Closed lists, this time placing the nonselected states, in order, at the right end of Open. Breadth-first search takes the first state A and looks at all of its next states, B, C, and D, putting them in that order on Open. Breath-first then takes the left-most state on Open, B, and considers its next states, only F, placing F at the *right end* of Open. Breadth-first search then selects the left-most state on Open, C, and puts all its possible next states, G and H in order, on the right end of Open. The search continues in this fashion until a solution is found or the entire graph is searched. Breadth-first search, although it can be computationally expensive, guarantees finding the shortest solution path, if a solution exists, and if all visited states are recorded to prevent cycles in the search. Figure 4.5 shows this search.

Fig. 4.3 Backtrack search. The numbers next to each state indicate the order in which that state is considered

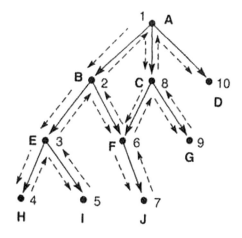

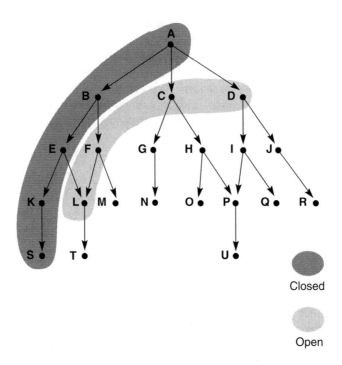

Fig. 4.4 The first five states of depth-first search. The order of states already visited, the Closed list, is: A B E K S, with S a dead end; L F C D are on Open

There are two components required for successful depth-first and breadth-first search. First, as noted above, is to keep track of every state visited so that later it can be eliminated as a possible next state. The second concern is complexity: the size of the graph to be searched determines how long it will take, and whether it is even possible to search the full space. Chess and Go, for example, have state space sizes that, as noted earlier, can never be exhaustively searched.

Best-first or *heuristic search* takes the "best" next state from each state considered in the state-space graph. Consider, for example, the game of tic-tac-toe, Fig. 1.7. The costs for an exhaustive search for tic-tac-toe are high but not insurmountable. Each of the nine first moves has eight possible continuations, which in turn have seven continuations, and so on through all possible board placements. Thus, the total number of states for exhaustive search as $9 \times 8 \times 7 \times \cdots \times 1$ or 9!, called 9 *factorial*, which is 362,880 paths.

Symmetry reduction decreases this search space. Many problem configurations are actually equivalent under symmetric operations of the game board. Using state symmetry, there are not nine possible first moves but actually three: move to a corner, to the center of a side, or to the center of the grid. The use of symmetry on the second level further reduces the number of paths through the space to $12 \times 7!$, as seen in Fig. 4.6. Symmetries such as this may be described as invariants, and when they exist, they can be used to reduce the search.

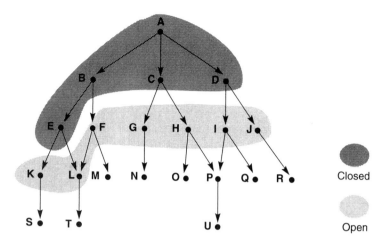

Fig. 4.5 Breadth-first search after five iterations. The order of the first five states visited, the Closed list, is: A B C D E and then F G H I J K L make up the Open list

A best-first search *heuristic* can, in the tic-tac-toe example, eliminate search almost entirely. If you are first move and play x, plan to go to the state in which x has the most possible winning opportunities. The first three states in the tic-tac-toe game are measured in Fig. 4.7. The best-first algorithm selects and moves to the state with the highest number of opportunities. In the case of states with equal numbers of potential wins, take the first such state found. In our example, x takes the center of the grid. Note that not only are the other two alternatives eliminated but so will be all their descendants. Two-thirds of the full space is pruned away with the very first move, as seen in Fig. 4.8.

After the first move, the opponent, o, can choose either of the two moves as seen in Fig. 4.8. Whichever state is chosen, the "most winning opportunities" heuristic is applied again to select among the possible next moves. As search continues, each move evaluates the children of a single node. Figure 4.8 shows the reduced search after three steps in the game, where each state is marked with its "most wins" value. It can be seen that for the first two moves of the x player, only seven states are considered, considerably less than the 72 considered in the exhaustive search. For the full game, "most possible wins" search has even larger savings when compared to exhaustive search.

Traditional approaches to making plans for a robot's actions offer another example of using the state-space technology. Sets of descriptions, often given by logic-based specifications, are used to characterize possible states of the world. An automated reasoning system is then often used to decide which next state to take. Suppose we have a robot arm that is asked to move blocks around on a table. Consider the state space of Fig. 4.9. The start state is described by the nine specifications: ontable(a), ontable(c), ontable(d), on(b,a), on (e,d), cleartop(b), cleartop(c), cleartop(e), and gripping(), indicating the robot arm is not holding any block.

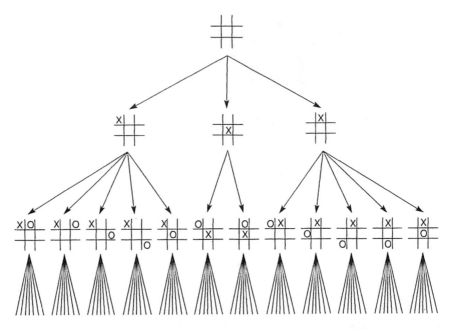

Fig. 4.6 The first three moves in the tic-tac-toe game where the state space is reduced by symmetry

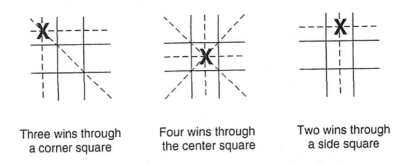

| Three wins through | Four wins through | Two wins through |
| a corner square | the center square | a side square |

Fig. 4.7 The "most wins" strategy applied to the first moves in tic-tac-toe

Suppose that the goal of the robot's task is to create a stack of blocks with block e on the table along with blocks d, c, and b and block a on the top of block e. That goal state can be described by the logic specifications: ontable(e), on(d,e), on(c,d), on(b,c), on(a,b), and gripping(). The search space would start as shown in Fig. 4.9, with the operators changing the states of the system until the goal state is found. The operators would have rules such as: to pick up a block, first remove any blocks stacked on top of it. For example, to pick up block d in the start state, block e must first be removed. Creating the ordered set of actions here that can make a goal situation possible is called *planning*. Further, a heuristic that determines which new state has a description closest to the goal's description can

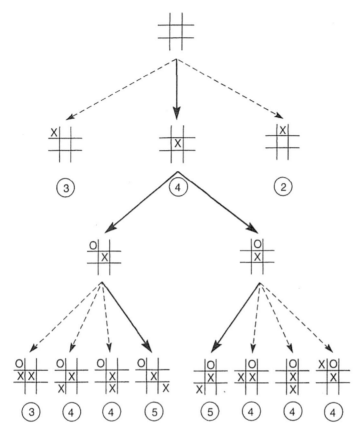

Fig. 4.8 The state space for tic-tac-toe was reduced by using best-first search. The "most wins" strategy is used, with the bold arrows indicating the best moves

radically simplify the search. Full details on how the logic rules are used to create the state space can be found in Luger (Luger 2009b, Sect. 8.4).

The *blocks world* example just described is what AI researchers often call a *toy problem,* designed primarily to demonstrate how planning should work in more difficult situations. This state-space planning technology does scale up for many more complex challenges. An example is the design of the controls for Livingstone, NASA's deep-space vehicle; different "states" of the propulsion system are presented in Fig. 4.10.

Williams and Nayak (1996, 1997) created a model of the propulsion system for the space vehicle and a set of logic-based reasoning rules to address possible adverse situations, such as a blocked valve or a disabled thruster. The spacecraft's computer controller will address these failings by changing the state of the propulsion system. As seen in Fig. 4.10, different control operations can take the space vehicle to different states of the thrusters.

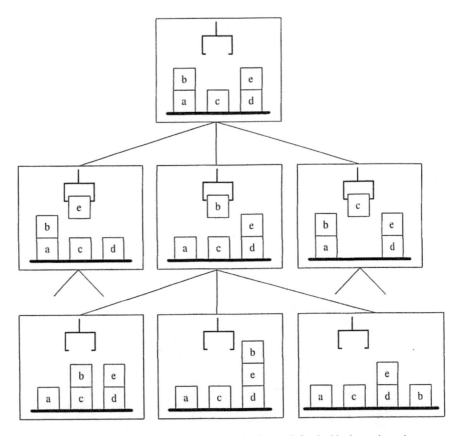

Fig. 4.9 The "start" state and possible next moves in the graph for the block-moving robot arm

The Williams and Nayak (1996, 1997) models for controlling deep-space vehicles were successful. This type of program might not be expected to operate well, however, in a world of constantly changing and less predictable states, such as that of a robot in unexpected situations or the constraints seen with self-driving cars (Brooks 1986, 1991; Thrun et al. 2007; Russell 2019).

4.1.3 An Example of State-Space Search: The Expert System

A final example of state-space problem-solving is the rule-based expert system. Production system problem-solving, described in Sects. 1.2.2 and 3.5, is an often-used architecture for rule-based expert systems. Newell and Simon developed the production system to model human performance in problem-solving, Sect. 3.5. Edward Feigenbaum, Herb Simon's PhD student at CMU, joined the faculty at Stanford University in 1965 as one of the founders of the Computer Science

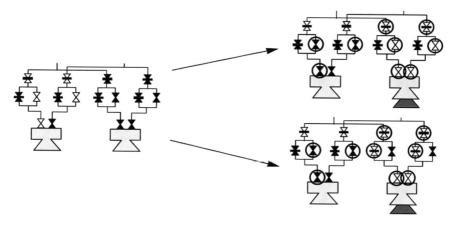

Fig. 4.10 The configuration of the propulsion system and possible next states dependent on the logic-based decision rules. The circled valves are opened/closed to produce the possible next states. This figure adapted from Williams and Nayak (1996)

Department. Feigenbaum led the development of early expert systems, including MYCIN for the diagnosis of meningitis and DENDRAL for the discovery of structure in chemical compounds. For this pioneering work, Ed Feigenbaum is considered the "Father of Expert Systems" and was awarded the ACM Turing award in 1994.

In the production system, Fig. 4.11, the knowledge base is represented as a set of *if… then …* rules. The premises of the rules, the *if* portion, corresponds to the condition, and the conclusion, the *then* portion, corresponds to a goal or action to be taken. Situation-specific data are kept in the working memory. The recognize-act cycle of the production system is either data-driven or goal-driven as we see next.

Many problem situations lend themselves to what is called *forward* or *data-driven* search. In an interpretation problem, for example, the data for the problem are initially given. It is the task of the program to determine the best hypothesis to explain the data. This suggests a forward reasoning process, where the facts are placed in working memory and the system then searches, using its if … then … rules, for possible next states in the process of determining a best possible solution.

In a *goal-driven* expert system, the problem's goal description is placed in working memory. The program then finds an if … then … rule whose *conclusion* matches that goal and places its *premises* in working memory. This action corresponds to working back from the problem's goal to supporting subgoals. The process continues in the next iteration, with these sub-goals becoming the new goals to match against the rules' conclusions. This process continues until sufficient subgoals in working memory are found to be true, indicating that the original goal has been satisfied.

In an expert system, if a rule's premises cannot be determined to be true by given facts or using rules in the knowledge base, it is common to ask the human user for help. Some expert systems specify certain subgoals that are to be solved by the user. Others simply ask the user about any subgoals that fail to match rules in the knowledge base.

Fig. 4.11 The production system at the start of the automobile diagnosis example, with the goal *what is the problem* in working memory

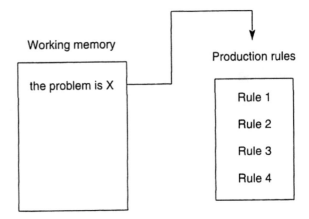

Consider an example of a goal-driven expert system with user queries when no rule conclusion is matched. This is not a full diagnostic system, as it contains only four simple rules for the analysis of automotive problems. It is intended to demonstrate the search of the goal-driven expert system, the integration of new data, and the use of explanation facilities. Consider the rules:

Rule 1:
   If
       the engine is getting gas, and
       the engine will turn over,
   then
       the problem is spark plugs.
Rule 2:
   if
       the engine does not turn over, and
       the lights do not come onthen
       the problem is battery or cables.
Rule 3:
   if
       the engine does not turn over, and
       the lights do come onthen
       the problem is the starter motor.
Rule 4:
   if
       there is gas in the fuel tank, and
       there is gas in the carburetor
   then
       the engine is getting gas.

To begin, in goal-driven mode, the top-level goal of determining the problem with the vehicle must match the then component of a rule. To do this, "the problem is X" is put as a pattern in working memory, as seen in Fig. 4.11. X is a variable that can match with any phrase, as an example, X can be the problem is battery or cables; variable X will be linked to the solution when the problem is solved.

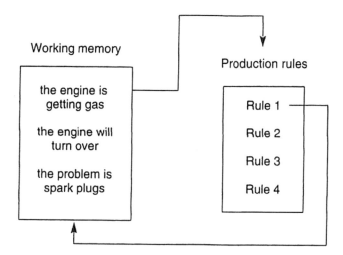

Fig. 4.12 The state of the production system after Rule 1 is used

Three rules match this expression in working memory: Rule 1, Rule 2, and Rule 3. If we resolve this rule conflict in favor of the first rule found, then Rule 1 is used. This causes X to be bound to the value spark plugs, and the premises of Rule 1 are placed in the working memory as in Fig. 4.12. The program has thus chosen to explore the possible hypothesis that the spark plugs are bad.

Another view is that the program has selected one or branch in an *and/or graph*. An and/or graph is a graph where some links between states are "or" transitions and the system can go to either one state or the other. The "and" transitions, connected by an arc as seen in Fig. 4.14, indicate that all anded transitions must be followed. The and/or graph reflects the "and," and the "or" of the if/then logic rule representations as can be seen for the four diagnostic rules presented earlier.

Note that there are two premises to rule 1, both of which must be satisfied to prove the conclusion true. These premises are the "and" branches of the search graph of Fig. 4.14. This represents the decomposition of the problem: to find whether the problem is spark plugs solve two subproblems, that is, find whether the engine is getting gas and whether the engine will turn over. The system then uses Rule 4, whose conclusion matches the engine is getting gas. This causes Rule 4's premises to be placed at the top of the working memory, as in Fig. 4.13.

At this point, there are three entries in working memory that do not match with any rule conclusions. The expert system will, in this situation, ask the user directly about these three subgoals. If the user confirms that all three of these are true, the expert system will have successfully determined that the car will not start because the problem is the spark plugs. In finding this solution, the system has searched the leftmost branch of the and/or graph of Fig. 4.14.

This is, of course, a very simple example. Not only is its automotive knowledge limited at best, but it also ignores a number of important aspects of actual implementations including that the rules are phrased in English rather than in a computer

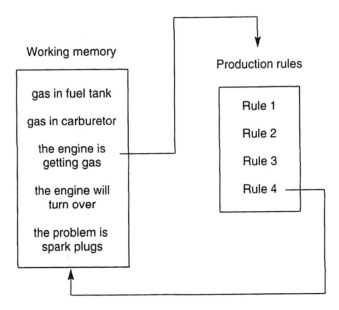

Fig. 4.13 The state of the production system after Rule 4 is used. Note that the newest results are placed on the top of older information in working memory

language. On finding a solution, an actual expert system will tell the user its diagnosis, although our example simply stops. If it had failed to determine that the spark plugs were bad, our expert system would have needed to back up to the top level and try Rule 2 next. Despite its simplicity, however, this example underscores the importance of production system-based search and its representation by the and/or graph as a foundation for expert system technology.

An important advantage of this expert system technology is its transparency in reasoning. First, all the rules are considered independent of each other, so in debugging an expert system, rules can simply be removed and replaced by "better" rules. This is an important example of the iterative refinement process mentioned in Chap. 1: when the program produces results that are "wrong" in some sense, replace them with better rules. The designer corrects his or her understanding of a problem by continuous improvement in the rules that generate solutions.

A second advantage of the expert system is the transparency of the reasoning process. For example, suppose the automotive expert system has an explanation facility, and assume that the consultation has reached the stage represented by the working memory configuration in Fig. 4.13. The dialogue begins by asking the user about the goals in working memory. User responses are in bold type.

gas in fuel tank?
yes
gas in carburetor?
yes
engine will turn over?
why

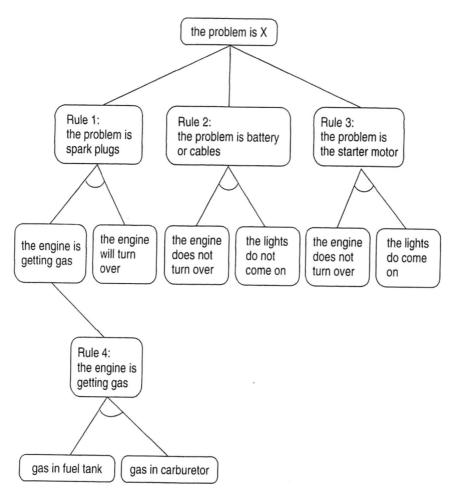

Fig. 4.14 The and/or graph that the expert system searches in determining that the problem is with the spark plugs. The "and" constraints are linked by an arc

Here the user enters a "why" query, i.e., the user asks: "why do you want to know whether the engine will turn over?" The system responds with a literal presentation of the rule under question:

It has been established that:
  the engine is getting gas,
  therefore if
  the engine will turn over,
  then the problem is spark plugs.

Because the user answered "yes" to the first two questions, Rule 4 is satisfied, verifying the first premise of Rule 1. When the "why" query was made, the system was trying to solve the second premise of Rule 1. Note that the explanation for the system's behavior is simply a restatement of the current rule under consideration, as this offers an explanation for why the program wants to know whether the engine will turn over. In the response to the "why" query, the system states that it has concluded that the engine is getting gas.

Suppose the user then asks:

how the engine is getting gas

The system will respond to "how" it concluded that the engine is getting gas. The response is a trace of the reasoning that led to this conclusion, working back from the goal along the rules that support it to the user responses:

```
This follows from rule 4:
    if
        gas in fuel tank, and
        gas in carburetor
    then
        engine is getting gas     gas in fuel tank was given by the user
        gas in carburetor was given by the user
```

Once again, the production system architecture provides an essential basis for these explanations. Each cycle of the control loop selects and uses another rule. The program may be stopped after each cycle and inspected. Because each rule represents a complete chunk of problem-solving knowledge, the current rule provides a context for the explanation. To summarize, the expert system answers "why" queries by showing the current rule that it is attempting to use; it answers "how" queries by showing the user the reasoning that led to that goal or subgoal.

We have just presented several examples using the symbol system approach to building AI programs. In the next section, we summarize further important examples of this technology. In Sect. 4.3, we critique the symbol-based approach, discussing its strengths and limitations from an epistemic perspective.

4.2 Symbol-Based AI: Continuing Important Contributions

Graphs, search, heuristics, and knowledge encoded in rules are all components of the symbol-based approach to AI. This technology of explicitly representing knowledge continues to be successful when addressing new challenges. In this section, we describe several AI programs indicative of the promising future for symbol-based AI.

Galileo's tool was his telescope. Without it, he was unable to see images of the planets, the moons of planets, and characterize their relationships. To the twenty-first century scientist, the computer offers such a supporting visualization tool. In our case, besides "seeing" previously unseen objects as Galileo did, we can also understand previously unrecognized relationships in large amounts of data, for example, patterns in DNA that are related to disease states.

A major tool for pattern recognition and analysis is the creation of machine learning algorithms. These techniques are made feasible with the speeds offered by modern computing and the storage afforded by the "cloud" and server farms. As an example, consider a relatively recent journal article by Marechal (2008) with keywords: chemogenomics, bioinformatics, biomarker, chemical genetics, cheminformatics, and machine learning. The article explores the interactions between functioning biological systems with the injection of molecular-level chemical agents. Computing enables this research with useful patterns identified using machine learning.

Many AI machine-learning algorithms are symbol-based, and we next describe a subset of these. We consider association-based or deep learning algorithms, in Chap. 5, and probabilistic learning in Chaps. 8 and 9. Symbol-based learning is built on the assumption that patterns in data can be described and can be explicitly represented and searched. Examples include the inductive building of decision trees, data classifiers, pattern recognition and identification, template-based learning, and more.

4.2.1 Machine Learning: Data Mining

One of the huge success stories of symbol-based AI, which also can present a distressing threat to human privacy and choice, is data mining technology. Decision tree analysis programs, such as ID3 (Quinlan 1986), are used on large sets of human data. The analysis of purchasing patterns, for example, is often used to predict a person's future needs and choices. We next demonstrate the ID3 algorithm analysis of a small sample of data.

Suppose a bank or department store wants to analyze the credit risk for new customer applications whose annual income is $50,000 or below. To proceed, the bank or store considers earlier records of customers in this same income group. It asks the new group of applicants for financial details to support their credit applications. The goal of the ID3 algorithm is to build up a profile of known customers' data in order to determine the risk for new customers that want credit. As an example, Table 4.1 presents the data of 14 earlier customers.

Table 4.1 The data of 14 lower income people that have already applied for credit

NO.	RISK	CREDIT HISTORY	DEBT	COLLATERAL	INCOME
1.	High	Bad	High	None	$0 to $15k
2.	High	Unknown	High	None	$15 to $35k
3.	Moderate	Unknown	Low	None	$15 to $35k
4.	High	Unknown	Low	None	$0 to $15k
5.	Low	Unknown	Low	None	Over $35k
6.	Low	Unknown	Low	Adequate	Over $35k
7.	High	Bad	Low	None	$0 to $15k

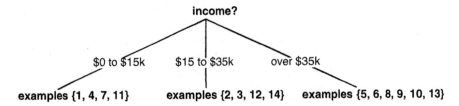

Fig. 4.15 The partial decision tree built using the INCOME factor. The example numbers at the end of each branch refer to the data of Table 4.1

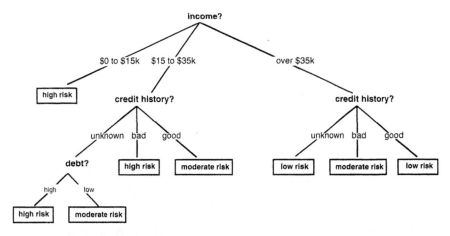

Fig. 4.16 The final decision tree produced from the data of Table 4.1 that is to be used for assessing the credit risk of new lower income customers

In Figs. 4.15 and 4.16, ID3 uses information theory (Shannon 1948) to build a decision tree that analyses the previous customers' data to determine credit RISK. The algorithm, using Shannon's formula, considers each of the four information sources, CREDIT HISTORY, DEBT, COLLATERAL, and INCOME, to determine which piece of information best divides the population in the question of credit RISK. INCOME does this best, see the partial decision tree of Fig. 4.15.

Since the group in the left-most branch of Fig. 4.15 all have high-risk credit, that part of the search is finished: If you make $15,000 or less in income, your credit rating is high RISK. The algorithm then considers the group on the middle branch to see which factor divides these people best for credit RISK and that factor is CREDIT HISTORY. The search continues until the decision tree of Fig. 4.16 is produced. Note that in Fig. 4.16 the COLLATERAL factor is not important. This helps minimize the amount of information needed for analysis of new customers in this group applying for credit: their amount of COLLATERAL is not useful for determining RISK. Full details of this algorithm are available (Luger 2009b, Sect. 10.3.2).

What we have just demonstrated is a very simple example of an important and powerful machine learning algorithm. This technology is now ubiquitous, used everywhere from your local department store when you use personal identification to apply for credit, to utilizing personal data from social media. Data from social media are easy to collect, as people describe their recent purchases, their likes and dislikes, and often political choices. Internet trolls also propose questionnaires and surveys to obtain information that they then use for purposes usually not disclosed to the user.

What does technology such as ID3 and other classifier algorithms say about individuals? It is important to understand that these classifiers say nothing deterministic about a particular individual. They do suggest what people in different groupings or classes tend to do. A particular person earning under $15,000 may, in fact, be an excellent credit risk; what the algorithm says is that this general group of earners tends not to be a good risk.

To address this uncertainty issue, many approaches to machine learning contain "confidence" or "likelihood" measures such as the *Stanford certainty factor algebra* used with MYCIN (Buchanan and Shortliffe 1984) and a number of early expert systems. This confidence measure offers support for heuristic search, for instance, examining most likely answers before all other possible answers are considered.

We see more certainty measures in later chapters: weighting values in connectionist networks, Chap. 5, and probability measures in Bayesian systems, Chap. 8. A large percentage of current machine learning algorithms are a combination of symbol-based, deep learning, and probabilistic systems.

4.2.2 Modeling the Physical Environment

Although the ID3 and other machine learning algorithms captured relational information "hidden" within collections of data, other symbol-based AI algorithms were designed to represent aspects of physical reality itself. Prospector (Duda et al. 1979) was created at SRI International as a consultation system for mineral exploration. The knowledge built into the program was a network of inference rules in the form of a production system that captured geologic information related to the discovery of minerals.

Prospector's rules represented the diagnostic skills of mineral exploration experts. It was intended to help the geologist identify the physical characteristics of a particular site that would correlate with the presence of mineral deposits. It was claimed to have predicted the existence of a previously unknown deposit of molybdenum in Washington State (Duda et al. 1979). Prospector's knowledge base was extensible in that it could be continually improved as its designers added new knowledge for other minerals.

Herb Simon, Pat Langley, and colleagues at Carnegie Mellon University (Bradshaw et al. 1983; Langley et al. 1987b) created the BACON programs, named after Francis Bacon the sixteenth-century philosopher and scientist. The goal of this

Table 4.2 The observations of planetary data and Bacon's discovery of D^3/P^2

Planet	D	P	D/P	D^2/P	D^3/P^2
Mercury	0.382	0.241	1.607	0.622	1.0
Venus	0.724	0.616	1.175	0.852	1.0
Earth	1.0	1.0	1.0	1.0	1.0
Mars	1.524	1.881	0.810	1.234	1.0
Jupiter	5.199	11.855	0.439	2.280	1.0
Saturn	0.539	29.459	0.324	3.088	1.0

This is the approximation of the relationship between a planet's distance from the sun, D, and its orbital period, P. Table is adapted from Langley et al. (1987b)

project was to build a program that could discover the mathematical laws, based on observed data, that describe the motions of the planets.

The BACON task was to discover the functional relationship existing between pairs, or within sets, of numbers. In pairs of numbers, is it possible to describe one number as some mathematical function of the other? As an example, taken from the BACON research (Langley et al. 1987b), consider observers finding data describing planetary motion; Table 4.2 shows an example of this. The second column, **D**, shows the distance in astronomical units of each planet in column 1 from the sun. The third column, **P**, shows the period, a measure of each planet's orbit. The goal of the BACON project was to discover the functional relationship between **D** and **P**.

The fourth, fifth, and sixth columns of Table 4.2 show the different relationships explored by BACON to capture the distance of a planet from the sun and the time, or period, of its orbit. BACON discovers **D^3/P^2** as the best approximation for this relationship, and this is, in fact, Kepler's third law of planetary motion. BACON's work was extended in further research to discover other laws of physics including Ohm's laws for electric circuits. A number of heuristics used to determine these mathematical relationships are described in Langley et al. (1987b).

The development of AI models for complex physical environments has always been a challenge that has produced many successful results. We presented the Williams and Nayak models for controlling vehicles in deep space in Sect. 4.1. In Chap. 8, we will see symbol-based models combined with probabilistic relationships to control the focus of particle beam accelerators and for monitoring the generation of electric power from sodium-cooled nuclear reactors.

4.2.3   Expertise: Wherever It Is Needed

An early use of symbol-based learning was in medical diagnostics with the recognition and treatment of meningitis with the Stanford Medical School based program, MYCIN (Buchanan and Shortliffe 1984). This early diagnostic system was important both for demonstrating the utility of the rule-based approach but also because its performance was shown to be equal to that of human medical diagnostic experts.

Medical expertise is often needed where there are few medical professionals available. Examples include the analysis of common clinical problems in third-world countries or in any situation where advice is needed for complex medical care delivery. Computer-based recommendation systems are ubiquitous in medical care, including the analysis of allergies, warnings on possible side effects of combining multiple prescriptions, and guidance systems that assist in complex surgeries.

Expert system-based diagnosis and recommendations have moved to almost all areas of medicine. Wearable devices give individual health updates in normal living as well as warning advice in areas of critical health monitoring, such as diabetes. Computer-based medical analysis including supporting lab testing for breast cancer and medical screening for disease states are now so common that they are no longer even seen as the products of artificial intelligence technology.

An important result of the early expert diagnostic programs is the ubiquitous presence of online medical analysis and recommendation systems. These programs include "Symptom Checkers" from WebMD, Isabel Healthcare, NetDoctor, and the Mayo Clinic (url 4.1). Further, there are also online health checkup programs including Symptomate and WebMD. (url 4.1). There are also computer programs for nutrition counseling, lactation services, and psychiatric therapy. One advice website claims that it deals with a medical question every 9 s (url 4.1).

There are many further examples of the use of computer-based diagnostic and recommendation systems. We describe five:

1. Oil well (mudding) advising, where the boring equipment and the compounds inserted at the drilling sites are automatically determined with no need for the presence of the geological/petroleum expert.
2. In automotive diagnosis, most service technicians plug your car into a high-end computer diagnostic system for analysis and recommendations.
3. For hardware and software troubleshooting, advisors, even if they handle simple questions directly, have as backup a computer-based advising system.
4. For complex advice and recommendation situations. As an example, a health insurance company with thousands of pages of different policy options based on age, sex, state of residence, and coverage, can use intelligent retrieval and recommendation programs. Similarly, financial advice and investment programs now assist both customers and financial advisors in finding appropriate options for customers.
5. Computer-based open-ended question answering programs help customers find information about important life choices, for example, answering concerns about joining the US Army (url 4.2).

The delivery of online diagnosis and remediation advice just discussed is but one of many complex technology areas where expert advice is available. Although many of the areas we mention started out as dedicated symbol-based expert systems, their knowledge is now so imbedded in diagnostic equipment and recommendation systems that they are simply seen as important assistive technology.

The current research projects also focus on issues including keeping online customers happy in their communication with automated advisors. How is the conversation going? Are the customers frustrated with the computer-based response system? How can the computer tell when it is best to connect the user with an actual human expert? Addressing such issues helps keep the online customer satisfied (Freeman et al. 2019).

> *Since no organism can cope with infinite diversity, one of the most basic functions of all organisms is the cutting up of the environment into classifications by which non-identical stimuli can be treated as equivalent...*
> —*ELEANOR ROSCH (1978)*

4.3 Strengths and Limitations of the Symbol System Perspective

First-generation AI, or good old-fashioned AI, GOFAI, as several commentators have described it, continues to be successful. Although many critics have called symbol-based AI a failure (Dreyfus 1992; Searle 1980, 1990; Smith 2019), it has performed well in situations appropriate for its use, many of which were presented in this chapter. Perhaps its critics are concerned because the symbol-based approach to AI could not produce *artificial general intelligence,* but this was not the goal of AI engineers.

Through continued use, however, the AI community has come to better understand both the strengths and the limitations of symbol-based AI. In this final section, we consider these issues. First, we note again that abstraction is the general process for creating symbol-based representations and for modeling changing time and rule applications as steps through a graph. Second, we present an issue related to the first point, the generalization problem. Finally, in asking why the AI community has not yet built a system with general intelligence, we discuss issues including symbol grounding, limited semantic transparency, and human intelligence as "embodied."

4.3.1 Symbol-Based Models and Abstraction

The abstractive process is at the core of the explicit symbol system approach to artificial intelligence. Symbols are identified to represent shared properties of multiple objects, structures, or situations. This abstractive process is much like that witnessed in Plato's cave (2008), where individual differences are ignored in the process of seeking pure forms. The symbol-based approach to AI assigns symbols to these abstracted entities and then uses algorithms to reason about their further properties and relationships.

A simple example is presented in Fig. 4.6, where different tic-tac-toe board positions, equivalent by symmetry, are represented by one state and used to create an efficient search for a solution. Another example was seen in Fig. 4.10, where the continuous processes of a vehicle traveling in outer space were abstracted into discrete states of the propulsion system. Changes in that system as time progressed were then represented by state transitions in the graph of possible next states for the propulsion system.

Another sophisticated use of abstraction is seen in the rule-based programs of Figs. 4.11, 4.12, 4.13, and 4.14, where human knowledge in complex environments is captured as a set of if-then rules that can be "run" in a computational environment. There are two issues here: First, can complex human knowledge and skills be represented as sets of pattern-action rules? Second, can the actions of skilled human problem-solving be captured by an organized sequence of applying rules that change "knowledge" states in a graph?

To take the knowledge-based approach to AI seriously, one must question what aspects of human knowledge are amenable to a condition-action reduction. When can the situations for the use of knowledge be represented by the conditions of rules? Is it possible to reduce skilled human action to explicit computational specifications? If human skill is used across time, for example in the improvisations of a talented musician, is this expressible by sequences of rules? Can various sensory modalities, such as the perception-based diagnostic skills of a physician, be reduced to a set of if-then rules?

The question is not whether rule-based-systems work. They have been very successful in a wide variety of applications and are now so commonly used that they are not always seen as part of the AI enterprise. The issue is to examine the edge cases to determine when the abstractions required to characterize complex situations and related actions are optimal for symbol-based representations.

In game playing, it may seem appropriate to describe positions as states of a graph and legal moves as state transitions. However, in creating a winning search strategy, it can be extremely difficult to represent a "sacrifice," where one player intends to lose a board position or piece in order to gain a longer term advantage over an opponent. In the Deep Blue chess program, described in Sect. 3.1.1, it proved necessary to program in higher level search strategies to both produce expert-level chess and to address the complexities of exhaustive search.

The clearest articulation of the symbol-based approach to problem-solving was Newell and Simon's research (1963, 1972, 1976) and their articulation of the physical symbol system hypothesis, presented in Chap. 3. Their production system architecture, augmented by an automated "learning" module called SOAR (Newell 1990), is arguably the closest that symbol-based AI has come to proposing a general "intelligent system." SOAR learns new rule pattern relationships within a problem domain and adds these rules to the current set of productions.

The abstractive process necessary to support symbol-based problem-solving of necessity ignores aspects of reality. This omitted reality can in the long term doom a computational project. Abstraction is, however, as Eleanor Rosch contends in the introductory quote of this section, our only method of coping with infinite diversity.

4.3.2 The Generalization Problem and Overlearning

The *generalization problem* is a crucial component of abstraction. Without an appropriate bias or extensive built-in knowledge, the process of abstraction can be totally misled in its attempt to find appropriate patterns in noisy, sparse, or even bad data. The generalization problem is difficult, important, and remains an open issue in artificial intelligence. Let's consider two classic problems in science.

First, consider Newton's second law of motion, *force* = *mass* × *acceleration*, or $f = m \times a$. In a practical sense, the law says the acceleration of an object is directly related to the force applied to the object and inversely related to its mass. Or alternatively, the more mass a system has, the less acceleration it will have, given a constant amount of applied force. The consistency of Newton's formulation is remarkable, both in our normal lives and in the motions of the planets in space. However, as an object gets accelerated to extreme velocities, as a particle, for example, in a particle beam accelerator, it was discovered that the particle's mass increased. Thus, the $f = m \times a$ generalization is not supported at extreme accelerations.

A second example comes from the discovery by astronomers of perturbations in the orbit of the planet Uranus. Scientists, in light of this new data, did not reject the laws of Newton and Kepler. Rather they used the perturbation data to postulate the existence, and consequent effect, of another body in orbit. Later, of course, the planet Neptune was discovered.

The point of these two examples is that all generalizations must at some time and in particular situations be "accepted" or "affirmed." As we suggest in later chapters, these generalizations are utilized by science and society when they are determined to be useful for some practical purpose. These generalizations may not be useful for other purposes, however, and must be reconsidered for new situations. Finally, as both examples show, when generalizations fail to fit new situations, the science itself is not discarded. Scientists make adjustments to equations or conjecture new relationships between variables. We discuss this methodology further in the concluding chapters.

We next offer an example of trying to determine *appropriate* generalizations. Suppose we are trying to find a functional relationship in two dimensions to describe a set of data collected from experiments. In Fig. 4.17, we present six points from a two-dimensional data set of experiments. To understand the problem of *overlearning*, we wish to discover a function that describes/explains not just these six points but also future data that might be collected from these experiments.

The lines across this set of points in Fig. 4.17 represent functions created to capture this generalization. Remember that once the relation function is determined, we will want to present it with new and not previously seen data points. The first function, f_1, might represent a fairly accurate least mean squares fit to the six data points. With further training, the system might produce function f_2, which seems an even "better" fit to the data. Further exploration produces a function f_3 that exactly fits the

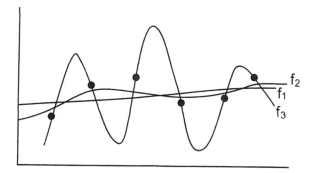

Fig. 4.17 Six data points and three functions that try to capture their two-dimensional relationship

given data but may offer terrible generalizations for further sets of data. This phenomenon is referred to as *overtraining* or *overlearning* a set of data.

One of the strengths of successful machine learning algorithms is that in many application domains they produce effective generalizations, that is, functional approximations that fit the training data well *and also* handle new data adequately. However, identifying the point where an automated learning algorithm passes from an undertrained to an overtrained state is nontrivial.

We conclude this chapter by addressing several further issues relating to symbol selection and the process of abstraction. When AI program designers use representations, whether symbols, nodes of networks, or any other construct for capturing "reality," they are attributing some "meaning" to these constructs. What is the nature of this "meaning" and how does an eventual solution then reflect back on the context that generated it?

4.3.3   Why Are There No Truly Intelligent Symbol-Based Systems?

There are many criticisms that can be leveled at *symbol-based AI* and the *physical symbol system* characterization of intelligence. The most salient criticisms, besides the limitations which abstraction entails, include the issues of semantic meaning or the *grounding* (Harnad 1990) of the symbols that are used by an intelligent program. Attempts to capture "meaning" with search through a pre-interpreted state space and to find "purpose" implicit in the use of heuristics to direct that search offers a questionable epistemic foundation for capturing intelligence. The notion of meaning in traditional AI is, at best, very weak.

Alfred Tarski's *possible world semantics* (1944, 1956) offers one approach to the attribution of meaning. Tarski's "meaning" is a product of formal logic, including the propositional and predicate logics. The goal of his semantics is to demonstrate that when certain conditions are met, logical reasoning rules, such as *modus ponens*, *modus tollens*, *resolution* and others, produce guaranteed correct results.

The possible worlds semantics assigns items from an application domain or possible world to symbols from a set of symbols such as names or numbers. It assigns variables to subsets of the sets of symbols. The results of actions, functions, are mapped to symbols within the set of symbols that reflect the result of these actions. For example, a number of men and women could each be represented by a symbol, such as their name. A variable, for example M, could represent all males in a situation. A function, such as *produce_child(tom, susan, mary)*, could reflect the fact that Tom and Susan produce a child named Mary. Finally, predicate relationships, such as *married (tom, susan)*, will have either *true* or *false* truth-values. With this apparatus in place, Tarski then formulates proofs that various reasoning rules always produce true results, given premises that are true.

Moving toward a more mathematics-based semantics, such as the Tarskian possible worlds approach, seems wrongheaded. It reinforces the rationalist project of replacing the flexible and evolving intelligence of an embodied agent with a world where clear and distinct ideas are always directly accessible and the results of reasoning. Although Tarski's semantics captures well a small and important component of human reasoning, such as the NASA deep-space propulsion engine of Sect. 4.1.3, thinking that this approach generalizes to all reasoning is delusional. Where are the insights of the artist or poet, or what Peirce (1958) calls the *abductive inference* of the trained doctor, determining the *best* explanation for a possible illness, given a particular set of symptoms?

A related issue, the *grounding* of meaning, has forever frustrated both the proponents and the critics of the AI and cognitive science enterprises. The grounding problem asks how particular symbols can be said to *have meaning* (Harnad 1990). Searle (1980) makes just this point in his discussion of the so-called *Chinese Room*. Searle places himself in a room intended for translating Chinese sentences into English. Searle receives a set of Chinese symbols, looks the symbols up in a large Chinese symbol cataloging system, and then reports back the appropriately linked sets of English symbols. Searle claims that although he himself knows absolutely no Chinese, his "system" can be seen as a Chinese-to-English translation machine.

There *is* a problem here. Workers in the research areas of machine translation and natural language understanding have argued that the Searle "translation machine," blindly linking one set of symbols to other symbols, produces minimal quality results. The fact remains, however, that many current intelligent systems have a very limited ability to interpret sets of symbols in a "meaningful" fashion. Would anyone be impressed if his or her computer printed out "I love you?" The problem, as the philosopher John Haugeland (1985, 1997) suggests, is that "computers just don't give a damn."

In fact, computers don't "know" or "do" anything besides producing the product of their program designers' instructions. A program's "recommendation" for medical therapy is simply a set of symbols representing the prior thoughts of its programmer. In itself, the running program understands nothing about medicine, health, illness, or death. It does not even know that it is a program!

In the areas of human language understanding, Lakoff and Johnson (1999) argue that the ability to create, use, exchange, and interpret meaning symbols comes from a human's embodiment within an evolving social context. This context is physical, social, and "right-now"; it supports and enables the human ability to survive, evolve, and reproduce. It makes possible a world of analogical reasoning, the use and appreciation of humor, and the experiences of music and art. Our current generation of symbol-based AI tools and techniques is very far away from being able to encode and utilize any equivalent "meaning" system. We address these issues further in Chap. 7.

As a result of this weak semantic encoding, the traditional AI search/heuristic methodology explores states and contexts of states that are pre-interpreted. This means that an AI program's creator "imputes" or "lays on" to the symbols of the program various contexts of semantic meaning. A direct result of this pre-interpreted encoding is that intelligence-rich tasks, including learning and language, can only produce some computed function of that interpretation. Thus, many AI systems have very limited abilities to evolve new meaning associations as they explore their environments. Even areas of symbol/search-based successes remain brittle, without multiple interpretations, and often have only limited ability to recover from their failures.

4.4   In Summary

Much of the early research in artificial intelligence may be characterized as symbol-based and search-enabled problem-solving. We presented graph theory as the basis of state-space search and described several basic algorithms for searching state-space graphs. The physical symbol system hypothesis of Newell and Simon, discussed in Sect. 3.4, can be seen as a motivation and supporting epistemology for using this approach.

Across its brief history, the artificial intelligence research community has explored the ramifications of the physical symbol system hypothesis and has developed its own challenges to that previously dominant view. As we see in Chaps. 5 and 6, models of computing based on the architecture of the animal brain as well as on the processes of biological evolution can also provide useful frameworks for understanding intelligence. In Chap. 5, we present the association-based tradition in psychology and the artificial intelligence representational response of semantic and connectionist networks. In Chap. 6, we present the genetic, evolutionary, and emergent approaches to representing intelligence.

Further Thoughts and Readings   Complete references for the suggested readings may be found in the Bibliography. Allen Newell and Herbert Simon at Carnegie Mellon University were in many ways the intellectual leaders of the "symbol-system" approach to AI:

Newell, A. and Simon, H.A. (1976). *Computer Science as Empirical Inquiry: Symbols and Search.*
Simon, H.A. (1981). *The Sciences of the Artificial.*
Newell, A. (1990). *Unified Theories of Cognition.*

There were many arguments pro and con over the early symbol-system approach to AI. Two among many of the protagonists are John Searle and John Haugeland. Brian Cantwell Smith offers a more current critique:

Searle, J.R. (1980). *Minds, Brains and Programs.*
Searle, J.R. (1990). *Is the Brain's Mind a Computer Program?*
Haugeland, J. (1985). *Artificial Intelligence: the Very Idea.*
Haugeland, J. ed. (1997). *Mind Design: Philosophy, Psychology, Artificial Intelligence.*
Smith, B.C. (2019). *The Promise of Artificial Intelligence: Reckoning and Judgment.*

Figure 4.11 was adapted from Williams and Nayak (1996). All other figures of this chapter were created for my own teaching requirements at the University of New Mexico. Several were used earlier in my AI and Cognitive Science books.

Programming Support   For those wishing to build computer programs that reflect many of the representations and search algorithms described in this chapter, the textbook *AI Algorithms, Data Structures, and Idioms in Prolog, Lisp, and Java* (Luger 2009b), is available on my website (url 4.3). Programs are presented there in what is called a *shell* form, where representations are proposed, and control algorithms are given. It is left to the programmer to produce the knowledge supporting the search, e.g., the rules of the *Missionaries and Cannibals* problem, and to choose and deploy a control strategy, e.g., heuristic search. There are also several control structures for building planning algorithms, rule-based expert systems, and machine learning programs. The programmer adds the domain knowledge appropriate for the application and can also refine the search strategies.

Chapter 5
Association and Connectionist Approaches to AI

A cat that once sat on a hot stove will never again sit on a hot stove, or on a cold one either...

—*MARK TWAIN*

Everything is vague to a degree you do not realize till you have tried to make it precise...

—*BERTRAND RUSSELL*

Contents

In Chap. 4, we presented symbol-based AI and described many of its successes. We also noted several limitations, including the necessary use of the abstractive process to create symbolic representations. Abstraction identifies and tokenizes, representing with specific symbols, similar objects, and properties. Associationist theories of meaning, following the empiricist tradition in philosophy, define objects in terms of

© Springer Nature Switzerland AG 2021
G. F. Luger, *Knowing our World*, https://doi.org/10.1007/978-3-030-71873-2_5

networks of relations to other objects. When a human perceives an object, it is mapped into a concept. This concept is part of the human's entire knowledge of the world and is connected through appropriate relationships with other concepts. The resulting network constitutes an understanding of the properties and behaviors of objects. Chapter 5 presents this associationist approach to artificial intelligence problem solving.

5.1 The Behaviorist Tradition and Implementation of Semantic Graphs

It was quite natural, historically, that early association-based representation had an explicit symbol-system beginning. Semantic and early neural networks both require fixed symbolic data for input values. Semantic networks also captured semantic associations using explicit symbol-based graph-like links. The reason semantic networks are presented in this chapter is because they were designed explicitly to capture the *meaning relationships* that enable intelligence. Section 5.1 has three parts. The first presents the philosophical and psychological foundations for association-based networks. In the second, we describe the early use of semantic networks. Finally, we present more recent applications of this technology.

5.1.1 Foundations for Graphical Representations of Meaning

Rationalist representations emerged from the efforts of philosophers and mathematicians to characterize the principles of correct reasoning. An alternative line of research comes from the efforts of psychologists, philosophers, neuroscientists, and linguists to describe the nature of human memory and understanding. This approach is concerned with the ways in which humans actually acquire, associate, and utilize knowledge and has proved particularly useful to the AI application areas of natural language understanding and pattern-oriented problem-solving.

Association-based network representations have almost as long a history as has logic. In the third century BCE, the Greek philosopher Porphyry (1887, translation) created tree-based type hierarchies (with their roots at the top!) to describe the relations that would become components of Aristotle's categories. Gottlob Frege (1879), see Sect. 2.9, developed a tree notation for logic expressions. Perhaps the earliest person to have a direct influence on contemporary semantic networks was Charles S. Peirce's system of graphs developed in the nineteenth century (Roberts 1973). Peirce's theory had the power of the predicate calculus, with an axiomatic basis and formal rules for reasoning.

Graphs have long been used in psychology to represent structures of concepts and associations. Selz (1913, 1922) was a pioneer in this work, using graphs to represent concept hierarchies and the inheritance of properties, for example, that all women inherit properties of being human and all humans the properties of mammals. He also developed a theory of schematic anticipation that influenced later AI work in frames and schemata. In more recent AI research, Anderson and Bower (1973), Norman et al. (1975), and others used networks to model human memory and performance.

Associationist theories of meaning, following the empiricist tradition in philosophy, define objects in terms of networks of relations to other objects. When a human perceives an object, it is mapped into a concept. This concept is part of the human's entire knowledge of the world and is connected through appropriate relationships with other concepts. The resulting network constitutes an understanding of the properties and behaviors of objects. For example, through experience, we may associate the concept of snow with cold, white, snowman, slippery, and ice. The generation of statements such as "snow is white" and "the snowman is white" emerge from this network of meaning associations.

There is psychological evidence that, in addition to their ability to associate concepts, humans also organize their knowledge hierarchically, with information kept at appropriate levels within the taxonomy. Collins and Quillian (1969), Fig. 5.1, modeled human information storage and management using a *semantic network*. The structure of this hierarchy was derived from the laboratory testing of human subjects. The subjects were asked questions about different properties of birds, such as, "Is a canary a bird?" or "Can a canary sing?" or "Can a canary fly?"

As obvious as the answers to these questions may seem, reaction time studies indicated that it took longer for subjects to answer, "Can a canary fly?" than to answer, "Can a canary sing?" Collins and Quillian explain this difference by arguing that people store information at its most generally usable level. Instead of trying to recall that canaries fly, robins fly, and swallows fly, the property of flying is stored with the concept "Bird." The test subjects knew that canaries, swallows, and robins are all birds and that birds usually can fly. More general properties such as eating, breathing, and moving are stored at the "Animal" level. Thus, trying to recall whether a canary can breathe should take longer than recalling whether a canary is yellow or can fly. Note also that answering a false sentence, e.g., "Does a canary have gills?" takes even longer suggesting that the entire hierarchy is searched for an answer that is not found.

The fastest human recall was for the traits more specific to the bird, i.e., that it can sing or is yellow. Handling exceptions also seemed to be done at the most specific level. For example, when subjects were asked whether an ostrich could fly, the answer was produced faster than when they were asked whether an ostrich could breathe. Thus, the hierarchy ostrich → bird → animal seems not to be traversed to get the exception information: It is stored directly with ostrich. This type of knowledge organization has been formalized in computer-based representation systems, including families of object-oriented languages.

Graphs, introduced in Sect. 4.1, provide a means for explicitly representing relations using arcs and nodes and provide an ideal vehicle for formalizing association-based theories of knowledge. A *semantic network* represents knowledge as a graph,

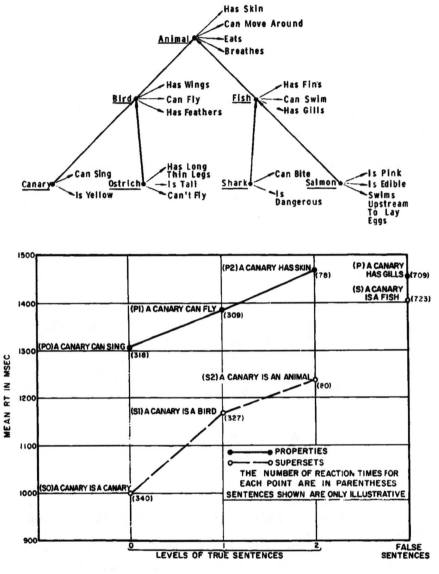

Fig. 5.1 A semantic network, taken from the Collins and Quillian (1969) research, and a record of response times for human information retrieval. In the bottom figure, the X-axis indicates the steps searched on the (upper) inheritance tree to make a response; the Y-axis measures the reaction time for the response

with the nodes corresponding to facts or concepts and the arcs to relations or associations between these concepts. Both nodes and links are generally labeled. An example semantic network describing the properties of "snow", "snowman", and "ice" appears in Fig. 5.2. We next describe the evolution and use of the semantic network representation.

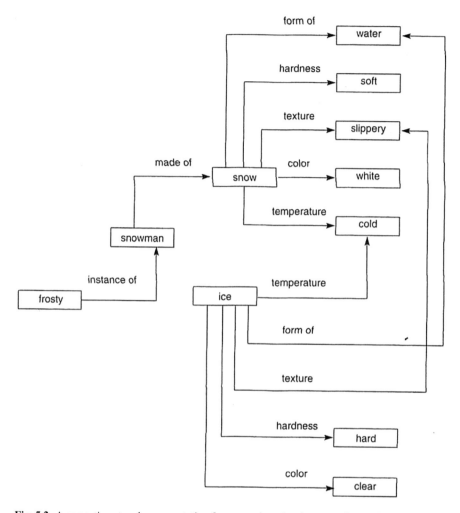

Fig. 5.2 A semantic network representation for properties related to snow, ice, and snowman

5.1.2 Semantic Networks

A major component of semantic network research was done to support computer-based human language understanding. Comprehending human language requires understanding human intentions, beliefs, hypothetical reasoning, plans, and goals. Human language also assumes an understanding of common sense, the ways in which physical objects behave, the interactions that occur between humans, the ways in which human institutions are organized, and much more. Because of these constraints, computer-based human language understanding has been a major driving force for research in association-based representations.

The first computer implementations of semantic networks were developed in the early 1960s for use in machine translation. Masterman (1961) defined a set of 100 primitive concept types and then used these to create a dictionary of 15,000 concepts. Wilks (1972) continued to build on Masterman's work in semantic network-based natural language systems. Shapiro's (1971) MIND program was the first implementation of a propositional calculus-based semantic network. Other early AI workers exploring network representations include Ceccato (1961), Raphael (1968), Reitman (1965), and Simmons (1966).

An influential program, illustrating many features of early semantic networks, was written by Quillian (1967). As seen in Fig. 5.3, Quillian defined English words in much the same way that a dictionary does: a word is described in terms of other words, and the components of that description are again described in the same fashion. Rather than formally defining words in terms of basic atoms of meaning, each description simply leads to other descriptions in an unstructured and sometimes circular fashion. In looking up a word, we traverse this relational network until we are satisfied that we understand the meaning of that word.

Each node in Quillian's network corresponds to a *word concept*, with associative links to other word concepts that form its definition. The knowledge base is organized into *planes*, where each plane is a graph that defines a single word. Figure 5.3 illustrates three planes that capture three different definitions of the word "plant": (1) a living organism; (2) a place where people work; and (3) the act of putting a seed in the ground to grow.

Quillian's program uses this knowledge to find relationships between pairs of English words. Given two words, it searches the graphs outward from each word in a breadth-first fashion, looking for a common concept or *intersection node*. The paths to this node then reflect the relationship between the word concepts. As an example, Fig. 5.4 shows the *intersection paths* between "cry" and "comfort". Using this path, the program concludes that: "cry 2" is, among other things, to make a sad sound. To "comfort 3" can be to "make 2" someone less sad. The numbers in the response indicate that the program has been selected from among different meanings of these words.

Quillian (1967) suggests that the network approach to semantics might provide a natural language understanding system with the ability to:

1. Determine the meaning of a body of English text by building up collections of these intersection nodes.
2. Choose between multiple definitions of words by finding the meanings with the shortest intersection path to other words in the sentence. For example, in Fig. 5.3, the meaning for "plant," in "Tom went home to water his new plant" is based on the intersection of the word concepts "water" and "plant."
3. Answer a flexible range of user queries based on the associations found between words of a query and the word concepts within the system.

After Quillian, researchers including Robert Simmons (1966), Charles Fillmore (1968, 1985), and Roger Schank and Larry Tesler (1969) addressed the need to establish a more precise set of semantic links to better capture human language use.

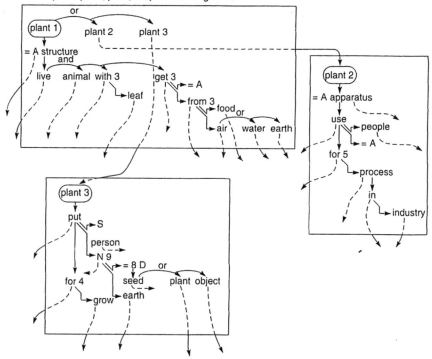

Plant:1) Living structure that is not an animal, frequently
           with leaves, getting its food from air, water, earth.
       2) Apparatus used for any process in industry.
       3) Put (seed, plant, etc.) in earth for growth.

Fig. 5.3 Three "planes" representing the different definitions of "plant" (Quillian 1967)

Simmons focused on the *case structure* of English verbs. In this verb-oriented approach, based on work by Fillmore, network links define the roles played by nouns and noun phrases in the action of the verb. Case relationships include *agent*, *object*, *instrument*, *location*, and *time*. A sentence is represented as a verb node with case links to nodes representing the participants in the action. This structure is called a *case frame*. In parsing a sentence, the program finds the verb and retrieves from its knowledge base the case frame for that verb. It then binds the values for agent, object, etc. to the appropriate nodes of this case frame.

Perhaps the most ambitious attempt to capture the deep semantic structure of language is Schank and Tesler's (1969) *conceptual dependency* theory. This theory offers a set of four primitives from which the world of meaning is built: *actions*, *objects*, *modifiers of actions*, and *modifiers of objects*. All possible action words are assumed to reduce to one of Schanks' primitive actions.

In succeeding decades, the semantic network approach became even more structured. For example, Frame systems were created at MIT by Marvin Minsky (1975). Roger Schank and his colleagues developed *scripts* (Schank and Abelson 1977), a

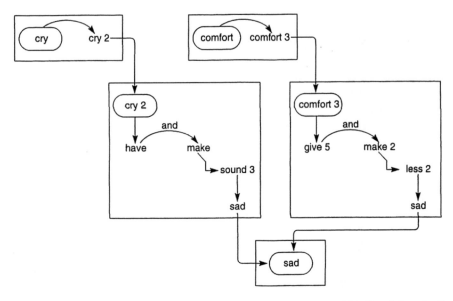

Fig. 5.4 An example of an intersection path between the concepts of "cry" and "comfort" (Quillian 1967)

network of associations that described well-understood events, such as a child's birthday party or going to a restaurant and ordering food. Schank's research group also created *memory organization packets* (Schank 1980) and *case-based reasoning* (Kolodner 1993), each a product of the semantic network approach to representation.

In 2003, Alan Kay was given the ACM Turing Award for his pioneering work in object-oriented design and programming languages. The product of Kay's research was a computer language, SmallTalk, that implemented many aspects of semantic network representations (Goldberg and Kay 1976), a precursor of many modern computer interface designs. For more detail and examples of semantic networks, scripts, and frames see Luger (2009b, Sect. 7.1).

5.1.3   More Modern Uses of Association-Based Semantic Networks

Semantic networks have matured in several directions from their early uses, for example, with John Sowa's (1984) theory of *conceptual graphs*. Sowa systematized the semantic network by describing two components of different types: *concepts* and *relations* between concepts. These two entities can only be connected to each other (this is called a *bipartite* relation) in the conceptual graph, see Fig. 5.5.

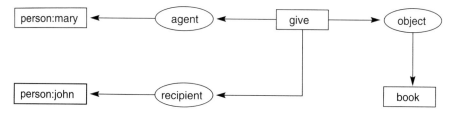

Fig. 5.5 Adapted from Sowa (1984). A conceptual graph for "Mary gave John the book"

As seen in Fig. 5.5, concepts can also have hierarchical relationships, where Mary and John are instances of person. Sowa's conceptual graph representation has been used quite successfully to represent human language expressions. Sowa (1984), as Shapiro (1971) before him, also demonstrated how the semantic network representation can be designed to be equivalent to the predicate calculus.

Two other outgrowths of the early semantic networks research are the *WordNet* and *FrameNet* representations. WordNet was created at Princeton University by George Miller and colleagues (Miller et al. 1990). It is a database of English-language words collected into sets of synonyms, called *synsets*, along with short definitions and examples of how that word is used. WordNet can be seen as both a dictionary and a thesaurus. The synsets are connected to other synsets by their semantic relationships. WordNet, public domain software, is used in situations including language-based information systems, word-sense clarification, information retrieval, text classification and summarization, and language translation.

Charles Fillmore (1985), the creator of *frame semantics*, and colleagues at the *International Science Institute* (*ISI*), at the University of California, Berkeley, built the FrameNet repository (Goddard 2011). A semantic frame is a conceptual structure describing events and relationships, including required participants. The FrameNet database contains over 1200 semantic frames, 13,000-word units, and more than 200,000 sentences. FrameNet is used in both linguistics analysis and language processing for tasks including question answering, paraphrasing, and information retrieval.

As an example of how WordNet and FrameNet might be used, consider an airline company developing an on-line customer advisor for purchasing travel tickets. When interacting with the customer, the advisor might hear any number of statements including: "I've got to get to Seattle," "John needs to fly to Seattle," "Can I travel to Seattle? I need a ticket," or "Do you fly to Seattle?" All these queries trigger a frame, having a template pattern: "customer" … travel to … "airport."

The particular passenger's name will then be bound to customer, airport will be bound to SEATAC, and the computer service advisor will continue using the frame semantics of … travel to … to query the customer for the time and date of flying, and, of course, the credit card information to pay for the trip. In this example, the template "customer" … travel to … "airport" would be from a collection of FrameNet-like templates created by the airline. The different word sets, "got to get to," "need a ticket to," "fly to," etc., can be seen as WordNet synsets for the concept of "travel to".

We next describe a different approach to association-based representations, neural or connectionist networks, and their use in deep learning.

5.2   Neural or Connectionist Networks

Section 5.2 has three parts. First, we describe early research in the area called "neuron nets" by the 1956 Dartmouth Workshop, including the work at MIT of McCulloch, Pitts, and Hebb. In the second section, we introduce backpropagation, the algorithmic advance that led to the widespread use of multi-layered neural networks. Finally, we describe more current uses, including deep learning.

5.2.1   Early Research: McCulloch, Pitts, and Hebb

Neural network architectures are often thought to be a recent development, but they have their origins in 1940s work in computing, psychology, and neuroscience. In the 1940s, both cellular automata and neurally inspired approaches to computation fascinated John von Neumann. Work in neural learning, especially that of Warren McCulloch and Walter Pitts (1943) and Donald Hebb (1949), influenced psychological theories of animal behavior as noted in Sect. 3.2. Finally, the 1956 Dartmouth AI workshop cited *neuron nets* as an important research task.

Neural Networks, often characterized as *neurally-inspired computation*, or *parallel distributed processing (PDP)*, like semantic networks, de-emphasize the explicit use of symbols and logic-based reasoning. Neural network approaches are designed to capture relations and associations in an application domain and interpret new situations in the context of previously learned relational patterns.

The neural net philosophy conjectures that intelligence arises in systems of simple interacting components, the biological or artificial neurons. This happens through a process of learning or adaptation by which the connections between components are adjusted as patterns in the world are processed. Computation in these systems is distributed across collections, or layers, of neurons. Problem-solving is parallel in the sense that all the neurons within the collection or layer process their inputs simultaneously and independently. These systems also tend to degrade gracefully because information and processing are distributed across nodes and layers and not localized to any single component of the network.

In connectionist models, however, there is a strong representational bias both in the creation of input parameters and in the interpretation of output values. To build a neural network, the designer must create a scheme for encoding patterns in the world as numerical or neural-based analog measures to be interpreted by the network. The choice of an encoding scheme plays a crucial role in the eventual success or failure of learning in the network. Patterns from a domain are encoded as numerical vectors. The connections *between* components are also represented by numerical

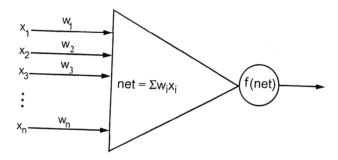

Fig. 5.6 An artificial neuron with input vector x_i, weights w_i for each input, and a threshold function f that determines the neurons' output value

values. Finally, the transformation of patterns is the result of numerical operations, usually, matrix multiplications and nonlinear mappings. These choices, necessary in the design and building of connectionist architectures, constitute the *inductive bias* of the system.

The algorithms and architectures that implement connectionist techniques are usually trained or conditioned rather than explicitly programmed. This fact is a major strength of the approach, as an appropriately designed network architecture and learning algorithm can often capture invariances in the world, even in the form of strange attractors, without being explicitly programmed to recognize them.

The tasks for which the neural/connectionist approach is well-suited include:

> *classification*, deciding categories or groups to which input values belong;
> *pattern recognition*, identifying structure or patterns in data;
> *memory recall*, including the problem of content addressable memory;
> *prediction*, such as identifying a disease from symptoms, causes from effects;
> *optimization*, finding the "best" organization of constraints;
> *control,* deciding between alternative choices in complex situations, and
> *noise filtering* or separating signal from the background as the network factors out the irrelevant components of a complex signal.

The basis of a network is the artificial neuron, introduced in Sect. 3.6, and shown in Fig. 5.6:

The minimal components of the artificial neuron are:

1. *Input signals* X_i. These signals may come from the environment or the activation of other neurons. Different models vary in the allowable range of the input values; typically, inputs are discrete, from the sets $\{0, 1\}$ or $\{-1, 1\}$.
2. A set of real-valued *weights,* w_i. These values describe connection strengths.
3. An *activation level,* $\Sigma w_i x_i$. The neuron's activation level is determined by the cumulative strength of its input signals where each input signal is scaled (multiplied) by the connection weight associated with that input. The activation level is computed by taking the sum of the weighted inputs, that is, $\Sigma w_i x_i$. The Greek sigma, Σ, indicates that these values are added.

4. *A threshold or a bounded non-linear mapping function, f.* The threshold function computes the neuron's output by seeing if it is above an activation level. The nonlinear mapping function produces either an on/off or a graded response for that neuron. See Fig. 5.9 for three different threshold functions.

The architecture of the neural network is described by properties including:

1. *The network topology.* The topology of the network is the pattern of connections between the individual neurons. This topology is a primary source of the net's inductive bias.
2. *The learning algorithm used.* A number of algorithms for learning are discussed in this section.
3. *The encoding scheme.* This encoding includes the interpretation placed on the data to the network, the input vector, and the results of its processing.

An early example of neural computing is the McCulloch and Pitts (1943) neurons. The inputs to the McCulloch–Pitts neuron are either *true*, +1, or *false*, −1. The activation function multiplies each input by its corresponding weight and adds the results; if this sum is greater than or equal to zero, the neuron returns 1, true, otherwise, −1, false. McCulloch and Pitts showed how these neurons could be constructed to compute any logical function.

Figure 5.7 shows McCulloch-Pitts neurons for computing the logical functions and ($\wedge$) and or ($\vee$). The *and* neuron, on the left, has three inputs: x and y are the values to be conjoined; the third input, sometimes called a bias, has a constant value of +1. The input data and bias have weights of +1, +1, and −2, respectively. Thus, for any input values of x and y, the neuron computes $x + y - 2$. Table 5.1 shows that if this value is less than 0, it returns −1, false, otherwise a 1, true. The or neuron, b on the right of Fig. 5.7, illustrates the neuron computing $x \vee y$. The weighted sum of input data for the $\vee$ neuron is greater than or equal to 0 unless both x and y equal −1 (are false).

Although McCulloch and Pitts demonstrated the power of neural computation, interest in neural network research only began to flourish with the development of practical learning algorithms. Early learning models drew heavily on the work of the psychologist Donald Hebb (1949), who speculated that learning occurred in brains through the modification of synapses. Hebb stated:

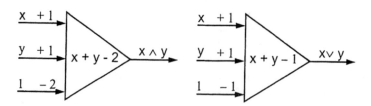

Fig. 5.7 McCulloch-Pitts neurons for functions *and*, on the left, and *or*, on the right

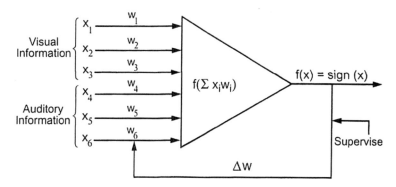

Fig. 5.8 An example of a Hebbian network, with no extra-network supervision, that learns a response for an unconditioned stimulus. ΔW adjusts the weights at each iteration of the data through the network

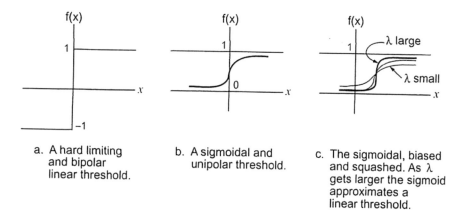

a. A hard limiting and bipolar linear threshold.

b. A sigmoidal and unipolar threshold.

c. The sigmoidal, biased and squashed. As λ gets larger the sigmoid approximates a linear threshold.

Fig. 5.9 An analysis of thresholding functions that produce realistic and useful error/success measurers

> When an axon of cell A is near enough to excite a cell B and repeatedly or persistently takes place in firing it, some growth process or metabolic change takes place in one or both cells such that A's efficiency, as one of the cells firing B, is increased.

Neural physiological research has confirmed Hebb's idea that temporal proximity of the firing of connected neurons can modify their synaptic strength, albeit in a more complex fashion than Hebb's intuition of "increase in efficiency." We next demonstrate *Hebbian learning*, which belongs to the *coincidence* class of learning laws. This learning produces weight changes in response to localized events in neural processing. We describe the learning laws of this category by their local time and space properties.

Table 5.1 The McCulloch-Pitts model for computing the logical *and* of Fig. 5.7a

x	y	$x + y - 2$	Output
1	1	0	1
1	0	−1	−1
0	1	−1	−1
0	0	−2	−1

Table 5.2 The signs (±) of inputs and the product of signs of node output values

O_i	O_j	$O_i{*}O_j$
+	+	+
+	−	−
−	+	−
−	−	+

Hebbian learning has been used in a number of network architectures. The effect of strengthening the connection between two neurons, when one contributes to the firing of another, may be simulated mathematically by adjusting the weight on their connection by multiplying a constant by the sign of the product of their output values. For example, suppose neurons i and j are connected so that the output of i is an input of j. We can define the weight adjustment, indicated by the Greek delta, Δ, on the connection between them, ΔW, as the sign of $c * (O_i * O_j)$, where c is a constant controlling the rate of learning.

In Table 5.2, O_i is the sign of the output value of neuron i, and O_j the sign of output j. From the first line of the table, when both O_i and O_j are positive, the weight change, ΔW, is positive when the learning rate c is positive. The result strengthens the connection between i and j when neuron i contributes to neuron j's activation.

In the second and third rows of Table 5.2, i and j have opposite signs. Since their signs differ, Hebb's model inhibits i's contribution to j's output value, when the learning rate c is positive. Therefore, the weight of the connection is adjusted by a negative amount. Finally, in the fourth row, i and j again have the same sign, −, so the strength of their connection is increased when the learning rate is positive. This weight adjustment mechanism, sometimes called rewarding *temporal behavior*, has the effect of reinforcing the path between neurons when they have similar signals and inhibiting them otherwise.

Neural network learning may be unsupervised, supervised, or some hybrid combination of the two. The examples seen so far in Sect. 5.2 are unsupervised, as the network and its weights transformed input signals to the desired output values. We next consider an example of unsupervised Hebbian learning where each output has a weight adjustment factor. Then, in Sect. 5.2.2, we present an example of supervised learning that uses the backpropagation algorithm.

In unsupervised learning, a critic is not available to provide the "correct" output value. As a result, the weights must be modified across multiple iterations, solely as a function of the input and output values of the neuron. The training of the Hebbian network of Fig. 5.8 has the effect of strengthening the network's responses to patterns that it has already seen and interpreting new patterns properly. Figure 5.8 demonstrates how Hebbian techniques can be used to model *conditioned response learning*, where an arbitrarily selected stimulus can be used to condition a desired response.

Pavlov's classic 1890s experiment offers an example of a conditioned response. A dog is brought food at the same time that a bell is rung. The dog salivates in expectation of his meal. The unconditioned response of the salivating animal is the presence of food. After a number of instances where the arrival of food is accompanied by the ringing bell, the bell is rung without any food. The dog salivates. The ringing bell produces the conditioned response in the dog!

The network shown in Fig. 5.8 demonstrates how a Hebbian network can transfer a response from a primary or unconditioned stimulus to a conditioned stimulus. In Pavlov's experiments, the dog's salivation response to food is transferred to the bell. The weight adjustment, ΔW, at each iteration of the network is described by the equation:

$$W = c * f(X, W) * X.$$

In this equation, c is the learning constant, a small positive decimal, whose use modulates the extent of the learning at each step, as described later in Fig. 5.9. $f(X, W)$ is the network's output at each iteration, and X is the input vector at that iteration.

The network of Fig. 5.8 has two layers, an input layer with six nodes and an output layer with one node. The output layer returns either +1, signifying that the output neuron has fired, or a −1, that it has not fired. The feedback (Supervise) monitoring the network, ΔW, takes each output of the network and multiplies it by the input vector and the learning constant to produce the set of weights for the input vector at the next iteration of the network.

We set the learning constant to the small positive real number, 0.2. In this example, we train the network on the pattern [1, −1, 1, −1, 1−1] which joins the two patterns, [1, −1, 1] and [−1, 1, −1]. The pattern [1, −1, 1] represents the unconditioned stimulus and [−1, 1, −1] represents the new stimulus.

Assume that the network already responds positively to the unconditioned stimulus but is neutral with respect to the new stimulus. We simulate the positive response of the network to the unconditioned stimulus with the weight vector [1, −1, 1], exactly matching the input pattern, while the neutral response of the network to the new stimulus is simulated by the weight vector [0, 0, 0]. Joining these two weight vectors gives the initial weight vector for the network, [1, −1, 1, 0, 0, 0].

The network is next trained on the input pattern hoping to induce a configuration of weights that will produce a positive network response to the new stimulus. The first iteration of the network produces the result:

$$W * X = (1*1) + (-1*-1) + (1*1) + (0*-1) + (0*1)$$
$$+ (0*-1) = (1) + (1) + (1) = 3, \text{and}$$

$$f(3) = sign(3) = 1.$$

Now the Hebbian network creates the new weight vector W^2:

$$W^2 = [1,-1,1,0,0,0] + 0.2*(1)*[1,-1,1,-1,1,-1]$$

$$= [1,-1,1,0,0,0] + [0.2,-0.2,0.2,-0.2,0.2,-0.2]$$

$$= [1.2,-1.2,1.2,-0.2,0.2,-0.2].$$

Next, the adjusted network sees the original input pattern with the new weights:

$$W * X = (1.2*1) + (-1.2*-1) + (1.2*1) + (-0.2*-1) + (0.2*1)$$
$$+ (-0.2*-1) = (1.2) + (1.2) + (1.2) + (+0.2) + (0.2) + (0.2)$$

$$= 4.2, \text{and}$$

$$sign(4.2) = 1.$$

Now the Hebbian network creates the new weight vector W^3:

$$W^3 = [1.2,-1.2,1.2,-0.2,0.2,-0.2] + 0.2*(1)*[1,-1,1,-1,1-1]$$

$$= [1.2,-1.2,1.2,-0.2,0.2,-0.2] + [0.2,-0.2,0.2,-0.2,0.2,-0.2]$$

$$= [1.4,-1.4,1.4,-0.4,0.4,-0.4].$$

It can now be seen that the weight vector product, $W * X$, will continue to grow in the positive direction, with the value of each element of the weight vector increasing by 0.2 in the + or – direction, at each training cycle. After ten more iterations of Hebbian training the weight vector will be:

$$W^{13} = [3.4,-3.4,3.4,-2.4,2.4,-2.4].$$

We now use this trained weight vector to test the network's response to the two partial patterns. We would like to see if the network continues to respond to the unconditioned stimulus positively and, more importantly, if the network has now acquired a positive response to the new conditioned stimulus. We test the network first on the unconditioned stimulus [1, −1, 1]. We fill out the last three arguments of the input vector with random 1, and −1 assignments; for example, we test the network on the vector [1, −1, 1, 1, 1, −1]:

$$sign(W * X) = sign((3.4*1) + (-3.4*-1) + (3.4*1) + (-2.4*1)$$
$$+ (2.4*1) + (-2.4*-1))$$

$$= sign(3.4 + 3.4 + 3.4 - 2.4 + 2.4 + 2.4) = sign(12.6) = +1.$$

The network still responds positively to the original unconditioned stimulus. We next do a second test using the original unconditioned stimulus and a different random vector in the last three positions [1, −1, 1, 1, −1, −1]:

$$sign(W * X)$$

$$= sign((3.4 * 1) + (-3.4 * -1) + (3.4 * 1) + (-2.4 * 1) + (2.4 * -1) + (-2.4 * -1))$$

$$= sign(3.4 + 3.4 + 3.4 - 2.4 - 2.4 + 2.4) = sign(7.8) = +1.$$

The second vector also produces a positive network response. With these two examples, the network's sensitivity to the original stimulus has been strengthened due to repeated exposure to that stimulus.

We next test the network's response to the new stimulus pattern, [−1, 1, −1], encoded in the last three positions of the input vector. We fill the first three vector positions with random assignments from the set {1, −1} and test the network on the vector [1, 1, 1, −1, 1, −1]:

$$sign(W * X) = sign((3.4 * 1) + (-3.4 * -1) + (3.4 * 1) + (-2.4 * 1)$$
$$+ (2.4 * 1) + (-2.4 * -1))$$

$$= sign(3.4 - 3.4 + 3.4 + 2.4 + 2.4 + 2.4)$$

$$= sign(10.6) = +1.$$

The pattern of the secondary stimulus is also recognized!

We do one final experiment, with the vector patterns slightly degraded. This could represent the stimulus situation where the input signals are altered, perhaps because a new food and/or a different sounding bell is used. We test the network on the input vector [1, −1, −1, 1, 1, −1], where the first three parameters are one digit off the original unconditioned stimulus and the last three parameters are one digit off the conditioned stimulus:

$$sign(W * X) = sign((3.4 * 1) + (-3.4 * -1) + (3.4 * 1) + (-2.4 * 1)$$
$$+ (2.4 * 1) + (-2.4 * -1)).$$

$$= sign(3.4 + 3.4 - 3.4 - 2.4 + 2.4 + 2.4) = sign(5.8) = +1.$$

Even this partially degraded stimulus is recognized!

What has the Hebbian learning model produced? We created an association between a new stimulus and an old response by repeatedly presenting the old and new stimuli together. The network learns to transfer its response to the new stimulus without any external supervision. This strengthened sensitivity also allows the network to respond in the same way to a slightly degraded version of the stimulus. This was accomplished by using Hebbian coincidence learning to increase the strength of the network's response to the total pattern. This had the effect of increasing the strength to an individual component of the pattern: an example of *self-organization* emerging from the use of Hebb's rule.

5.2.2 Backpropagation Networks

Early neural networks, inspired by the research of Hebb and others, were intended to characterize aspects of human cortical activity. McCulloch and Pitts (1943) extended these arguments to show that networks of neurons could compute any Boolean function and suggested further that their networks were equivalent to Turing's machine.

In 1958, the neurobiologist Frank Rosenblatt (1958) continued in this tradition of neural emulation with his creation of the *perceptron,* a family on networks designed for more general problems in pattern recognition. Rosenblatt's 1958 paper was titled *The Perceptron: A Probabilistic Model for Information Storage and Organization in the Brain.* Encouraged by early successes, perceptrons were touted to soon be able to see images, beat humans at chess, and produce new copies of themselves (Olazaran 1996).

A decade later, Minsky and Papert's book *Perceptrons* (1969) described limitations within these early families of neural networks. For example, *Perceptrons* showed constraints on what a single layer perceptron network could compute. One problem that could not be solved by the current single-layer networks was the *exclusive-or*, considered later in this section. Olazaran (1996), a historian of the "perceptron controversy," has suggested that the limitations implied in the *Perceptrons* book helped produce a shift in research funding toward the newer and then very promising work in symbol-based AI, presented in Chap. 4.

After the perceptron controversy, research work did continue in the neural network tradition, with new architectures developed by engineers, physicists, and others (Grossberg 1982; Hecht-Nielsen 1990; Hopfield 1984; Luger 2009b, Chap. 11). In the mid-1980s, new research within the AI tradition produced Boltzmann machines (Hinton and Sejnowski 1983) and backpropagation networks (Rumelhart et al. 1986a). These architectures addressed the limitations suggested by the *Perceptrons* book and returned research in neural networks to be a critical force in the then current AI world view.

We next describe supervised learning in a backpropagation network. The neurons in the networks of the 1980s, seen previously in the multilayer perceptron of Fig. 3.2, are connected in layers, with units within layer n passing their activations only to neurons in layer $n + 1$. Multilayer signal processing means that errors deep in the network can spread and evolve in complex, unanticipated ways throughout the connected layers. Thus, the analysis of the source of final output error back into the network is complex. Backpropagation is an algorithm for apportioning this blame and adjusting the network's weights accordingly.

The approach taken by the backpropagation algorithm is to start at the output layer and *propagate* output error backward through the hidden layers. For output nodes, this is easily computed as the difference between the desired and the actual output values. For nodes in the hidden layers, it is considerably more difficult to determine the portion of the error for which each node is responsible.

In all our previous examples, the learning measure for each neuron has been discrete and limited to either a 1 or −1; it has not been a continuous function where there can be a more useful measure of error or success. Figure 5.9 shows several *thresholding* functions that produce useful measures of error. The linear bipolar threshold function, Fig. 5.9a, is similar to that used by the perceptron. Two continuous *sigmoidal* functions are shown in Fig. 5.9b, and c. These functions are called sigmoidal because their graph is an "S" shaped curve.

A common sigmoidal activation function, Fig. 5.9c, called the *logistic* function, is given by the equation:

$$f(\text{net}) = 1/\left(1 + e^{-\lambda * \text{net}}\right), \text{where net} = \Sigma x_i w_i.$$

As in previously defined functions, x_i is the input online i, w_i, w_i is the weight online i, and λ, a "squashing parameter" used to fine-tune the sigmoidal curve. As λ gets large, the sigmoid approaches a linear threshold function over $\{0,1\}$; as it gets closer to 1, it approaches a straight line.

These sigmoidal activation functions plot the input values, on the x-axis, to produce the scaled activation level or output of the neuron as $f(x)$. The sigmoidal activation function is continuous and thus differentiable, which allows a more precise measure of error. Similar to the hard limiting threshold function, the sigmoidal activation function maps most values into regions close to their limiting values, in the sigmoidal case, 0 or 1. However, there is a region of rapid but continuous transition between 0 and 1. In a sense, it approximates a thresholding behavior while providing a continuous output function. The use of λ in the exponent adjusts the slope of the sigmoid shape in the transition region. A weighted *bias* shifts the function along the x-axis.

The historical emergence of networks with continuous activation functions suggested new approaches to error reduction learning. The Widrow and Hoff (1960) learning rule is independent of the activation function, minimizing the squared error between the desired output value and the network activation, $\text{net}_i = WX_i$. Perhaps the most important learning rule for continuous activation functions is the *delta rule* (Rumelhart et al. 1986a) and its extension to the *backpropagation* algorithm.

Intuitively, backpropagation is based on the idea of an error surface, as illustrated in Fig. 5.10. This error surface represents cumulative error over a data set as a function of network weights. Each network weight configuration is represented by a point on the surface as seen in Fig. 5.10 for a two-dimensional space. In realistic situations, the error search will be on much higher dimensioned space, where the dimension of the error surface is the number of weights on a particular layer plus the error measure. On this n-dimensional error surface, given the set of weights, the learning algorithm must find the direction on this surface that most rapidly reduces the error for each dimension. This is called *gradient descent learning* because the gradient is a measure of slope, as a function of a direction (a *partial derivitive*), for a point on the surface.

The logistic function, described above, is used for three reasons: First, the sigmoid's continuous shape has a derivative, or measurable change in the curve, at every point on the curve. This is necessary for error estimation and attribution. Second, since the value of the derivative is greatest where the sigmoidal function is changing most rapidly, the assignment of the most error is attributed to those nodes whose activation was least certain. Finally, the derivative of the logistic function, f', is easily computed by a subtraction and multiplication:

$$f'(\text{net}) = \left(1/\left(1 + e^{-\lambda * \text{net}}\right)\right) = \lambda\left(f(\text{net}) * \left(1 - f(\text{net})\right)\right).$$

A complete derivation of the delta rule with further examples of backpropagation training may be found in Luger (2009b, Sect. 11.2.3).

We next demonstrate the backpropagation algorithm solving one of the classic problems in neural net lore. As previously noted, in the mid-1960s when perceptron learning was the generally accepted neural network paradigm, Minsky and Papert wrote *Perceptrons* (1969). Among the limitations claimed in this book was that the perceptron algorithm could not solve the *exclusive-or* problem.

The *exclusive-or* (*XOR*) function in logic produces *true* when either of its two input values is *true* and *false* when both input values are either *true* or *false*. It was not until the creation of the Boltzmann machine (Hinton and Sejnowski 1983), the generalized delta rule, and the backpropagation algorithm that the exclusive-or problem was solved.

Figure 5.11 shows a network with two input nodes, one hidden node, and one output node. The network also has two bias nodes, the first connected to the hidden node and the second to the output node. The net values for the hidden and output

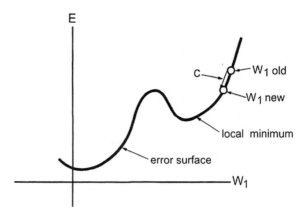

Fig. 5.10 An error surface in two dimensions. The dimension of a problem's error space is the number of weights involved plus the error measure. The learning constant c controls the step size taken on the error surface before the next iteration of network learning. The goal is to find the value of W_1 where E is at a minimum

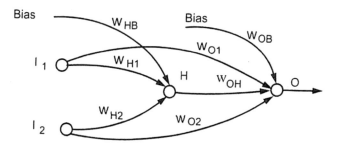

Fig. 5.11 One backpropagation neural network that solves the *exclusive-or* problem. The W_{ij} are the weights, and I the input nodes, H the hidden node, and O the output node

nodes are calculated in the usual manner, as the vector product of the input values times their trained weights. The bias is added to this sum. The weights and the biases are trained using the backpropagation algorithm with the sigmoidal activation function. Note that the input nodes are also directly linked, with trained weights, to the output node. This additional linking can often let the network designer get a network with fewer nodes in the hidden layer and quicker convergence. There is nothing unique about the network of Fig. 5.11; any number of different networks could be used to compute a solution to the *XOR* problem.

This randomly initialized network was trained with multiple instances of the four patterns that represent the truth-values of the exclusive-or function. We use the symbol "→" to indicate that the value of the function is 0 or 1. These four values, as just described, are:

$$(0,0) \rightarrow 0; (1,0) \rightarrow 1; (0,1) \rightarrow 1; (1,1) \rightarrow 0.$$

A total of 1400 training cycles, using these four instances produced the following values, rounded to the nearest tenth, for the weight parameters of Fig. 5.11:

$$W_{H1} = -7.0; W_{H2} = 2.6; W_{O1} = -5.0; W_{OH} = -11.0; W_{H2} = -7.0; W_{OB} = 7.0;$$

$$W_{O2} = -4.0.$$

With input values (0, 0), the output of the hidden node is:

$$f(0*(-7.0)+0*(-7.0)+1*2.6) = f(2.6) \rightarrow 1.$$

The output of the output node for (0, 0) *is*:

$$f(0*(-5.0)+0*(-4.0)+1*(-11.0)+1*(7.0)) = f(-4.0) \rightarrow 0.$$

With input values (1, 0), the output of the hidden node is:

$$f\bigl(1*(-7.0)+0*(-7.0)+1*2.6\bigr)=f(-4.4)\rightarrow 0.$$

The output of the output node for $(1, 0)$ is:

$$f\bigl(1*(-5.0)+0*(-4.0)+0*(-11.0)+1*(7.0)\bigr)=f(2.0)\rightarrow 1.$$

The input value of $(0, 1)$ is similar. Finally, we check the network with input values of $(1, 1)$. The output of the hidden node is:

$$f\bigl(1*(-7.0)+1*(-7.0)+1*2.6\bigr)=f(-11.4)\rightarrow 0.$$

The output of the output node for $(1, 1)$ is:

$$f\bigl(1*(-5.0)+1*(-4.0)+0*(-11.0)+1*(7.0)\bigr)=f(-2.0)\rightarrow 0.$$

The result demonstrates that the feedforward network of Fig. 5.11, using back-propagation learning, made a nonlinear separation of exclusive-or data points. The threshold function f is sigmoidal of Fig. 5.9c, the learned biases have translated it very slightly along the positive direction of the x-axis.

In concluding this example, it is important to understand what the backpropagation algorithm produced. The search space for the *exclusive-or* network has eight dimensions, represented by the seven weights of Fig. 5.11 plus the error of the output. Each of the seven weights was initialized with random values. When the initial output was produced and its error determined, backpropagation adjusted each of the seven weights to decrease this error. The seven weights are adjusted again with each iteration of the algorithm, moving toward values that minimize the error for computing the *exclusive-or* function. After 1400 iterations, the search found values for each of the seven weights that let the error approach zero.

Finally, an observation. The *exclusive-or* network was trained to satisfy four exact patterns, the results of applying the *exclusive-or* function to true/false pairs. In modern deep learning situations training to solve exact situations is rarely the case. Take, for example, a program that scans X-ray images to detect disease situations. Another example is a network that scans metal welds looking for bad metal binding. Such systems are called *classifiers*, and they examine new, previously unseen, situations to determine if there are potential problems.

Classifiers are usually trained on labeled data. For example, a radiologist might have thousands of X-rays that capture tumors and others that are tumor-free. Likewise, the welder may have thousands of examples of acceptable and unacceptable welds. Once these networks are trained, however, they will be considering totally new situations, examples they have never considered before. The classifier must decide each new situation and label it as either good or not. This is the situation for deep learning classifiers, which we consider next.

5.3   Neural Networks and Deep Learning

In Sect. 5.2, we presented many of the early and classic projects in building neural networks. These projects included the development of McCulloch-Pitts neurons, a Hebbian learning network, a multilayer perceptron network, and a backpropagation weight adjustment algorithm that solved the *exclusive-or* problem.

With the successes of the backpropagation algorithm and the availability and affordability of vastly increased computing resources, the challenge turned to building networks with both more and larger hidden layers. Rina Dechter (1986) first named this project *deep learning*. The approach is also called *hierarchical learning* or *deep structural learning*.

When using multiple layer neural networks, the intuition is that each layer of the network converges to "generalizations" or "concepts" from previous layers that are then analyzed and refined by the next processing layer. Thus, nodes at deeper layers in the network can be seen to correspond to levels of abstractions and compositions of earlier layers that refine the original input into useful results. Although it is not always clear what these "concepts" might be, they often lead to successful solutions. We have more discussion on this "black-box" aspect of neural networks in Sect. 5.4.

As deep neural networks became more ubiquitous, it was proven that, given enough nodes in a layer and a sufficient number of hidden layers with appropriate connectivity, these networks were Turing machine equivalent (Kolmogorov 1957; Hecht-Nielsen 1989; Siegelman and Sontag 1991). This equivalence means that appropriately designed networks can approximate arbitrarily mappings between any set of inputs and outputs. Networks can model any complex non-linear function, that is, any polynomial function.

But in practice, discovering appropriate networks for solving tasks has often proven to be quite difficult. Finding the optimum set of network nodes and layers, as well as determining hyper-parameters such as activation functions and learning rates appropriate for a complex task, seemed to limit the utility of deep network problem-solving. Three researchers working independently but often together developed conceptual foundations, obtained surprising results through experiments, and made important engineering advances that led to breakthrough insights supporting the development of deep learning networks.

In 2018, Yoshua Bengio, Geoffrey Hinton, and Yann LaCun were given the Association for Computing Machinery's *Turing Award* for their conceptual and engineering breakthroughs that made deep learning a critical component of modern computing. In the 1990s, LeCun and Bengio (1995) created probabilistic models of sequences, combining neural networks with probabilistic techniques such as hidden Markov models (Sect. 8.2). This technology was later used for machine reading of handwritten checks. Later Benjio et al. (2003) introduced high-dimensional word embeddings that represented word meanings (Sect. 5.3.4). Since 2010, Bengio's research included *generative adversarial networks* or *GANs* (Goodfellow et al. 2014) that supported quantitative improvements in computer vision technology.

In 1983, Geoffrey Hinton and his colleague Terrance Sejnowski (1983) proposed the *Boltzmann machine*, an algorithm for distributing errors back across the hidden nodes of the multi-layer perceptron. The Boltzmann machine was also the precursor of the backpropagation algorithm seen in the previous section. Hinton (Rumelhart et al. 1986a), along with his colleagues David Rumelhart and Ronald Williams, also created the backpropagation algorithm. In 2017, Hinton and his colleagues (Krizhevsky et al. 2017) offered improvements to convolution-based networks that supported the analysis of objects in a visual field.

In the 1980s, Yann LeCun (1989) showed how to make deep learning more efficient by adopting technologies such as convolution layers in networks. His research also helped improve the efficiency of the backpropagation algorithm. LaCun showed how different network modules could be used efficiently in problem-solving. He and his colleagues also demonstrated how hierarchical features could be learned by networks as well as how the information in symbol structures such as graphs could be integrated into networks.

The research of Bengio, Hinton, and LaCun produced many of the engineering breakthroughs that made modern deep learning models successful. We next describe the importance of convolution components in networks. As just noted, Geoffrey Hinton and his colleagues (Bishop 2006; Hinton, et al. 2006; Krizhevsky et al. 2017) applied convolutional networks to image-processing tasks. The network they created, *AlexNet*, won the ImageNet Large Scale Visual Recognition Challenge in 2012 with a score more than 10% better than any competitor.

A network layer is called *convolutional* when it is based on the mathematical notion of an operation of two functions that produces a third function which expresses how the shape of one is modified by the other. Convolution refers both to the resulting function and to the process of computing it. Convolution produces filters that can identify edges and other detail that support image recognition. The design of convolutional neural networks was inspired by the research of neuroscientists Hubel and Wiesel (1959) and evolved from earlier networks designed by Fukushima (1980) and LeCun (1989).

AlexNet contains 5 convolutional network layers and 3 fully connected layers to process each 227 by 227 pixel, or "picture element," image. The network contains 6.3 million parameters and requires 1.1 billion computations to process each image. AlexNet takes 90 runs of the full data set on two GPX580 GPUs to converge. This training process can take 5 or 6 days. (See url 5.3 for further information on convolutional network processing of visual images.)

In fact, the training costs of applying error reduction algorithms to large numbers of nonlinear processing units in these hidden layered architectures are immense and often not possible on "normal" stand-alone computing devices. As an example, it is estimated that in 2018 the computation cost for training the AlphaGo Zero program, Sect. 5.3.1, was about $25 M. The hardware for training AlphaGo Zero consisted of 19 central processors using 64 graphics processors (url 5.4). These costs ignore the Google DeepMind research team's salaries and workspace expenses.

A further example of a cost estimate for training a deep learning language model such as Google's BERT (Devlin et al. 2019, Sect. 5.3.4) is just over $60 k (url 5.5).

The larger computational cost for training large networks made deep learning prohibitive until large server farms, cloud computing, and other cluster-based environments became generally available. Many industry and university research groups do build their own deep learning models but, more often, use a pretrained model from a public domain library. These pretrained models allow the programming team to replace the output layer of the trained network with their own specific output requirements. As a result, models can be run on almost any reasonably robust workstation with acceptable times and costs.

The AlphaGo program, introduced in Sect. 3.1, used deep learning along with *reinforcement learning* (Sutton and Barto 2018). We have previously described two techniques that support neural network algorithms, supervised and unsupervised learning. In supervised learning, as seen with backpropagation, the error of output values is used to condition the weights that produced that error. Unsupervised learning classifies data according to intrinsic properties of the data itself.

Reinforcement learning takes a third approach. Given a decision at any learning cycle where there is no immediate error estimate, the program takes the resulting action and tests it in the environment, for example, in a board game. The reinforcement learner then records the new state of the environment along with a measure of the success or failure of that new state. Samuel's (1959) checker playing program, Sect. 3.2.3, where the "weights" on parameters that led to selecting the next board positions were conditioned by the results of their choices, is an early use of reinforcement learning in computer game playing. Reinforcement is part of an associationist or behaviorist approach to learning in that it remembers and rewards states that are on paths that are components of useful solutions.

Figure 5.12 gives an example of a task appropriate for reinforcement learning. When most of us learned to play tic-tac-toe, we worked to discover intermediate states in the game that would lead to a successful outcome. We learned that the middle board position was a best-first move because it was on more possible winning paths, see Fig. 4.7. We learned that a "fork" position, the bottom game position of Fig. 5.12 where x's opponent can only block one of two winning patterns, was a desirable intermediate state. The reinforcement algorithm learns these and similar patterns through playing and analyzing the intermediate results of steps within games.

Deep learning techniques have been applied to tasks in visual pattern recognition, classification, natural language processing, bioinformatics, drug research, toxicology, and many other information processing domains. We next describe in more detail four interesting applications that use deep learning technology.

5.3.1 AlphaGo Zero and Alpha Zero

AlphaGo Zero is a later version of the original AlphaGo program, Sect. 3.1.3, created by Google's DeepMind research group. Its major strength was that it taught itself how to play go without any experience against human players. It was simply

Fig. 5.12 A sequence of
tic-tac-toe moves with
dashed lines represents
possible choices of the
player with the first move.
Solid lines indicate the
move selected.
Reinforcement learning
rewards decisions that are
part of successful move
patterns

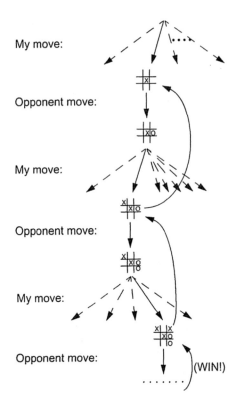

given the rules of the game and then started playing against a version of itself. After 40 days and 29 million games, the program proved to be better than all earlier versions of AlphaGo (Silver et al. 2017). This result is interesting, in that it demonstrates that knowing only the rules of a game and playing against itself, the program quickly learns to exceed the best human players.

AlphaZero, also created by Google's DeepMind research group, takes the deep learning coupled with reinforcement learning algorithms a very important step beyond AlphaGo Zero. The neural net reinforcement learning architecture is made general enough to play several different games.

AlphaZero, besides playing go, plays chess and shogi as well. It was able to outperform all chess and shogi programs and a version of AlphaGo Zero with only 3 days of training (url: 5.6). AlphaZero also, given only the rules of go, learned skilled performance by repeatedly playing against itself. Choosing a next move AlphaZero searched 1000 times fewer states than did its computer-based opponents (url: 5.6).

5.3.2 Robot Navigation: PRM-RL

We saw earlier, Sect. 4.1.2, how AI planning and robotics programs used the state space and search to discover paths that allowed a robot to accomplish a task. Modern robotics has taken these earlier search-based approaches to entirely new levels, including using deep learning coupled with reinforcement learning to support exploring environments. At Google Brain, Faust and her colleagues (2018) created a robot navigation system called PRM-RL that uses *probabilistic roadmaps* and *reinforcement learning* to find paths in complex environments.

A probabilistic roadmap planner (Kavraki et al. 1996) has two phases: First, a graph-based map is built that approximates the movements that the robot can make within its environment. To build this roadmap, the planning algorithm first constructs a set of possible partial paths by considering links between accessible locations it discovers in the environment. In the second phase, the actual goal for the robot is linked to the graph and the algorithm determines the shortest path to that goal.

The reinforcement learning component of PRM-RL is trained to execute point-to-point tasks and to learn constraints, system dynamics, and sensor noise independent of the ultimate task environment of the robot. In the testing environment, the PRM-RL program builds a roadmap using reinforcement learning to determine connectivity. The reinforcement learning algorithm joins two configuration points only when the search finds point-to-point connectivity between them that avoids all obstacles. Figure 5.13a shows the training map within a 23 × 18 m building floor plan. Figure 5.13b shows the testing environment, a 134 × 93 m floor plan of a building.

All these approaches are, as mentioned earlier, computer time and cost-intensive. Because of this complexity, a major challenge to deep reinforcement learning is analyzing frequently long successful search paths and identifying appropriate states within that search to "reinforce." It is also very impressive that Google's PRM-RL robot can be trained in one environment and then transfer that learning to a new and different situation, as seen in Fig. 5.13.

5.3.3 Deep Learning and Video Games

Deep learning algorithms that play video games use similar approaches to those of Google's AlphaZero. The input values for the network are the game's pixelated video screen and the current game score. There is no model for the game situation as would be needed in a symbol-based approach. For example, the symbolic approach would represent the agent that is playing and learning the game, the target goals, and the tools or weapons for achieving these goals, as well as rules for attack, defense, escape, and so on.

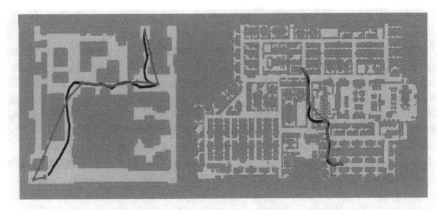

a. Training environment (23 m by 18 m)   b. Testing domain (134 m by 93 m)

Fig. 5.13 (**a**) Is the training environment for the robot and (**b**) the testing environment. The heavier line indicates the actual path taken by the robot. Adapted from (Faust et al. 2018)

Given only the current pixelated screen and current game score, reinforcement learning analyzes the state of the player and the game choices available. In video games, these choices can be very large, estimated at about 10^{50}, while the maximum number of choices a Go player has is about 10^2. The video game choices are in multiple categories, including movement, weapon use, and defensive strategies. The reinforcement algorithm has probabilistic estimates of the quality of each of these choices, given the current state of the game. These probabilistic measures are determined by the previous successes of making that choice, given that state.

When the reinforcement learning begins, there is very little reward information and the agent's moves will seem very exploratory and erratic. As multiple games are played, the reward algorithm gets more "success" information, the agent's choices improve, and eventually so does winning. The learning process for a video game-playing computer requires multiple millions of games of a program playing against a version of itself and can cost several millions of 2018-dollars.

Deep learning video game programs including Google's DeepMind's AlphaStar program playing StarCraft II (Gristo 2019; Arulkumaran et al. 2020) have successfully outperformed humans in single-player games. AlphaStar achieved Grandmaster status in August 2019. A single agent game program, with full explanations and code that uses Q-leaning, a model-independent reinforcement learning algorithm, to play the video game Snake can be found at url 5.7.

Many interesting video games require teamwork. Jaderberg et al. (2019) designed a program that plays Quake III Arena in Capture the Flag mode. Its agents learn and act independently to cooperate and compete with other agents. Again, the reinforcement learner uses only the pixelated screen images and the game score as input. The population of reinforcement learning agents is trained independently and in parallel. Each agent learns its own internal reward pattern to support its active interactions within the game environment.

5.3.4   Deep Learning and Natural Language Processing

From the early 1990s until about 2015, the traditional computer methods used to understand human language, summarize documents, answer questions, and to translate speech and text from one language to another were probabilistic. We see examples of this probabilistic approach in Sect. 8.3. More recently, alternative technologies, including deep learning, address these same human language tasks.

How do you offer human language input values to a neural network? Earlier, Sejnowski and Rosenberg (1987) created a neural net program called NETtalk that could read a sequence of letters from English text and learn appropriate pronunciation and emphasis for that text. Although this worked well for English pronunciation, their approach did not scale to determining document similarity or other more complex tasks such as translation between languages.

In 1988, Scott Deerwester and his colleagues (1990) patented a technique called *latent semantic analysis (LSA)*. The insight behind LSA was that similar documents are likely to contain similar sets of words. The task of calculating sets of similar words is accomplished using a very large matrix. Each column in the matrix represents a document, while each row gives the number of times each individual word of that document is used, alphabetically ordered.

The row–column intersection point of the matrix gives the number, normalized, with emphasis for rarer words, of times that word appeared in the document of that column. Before the matrix is created, common words, often called *stop words*, e.g., a, the, to, and, for, etc., are removed from consideration. Since these common words appear in almost all documents, removing them improves document comparisons. The matrix, however, remains very large for most interesting tasks and is *sparse*, having zero for a large number its elements.

Various mathematical techniques may be used to simplify this matrix, for example, *singular value decomposition* can reduce the number of rows while preserving the integrity of document similarity. Finally, each column of the matrix is seen as a one-dimensional vector representing a particular document. When these document vectors are positioned in a multiple dimensioned space, the distance between the vectors, often represented as the cosine of the angle between them, is used to determine the similarity of any two of the documents.

There are related language tasks, such as to determine when two words may have similar meanings (Mikolov et al. 2013). For example, *word2vec* creates a vector, called an *embedding*, for individual words. These vectors are made up of the words in a fixed size "window" of words surrounding that word in a document. It is then assumed that words surrounded by similar words are closer in meaning than those words that are not. This word similarity technology, where different words are determined to have roughly equivalent meanings, can then be used to reduce the total number of different words in a document vector.

A *language model* characterizes how the components of a language work together in communication. These models capture relationships including noun–verb agreement, proper use of adjective and adverbs, how clusters of words are often used together, and much more. Many deep learning–based language models are currently available, with perhaps two, Google's BERT (Devlin et al. 2019) and OpenAI's GPT-3 (Brown et al. 2020), most widely used.

Deep learning neural language models are trained networks that capture the relationships between words in a language. There are a number of regimens for training these models. One more traditional approach asks, given the n words that precede an unknown token word, what is the most likely word that token would be. Google's BERT (Devlin et al. 2019), also considers the n words that follow that unknown token to determine what word is most likely to precede these n words.

Training takes place by giving these learning networks an extremely large number of sentences, for example, all of the Wikipedia corpus. As of December 2020, this corpus had more than six million articles with almost four billion words. Other large corpora include the *Google Books Corpus*, the *International Corpus of English*, and the *Oxford English Corpus*. The original BERT training took about 4 days on four cloud TPUs. A TPU is a *tensor processing unit*, a special-purpose processor built by Google for training the very large vectors used with deep neural networks. Google search engines are currently supported by the BERT technology.

OpenAI has taken the BERT approach to language models one important step further. After creating a standard language model similar to BERT, GPT-3, the *Generative Pre-Trained Transformer number 3* (Brown et al. 2020) adds a second, task-specific, training set. The primary training is task-agnostic and is just a general-purpose language model similar to BERT. With the addition of task-specific training, GPT-3 can focus on targeted applications. For example, if the task-specific training is the writing of a specific author, the user can request what that author thinks about a particular topic. GPT-3's response, in the words and style of that author, is often cogent and believable.

GPT-3 is, at the present time, the most powerful language model yet created. Differing from BERT, it uses only next word prediction to build its model. GPT-3 is an autoregressive language model that has more than 175 billion parameters, the values the network tries to optimize during training, and has been estimated to cost about \$4.6 million to train. A strength of GPT-3 is that with minor secondary training for specific tasks, such as the sentences of a particular author, it performs well on tasks related to that secondary training. Examples include translation between languages, question answering, giving the meaning for novel words, and even performing simple arithmetic. GPT-3 has also produced impressive answers for the Turing test described in Sect. 2.10.

Although BERT and GPT-3 produce impressive language models successful at multiple tasks, they only reflect the patterns found in human language. There is no semantics in the human sense, as we discuss in Sect. 5.4 and Part III, only the presentation of the patterns of words found in human communication. As Will Douglas Haven (2020a) claims in an MIT Technology Review, GPT-3 is completely mindless, capable of producing total nonsense, and even at times racist and sexist utterances.

We have only touched the surface of how deep learning has assisted in human language analysis. There are successes if further language tasks, including finding documents that are similar such as patents (Helmers et al. 2019), producing document translations (Wu et al. 2016), and for answering questions about speech and text (Zaman and Mishu 2017).

These four applications of deep learning technology offer a very small sample from this research domain. There are now many other network architectures available for solving problems. Among these are *Hopfield networks* with *auto-associative memories*, *Kohonen networks* that learn prototypes, and *bi-directional associative memories* or *BAM* networks. A discussion of these and other architectures can be found in Hecht-Nielsen (1990). Ian Goodfellow and colleagues (2014) have an important deep learning textbook. A summary of many deep learning applications can be found in Samek et al. (2019). We conclude this chapter by considering epistemic issues related to association-based representations and the connectionist technology.

5.4 Epistemic Issues and Association-Based Representations

This chapter presented two approaches to building association-based representations for AI problem-solving, semantic networks and neural or connectionist networks. Both approaches have matured since their introduction and have successfully met many challenges.

There remain, however, epistemic issues. We next describe three: the inductive biases implicit in semantic and neural networks, the need for transparency and accountability for network results, and issues related to the generalization of successful solutions to related domains. Second, we compare the associationist systems of this chapter with the symbol-based problem-solving of Chap. 4. Finally, we ask why, given the current state of neural network technology, researchers have not yet built the equivalent of an animal brain.

5.4.1 Inductive Bias, Transparency, and Generalization

Although the semantic and neural network technologies have been very successful, significant research questions remain. These issues must not be seen as negative criticism of associative representations but as how continuing research can make them even more useful.

The design of a semantic or neural network is a function of the expectations of the builder, the problems to be addressed, and the data available for training and using that network. The design of the network offers both support for and limitations on possible results. For example, appropriate selection of *hyperparameters* mediates finding solutions. Hyperparameters include the overall network architecture, i.e., the number and sizes of the network's layers. They also include the learning rate, Sect. 5.2.2, the *batch* or amount of data in training sets, and the number of *epochs*, or times the full data set is used in training, and even the random values selected for initializing the weights.

There are often few guidelines for making decisions on architectures or other hyperparameters in building one's own network for complex tasks. "Best" engineering decisions are often based on training times and having data sufficient for convergence. In natural language situations, e.g., using Google's BERT (Devlin et al. 2019), the networks are pretrained for release to users who are able to use the trained BERT for their own specific tasks.

Researchers at Google (D'Amour et al. 2020) have noted that many pretrained language and other models used in deep learning have failed when applied to novel situations that the model is intended to represent. These researchers have also shown that some of these same models come to different convergence points when training begins with different random variables or when other model meta-parameters, such as learning rate or training schedule, are changed.

This type of hyperparameter-based failure phenomenon has also been noted by Heaven (2020b) and is attributed to the underspecification of these trained models. Underspecification means that the model does not exhaustively capture (learn) the details of the intended situation, and thus, there might well be infinitely more models that could do as well or better. In a GPT-3 environment, even with 175 billion parameters, underfitting, when it is understood, is not a fatal flaw. But users must be aware that even this large a model can still underfit the situation that it is trying to represent and explain.

Another interesting aspect of deep neural network training is that the error minimization search only considers spaces represented by continuous functions. This is just an obvious consequence of using the backpropagation algorithm and related error minimization techniques in multidimensional search spaces. As yet machine learning algorithms have little ability to jump to alternative contexts or new models of an environment. We address this topic again in Sects. 9.2 and 9.3.

An example of the limitations of error minimization search on continuous function models is to ask the question whether our algorithms are even searching the appropriate space: Exactly what hill are we climbing? For example, as pointed out by Bender and Koller (2020), using BERT or GPT-3 to find similar documents by comparing noun-phrase, word, or even the patterns of characters of these documents can be misleading, if not wrongheaded. No patterns discovered in the text can capture the semantics, meaning, or truths intended by these documents' creators. Meaning and truth, as we see in Chap. 7, are referential tools of a purpose-driven agent and not equivalent to patterns of symbols. There may be co-relations between documents, of course, as described in Sect. 5.3 on deep learning and natural language understanding, but patterns in text may coorelate with do not imply that there are similar patterns in the meanings of documents.

As the deep learning technology enters human society to provide critical services, it will need to be accepted and trusted by its users. The human must be able to understand the reasoning of the program, that is, its results must be transparent. For the Alpha Zero game programs of Sect. 5.3.1, this transparency is straightforward: a reinforcement-conditioned data structure selects sequences of optimal moves in the game tree. This is a fully transparent explanation. Similarly, using Google's BERT, or other pre-trained networks, to determine the similarity of word patterns in different documents is a transparent process.

When deep learning produces results that impact human values or decision making, however, the transparency of the decision process becomes even more important. These human-critical decisions can relate to health care, home and work environments, facial recognition, privacy, financial credit, and much more. One interesting approach is that of Ribeiro et al. (2016), where a second layer learning process, called *model agnostic interpretability*, attempts to further analyze and explain the results of earlier applied deep learning algorithms. Research addresses transparency issues in vision systems (Iyer et al. 2018) and in medical information processing (Chen and Lu 2018). From the AI Lab at MIT, Gilpin et al. (2019) critique the entire process of deep learning transparency in their article, *Explaining Explanations: An Approach to Evaluating Interpretability of Machine Learning*. We discuss the issue of transparency in AI programs further in Sect. 7.1.

For deep learning networks, the generalization problem asks how one successful solution process can be extended to other related problems. A number of researchers are considering this issue. As we have seen in the game playing of Sect. 5.3, tree search, supported by decision policies from reinforcement learning, constitutes a general-purpose decision-making approach that can be applied in many different environments. We saw these techniques applied not just to board games but to robot path planning and video games as well.

At Berkeley, the research of Finn and her colleagues (2017) explores relaxation in training of the top-level weights of a model's parameters so that when trained with new examples from a related domain, learning continues to succeed. This model-agnostic approach can be applied in any gradient descent domain, Sect. 5.2.2.

Animals and humans seem to have the ability to continually acquire and integrate knowledge throughout their lifetimes. This *lifelong learning* remains a challenge for deep learning networks. Parisi et al. (2019) summarize this challenge and review the literature related to continual learning. *Incremental learning*, another approach to lifelong learning, is also an area of continuing research. Castro et al. (2018) examine *catastrophic forgetting*, a decrease in the overall performance of a successful system as new classes of data are incrementally added. Castro and colleagues address this by adding new data along with small data samples from previous training, allowing the learner to incrementally learn new classes.

5.4.2 Neural Networks and Symbol Systems

In this brief section, we continue discussing the symbol-based-connectionist controversy. As we have shown, a significant alternative to the explicit symbol-based approach of Chap. 4 is the neural networks technology. Because the "knowledge" in a neural network is distributed across the structures of that network, it is often difficult, if not impossible, to isolate individual concepts to specific nodes and weights of the network. In fact, any portion of the network may be instrumental in the representation of different concepts.

Neural network architectures shift the emphasis of AI away from the problems of symbolic representation and logic-based reasoning to learning by association and adaptation. Neural networks do not require that the world be cast as an explicit symbolic model. Rather, the network is shaped by its interactions with the world, reflected through its training experience. This approach has made a number of contributions to our understanding of intelligence. Neural networks offer a plausible model of the mechanisms underlying the physical embodiment of mental processes and a viable account of learning and development. They demonstrate how simple and local adaptations can shape a complex system in response to data.

Neural nets, precisely because they are so different, can answer a number of questions that challenge the expressive abilities of symbol-based AI. An important class of such questions concerns visual, auditory, and tactile perception. Nature is not so generous as to deliver our perceptions to a processing system as neat bundles of predicate calculus expressions. Neural networks offer a model of how we might recognize "meaningful" patterns in the chaos of sensory stimuli.

Because their representation is distributed, neural networks are often more robust than their symbolic counterparts. A properly trained neural network can effectively categorize novel instances, exhibiting a human-like perception of similarity rather than strict logical necessity. Similarly, the loss of a few neurons need not seriously compromise the performance of a large neural network. This often results from the redundancy inherent in most neural network models.

Perhaps the most appealing aspect of connectionist networks is their ability to learn. Rather than constructing a detailed symbolic model of the world, neural networks rely on the plasticity of their own structure to adapt directly to external experiences. They do not construct a model of the world so much as they are shaped by their experience within the world. Learning is one of the most important aspects of intelligence. It is also the problems of learning that raises some of the hardest and most interesting questions for further research.

A number of researchers continue to ask how the symbolic and connectionist representational modalities might converge. See, for example, Hinton (2007), Friston (2009), and Mao et al. (2019). For those who feel uncomfortable with two seemingly incommensurable models of intelligence, the science of physics functions well with the intuitively contradictory notion that light is sometimes best understood as a wave and sometimes as a particle. Perhaps both viewpoints may well be subsumed by some higher order theory. Most importantly, however, both approaches deny philosophical dualism and place the foundations of intelligence in the structure and function of physically realized devices.

5.4.3   Why Have We Not Built a Brain?

The current generation of engineered connectionist systems bares very little resemblance to the human neuronal system. Because the topic of *neural plausibility* is a critical research issue, we begin with that question and then consider human development and learning. Research in cognitive neuroscience (Squire and Kosslyn 1998; Gazzaniga 2014; Gazzaniga et al. 2018; Hugdahl and Davidson 2003) brings new insight into the understanding of human cognitive architecture. We describe briefly some findings and comment on how they relate to the AI enterprise. We consider issues from three levels: first, the individual neuron; second, the level of neural architecture; and finally cognitive representation or the *encoding* problem.

First, at the level of the individual neuron, Shephard (2004) and Carlson (2010) identify multiple different types of neuronal architectures for cells, each of which is specialized as to its function and role within the larger neuronal system. These types include *sensory receptor* cells typically found in the skin and passing input information to other cell structures, *interneurons* whose primary task is to communicate within cell clusters, *principle* neurons whose task is to communicate between cell clusters, and *motor neurons* whose task is system output.

Neural activity is electrical. Patterns of ions flowing into and out of the neuron determine whether a neuron is active or resting. The typical neuron has a resting charge of -70 mV. When a cell is active, certain chemicals are released from the axon terminal. These chemicals, *neurotransmitters*, influence the postsynaptic membrane, typically by fitting into specific receptor sites, initiating further ion flows. Ion flows, when they achieve a critical level, about -50 mV, produce an *action potential*, an all-or-none triggering mechanism indicating that the cell has fired. Thus, neurons communicate through sequences of binary codes.

Postsynaptic changes from the action potential are of two sorts, *inhibitory*, found mainly in interneuron cell structures, or *excitatory*. These positive and negative energy potentials are constantly being generated throughout the synapses in the dendritic system. Whenever the net effect of all these events is to alter the membrane potentials of related neurons from -70 mV to about -50 mV, the threshold is crossed, and ion flows are again initiated into those cells' axons.

On the level of neural architecture, there are approximately 10^{10} total neurons in the cerebral cortex, a thin convoluted sheet covering the entire cerebral hemisphere. Much of the cortex is folded in on itself, increasing the total surface area. From the computational perspective, we need to know not only the total number of synapses, but also the *fan-in* and *fan-out* parameters of neurons, that is, the measure of their interconnections. Shephard (2004) estimates both these numbers to be about 10^5.

Finally, aside from the differences in the cells and architectures of neural and computer systems, there is a deep problem of cognitive representation. We are ignorant, for example, of how even simple memories are encoded in the cortex. How is a face recognized, and how, with recognition of that face, one module of cortex is linked to other modules, such as the limbic system, that produce feelings of joy, sadness, or anger? We know a large amount about the physical/chemical aspects of neural connectivity in the brain, but relatively little about how the neural system encodes and processes patterns within that brain.

The ability of connectionist networks to converge on a meaningful generalization from a set of training data has proven sensitive to the number of artificial neurons, the network topology, the training data, and the specific learning algorithms used. There is increasing evidence that human infants also inherit a range of "hardwired" cognitive biases that enable learning of languages and commonsense physics (Elman et al. 1998). At birth, animal brains have highly structured neural networks evolved through evolutionary constraints and by prenatal experiences.

It follows that one of the more difficult questions facing researchers in both the neural network and the symbolic-learning computing communities is the role of innate knowledge in learning. Can effective learning ever occur on a *tabula rasa*, or *blank slate*, starting with no initial knowledge and learning entirely from experience? Or must learning start out with some prior bias or expectations? Research attempting to understand the role of inductive bias to both initial learning and integrating new knowledge and relationships continues both in human and in computational systems. We discuss several further challenges to capturing human information processing with computational tools again in Sect. 9.5.

5.5   In Summary

Association-based models of intelligence have taken two forms within the AI research community. The first, based on the behaviorist traditions of early twentieth-century psychology, is the semantic network, used for answering questions and other natural language understanding tasks. These hierarchical and generalization-based representations capture many of the assimilated world knowledge or schemata that Kant and Bartlett have suggested as components of how humans interpret their world.

Neural or connectionist representations also capture important aspects of associative learning. We saw early examples of neural networks inspired by both Hebb and by McCulloch and Pitts. We reviewed supervised learning using the backpropagation algorithm and solved the XOR problem. We discussed issues related to larger systems with multiple hidden layers called *deep learning* networks. We discussed deep learning networks solving a variety of problems.

Finally, we described several responses to the mechanical implementation of association-based theories, including the problems of innate biases, the importance of transparency, and of creating generalizations. We discussed issues involved in building a human brain.

Further Thoughts and Readings   Complete references for the suggested readings may be found in the Bibliography.

Collins A. and Quillian, M.R. (1969). "Retrieval time from semantic memory."

Schank, R.C. and Colby, K.M., ed. (1973). *Computer Models of Thought and Language.*
Sowa, J.F. (1984). *Conceptual Structures: Information Processing in Mind and Machine.*

This volume had major influence in neural net research in the late1980s:

Rumelhart, D.E., McClelland, J.L., and The PDP Research Group. (1986a). *Parallel Distributed Processing.*

I thank Prof. Thomas Caudell and Dr. Chayan Chakrabarti for comments on this chapter.

We acknowledge Elsevier's copyright for Figs. 5.1, 5.3, and 5.4 and thank them for permission for our reuse. Figure 5.1 is from Collins and Quillian (1969), and Figs. 5.3 and 5.4 from Quillian (1967). Figure 5.13 is adapted from Faust et al. (2018). Many of the neural net examples and figures were first used in (Luger 1995). We thank Elsevier for permission for their reuse.

Programming Support   Computer code for building semantic network hierarchies and other object-oriented representation systems is available in Luger (2009b), AI Algorithms, Data Structures, and Idioms in Prolog, Lisp, and Java, see url 4.3. There are a number of neural network software building and visualization tools available, many found on the internet under "software for building neural networks." A demonstration of, and code to create a simple deep learning video game, *snake*, may be found at url 5.7.

Chapter 6
Evolutionary Computation and Intelligence

What limit can we put to this power, acting during long ages and rigidly scrutinizing the whole constitution, structure, and habits of each creature—favoring the good and rejecting the bad? I can see no limit to this power in slowly and beautifully adapting each form to the most complex relations of life....
—CHARLES DARWIN, On the Origin of Species.

Contents

Chapter 6 has four parts. Section 6.1 introduces genetic and evolutionary computing. Section 6.2 describes *genetic algorithms* and *programming* and gives several examples of their uses. In Sect. 6.3, *artificial life*, or *a-life*, is explored, and Sect. 6.4 considers genetic and evolutionary approaches to creating intelligent programs from an epistemic perspective. We conclude, Sect. 6.5, with some summary thoughts on Part II.

© Springer Nature Switzerland AG 2021
G. F. Luger, *Knowing our World*, https://doi.org/10.1007/978-3-030-71873-2_6

6.1   Introduction to Evolutionary Computation

Just as connectionist networks received much of their early support and inspiration from the goal of creating artificial neural systems, other biological analogs have influenced the design of search and learning algorithms in AI. This chapter considers algorithms patterned after the processes underlying evolution: shaping a population of individuals through the survival and reproduction of its most fit members. The power of selection across a varying population of individuals is demonstrated in natural evolution with the emergence of species with increasing complexity. These selection processes are also replicated computationally with research, including cellular automata, genetic algorithms, genetic programming, and artificial life.

Evolutionary computing simulates nature's most elegant and powerful form of adaptation: the production of complex plant and animal life forms. Charles Darwin saw "...no limit to this power of slowly and beautifully adapting each form to the most complex relations of life..." Through this simple process of introducing variations into successive generations and selectively eliminating less-fit specimens, adaptations of increasing capability and diversity develop in a population. Evolution occurs in populations of embodied individuals, whose actions affect others and who are, in turn, affected by others. Thus, selective pressures come not only from the outside environment but also from interactions between members of a population. An ecosystem has many members, each with roles and skills appropriate to their own survival, but more importantly, whose cumulative behavior shapes and is shaped by the rest of the population.

Despite their simplicity, the processes underlying evolution have proven remarkably general. Biological evolution produces species by selecting among changes in the genome. Similarly, cultural evolution produces knowledge by operating on socially transmitted and modified units of information, sometimes referred to as *memes* (Dawkins 1976). Genetic algorithms and other evolutionary analogs produce increasingly capable solutions by operating on populations of candidate problem solutions.

The history of evolutionary computing goes back to the very beginning of computers themselves. John von Neumann, in a series of lectures in 1949, explored the question of what level of organizational complexity was required for self-replication to occur (von Neumann and Burks 1966). Burks (1970) states von Neumann's goal as "...not trying to simulate the self-reproduction of a natural system at the level of genetics and biochemistry." Rather, von Neumann wished to "abstract from the natural self-reproduction problem its logical form."

By removing chemical, biological, and mechanical details, von Neumann was able to represent the essential requirements for self-replication. Von Neumann designed, although it was only built in the 1990s, a self-reproducing automaton that consisted of a two-dimensional cellular arrangement that contained a large number of individual 29-state automata. The next state for each automaton was a function of its current state and the states of its four immediate neighbors. We see detailed examples of this neighbor-cell interaction phenomenon in Sect. 6.3.

von Neumann designed his self-replicating machine, estimated to contain at least 40,000 cells, to have the functionality of a Universal Turing Machine. Von Neumann's computation device was *construction universal*, in that it was capable of reading an input tape, interpreting the data on the tape, and through the use of a construction arm, building the configuration described on the tape in an unoccupied part of the cellular space. By putting a description of the constructing automaton itself on the tape, von Neumann proposed the creation of a self-reproducing system (Arbib 1966).

Later, Codd (1968) reduced the number of states required for a computationally universal, self-reproducing automaton from 29 to 8 but required an estimated 100,000,000 cells for the full design. Then, Devore simplified Codd's machine to occupy only about 87,500 cells. In more modern times, Langton created a self-replicating automaton, without computational universality, where each cell had only eight states and occupied just 100 cells (Langton 1995; Hightower 1992; Codd 1992). It was not until the early 1990s that a Princeton University undergraduate student, Umberto Pesavento (1995), actually built von Neumann's machine! Further descriptions of the research efforts on self-reproducing automata can be found in the proceedings of the a-life conferences (see alife.org/conferences).

Because of John von Neumann, the formal analysis of self-replicating machines has deep roots in the history of computation. It is also not surprising that the 1956 Dartmouth summer workshop on artificial intelligence had *self-improvement* as one of its computational tasks, where research hoped to build intelligent machines that could, somehow, make themselves "better." In Sect. 6.3, we extend, with more examples, the a-life research that von Neumann began.

But first, in Sect. 6.2, we describe a natural follow-on of the ideas in self-organizing and reproducing machines, research in genetic algorithms (Holland 1975). Like neural networks, genetic algorithms are based on a biological meta-phor: They view computer-based search and learning as a competition among a population of evolving candidate solutions for a problem. A "fitness" function evaluates each solution to decide whether it will contribute to the next generation of solutions. Then, through operations analogous to gene transfer in sexual reproduction, the algorithm creates a new population of candidate solutions. We next describe genetic algorithms and genetic programming in more detail.

6.2   The Genetic Algorithm and Examples

To solve problems, the genetic algorithm has three distinct stages: First, individual potential solutions for a problem are created. As we will see in our examples, these solutions are encoded in representations amenable to genetic operators. In the second stage, a *fitness* function judges which individuals of this population are the "best" life forms, that is, most appropriate for the eventual problem solution. These successful individuals are favored for survival and are then used to produce the next generation of potential solutions, which are then produced by the genetic operators.

This next generation is built from components of their parents, as we will see in examples. Eventually, a "best" solution for the problem is selected from the latest generation of possible solutions.

We now present a high-level description of the genetic algorithm. This description is called *pseudo-code* because it is not intended to be run on a computer, but, like a cooking recipe, to indicate each step to a solution and when it is to be taken:

```
Let P(t) be a list of n possible solutions, x₁ᵗ , at time t:
        P(t)={x₁ᵗ, x₂ᵗ, ...xₙᵗ}

        procedure genetic algorithm;
        begin
            set time t to be 0;
            initialize the population P(t);
            while the termination condition of the problem is not met do
            begin
                evaluate fitness of each member of population P(t);
                select pairs, based on fitness, from population P(t);
                use genetic operators to produce children of the
                pairs;
                replace, based on fitness, weakest members of P(t);
                set new time to be t +1
            end
        end.
```

This pseudo-code algorithm offers a framework of genetic problem-solving; actual genetic algorithms implement that framework in different ways. Specific questions that need clarifying include: What percentage of the potential solution population is kept for producing the next generation? Which genetic operators are used to produce the next generation? How are the genetic operators applied? After applying the operators, can the best candidates from one generation be passed on to the next? Often, the procedure "replace the weakest candidates of a generation" is implemented by simply eliminating a fixed percentage of the weakest solution candidates.

More sophisticated genetic algorithms can order a population by fitness and then associate an "elimination probability" measure with each descendent. The probability of elimination could be, for instance, an inverse function of its fitness. The replacement algorithm then uses this measure as a factor in selecting candidates to eliminate. Although the probability of elimination would be very low for the fittest members of the society, there is a chance that even the best individuals could be removed. The advantage of this scheme is that it may save some individuals whose overall fitness is poor but that include some genetic material, which can contribute to a more successful solution over generations. This algorithm is called *Monte Carlo, fitness proportionate selection,* or *roulette wheel.*

We next describe and give examples of several genetic operators. First, we must select representations for solutions that are amenable to these genetic operators. A common approach is to represent each candidate solution as a series of *binary integers*, or *bits*. These are 0 and 1, plus we add the pattern #, to represent either a 0 or a 1. Thus, the pattern 1##00##1 represents all strings of eight bits that begin and end with 1 and that have two 0 s in the middle.

The genetic algorithm begins by creating, often randomly, a population of candidate solution patterns. Evaluation of a candidate assumes a fitness function that returns a measure of each candidate's "quality" at a particular time. A common method for determining a candidate's fitness is to test it on a set of problem situations and calculate the percentage of correct results. Using such a fitness function, the evaluation assigns each candidate a value that is the average fitness over all the problem situations. It is also common for the fitness measure to change across time periods so that it becomes a function of the stage of the overall problem solution.

After evaluating each candidate, the algorithm selects pairs of these candidates for a recombination procedure that produces the next generation. Recombination uses *genetic operators* to produce new solutions by combining components of their parents. As with natural evolution, the fitness of a candidate determines the extent to which it reproduces, with those candidates having the highest fitness given a greater probability of reproducing.

A number of genetic operators produce offspring that preserve features of their parents; the most common of these is *crossover*. Crossover takes two candidate solutions and divides them, swapping components to produce two new candidates. Figure 6.1 illustrates crossover on two bit string patterns of length 8. The operator splits the strings in the middle and forms two children whose initial segments come from one parent and the remainder comes from the other. Note that splitting the candidate solution in the middle is an arbitrary choice. This split may be at any point in the representation, and indeed, this splitting point can be randomly adjusted or changed during the solution process.

For example, suppose the task of a problem is to create a set of bit strings beginning and ending with a 1. Both the parent strings in Fig. 6.1 would have performed relatively well on this task. However, the first offspring would be much better than either parent: It would not have any false results and would fail to match fewer strings that were actually in the solution class. Note also that its sibling is worse than either parent and will probably be eliminated over the next few generations.

Mutation is often considered the most important genetic operator. Mutation takes a single candidate and randomly changes some aspect of it. For example, mutation

Fig. 6.1 Using the crossover genetic operator on two bit strings of length 8. #, don't care, indicates that either a 0 or 1 can be in that location

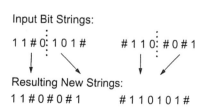

Input Bit Strings:

1 1 # 0 1 0 1 #   # 1 1 0 # 0 # 1

Resulting New Strings:

1 1 # 0 # 0 # 1   # 1 1 0 1 0 1 #

may select a bit in the pattern and change it, switching a 1 to a 0 or #. Mutation is important because the initial population may exclude an essential component of a solution. In our example, if no member of the initial population has a 1 in the first position, then crossover, because it preserves the first four bits of the parent as the first four bits of the child, cannot produce an offspring that does. Mutation would be needed in this situation to change the values of these bits. Other genetic operators, for example, *inversion*, or reversing the order of bits, could also accomplish this task.

The genetic algorithm continues until some termination requirement is met, where one or more candidate's solution's fitness exceeds some threshold. In the next section, we present the genetic algorithm's representations, operators, and fitness evaluations for the *traveling salesperson problem*. We then give examples of genetic programming.

6.2.1   The Traveling Salesperson Problem

The Traveling Salesperson problem, or *TSP*, is a classic problem in computer science. The statement of the problem is simple:

> A salesperson is required to visit N cities as part of a sales route. There is a cost, e.g., mileage or air fare, associated with each pair of cities on the route. Find the least cost path to start at one city, visit all the other cities exactly once, and return to the starting city.

The state-space search, Sect. 4.1, for the TSP has $N!$, or $N \times (N - 1) \times (N - 2) \ldots \times 1$ states, where N is the number of cities to be visited. For a large number of cities, exhaustive search is impossible; heuristic approaches are often used to discover a good enough, but perhaps not optimal, solution.

The TSP has some important applications, including circuit board drilling, X-ray crystallography, and routing in VLSI fabrication. Some of these problems require visiting tens of thousands of points (cities) with a minimum cost path. One question for the analysis of the TSP class of problems is whether it is worth running an expensive computer for many hours to get a near-optimal solution or run a cheap computer for a few minutes to get "good enough" results. The TSP is a complex problem and an excellent test bed for evaluating different search strategies.

How might we use a genetic algorithm to solve this problem? First, we must choose a representation for the path of cities visited. We also have to create a set of genetic operators that produce new paths. The design of a fitness function, however, is very straightforward: All we need to do is to evaluate the cost of traveling on each path. We can then order the paths by their cost, the cheaper the better.

Let's consider some obvious representations that turn out to have important ramifications. Suppose we have nine cities to visit, 1, 2, ..., 9, and we make the representation of a path to be the ordered listing of these nine integers. Next, we make each city a four-bit pattern, 0001, 0010, ..., 1001. Thus, the pattern:

$$0001 0010 0011 0100 0101 0110 0111 1000 1001$$

represents a visit to each city in the order of its numbering. We have inserted spaces into the string only to make it easier to read. Next, consider the genetic operators. Crossover is definitely out, since the new string produced from two different parents would most probably not represent a path that visits each city exactly once. In fact, with crossover, some cities could be removed while others would be visited more than once.

For mutation, suppose the leftmost bit of the sixth city, 0110, is mutated to a 1. 1110, or 14, is no longer a legitimate city. Inversion, and swapping cities, i.e., the four bits in the city pattern, within the path would be acceptable genetic operators but would these be powerful enough to obtain a satisfactory solution? One way to look at the search for the minimum path is to generate and evaluate all possible orderings, or permutations, of the N elements of the city list. The genetic operators must be able to produce all these permutations.

Another approach to the TSP is to ignore the bit pattern representation and give each city an alphabetic or numeric name, e.g., 1, 2, ..., 9; make the path through the cities an ordering of these nine digits, and then select appropriate genetic operators for producing new paths. Mutation, as long as it was a random exchange of two cities in the path, would work, but the crossover operator between two paths would be useless. The exchange of pieces of a path with other pieces of the same path, or any operator that shuffled the letters of the path, without removing, adding, or duplicating any cities, would also work. These approaches, however, make it difficult to combine into offspring the "better" elements of the two different parents' paths between the cities.

A number of researchers, including Davis (1985) and Oliver et al. (1987), created crossover operators that overcome these problems and support work with the ordered list of cities visited. For example, Davis has defined an operator called *order crossover*. Suppose we have nine cities, 1, 2, ..., 9, and the order of the integers represents the order of visited cities. Order crossover builds offspring by choosing a subsequence of cities within the path of one parent. It also preserves the relative ordering of cities from the other parent. First, select two cut points, indicated by a "‖", which are randomly inserted into the same location of each parent. The locations of the cut points are random, but once selected, the same locations must be used for both parents. For example, for two parents $p1$ and $p2$, with cut points after the third and seventh cities:

$$p1 = (192\|4657\|83).$$

$$p2 = (459\|1876\|23).$$

Two children, or new lists of cities to visit, $c1$ and $c2$ are produced in the following way. First, the segments between cut points are copied into the offspring:

$$c1 = (x\,x\,x\,\|4657\|x\,x).$$

$$c2 = (x\,x\,x\,\|1876\|x\,x).$$

Next, starting from the second cut point of one parent, the cities from the other parent are copied in the same order, omitting cities already present. When the end of the string is reached, continue on from the beginning. Thus, the sequence of cities from $p2$ is:

$$234591876.$$

Once cities 4, 6, 5, and 7 are removed, since they are already part of the first child, we get the shortened list 2, 3, 9, 1, and 8, which then makes up, preserving the ordering found in $p2$, the remaining cities to be visited by $c1$:

$$c1 = (239\|4657\|18).$$

In a similar manner, we can create the second child $c2$:

$$c2 = (392\|1876\|45).$$

To summarize, for the order crossover operator, pieces of a path are passed on from one parent, $p1$, to a child, $c1$, while the ordering of the remaining cities of the child $c1$ is inherited from the other parent, $p2$. This supports the obvious intuition that the ordering of cities will be important in generating the least costly path, and it is therefore crucial that pieces of this ordering information be passed on from fit parents to their children.

The order crossover algorithm also guarantees that the children will be legitimate, visiting all cities exactly once. If we wished to add a mutation operator to this result, we would have to be careful, as noted earlier, to make it an exchange of cities within the path. The inversion operator, simply reversing the order of all the cities in the tour, would not work, as there is no new path when all cities are inverted. However, if a piece within the path is cut out and inverted and then replaced, it would be an acceptable use of inversion. For example, using the cut ‖ indicator as before, the path:

$$c1 = (239\|4657\|18),$$

becomes, with inversion of the middle section,

$$c1 = (239\|7564\|18).$$

A new mutation operator could be defined that randomly selected a city and placed it in a new randomly selected location in the path. This mutation operator could also operate on a piece of the path, for example, to take a subpath of three cities and place them in the same order in a new location within the path. Once appropriate genetic operators are chosen to produce children that preserve the constraint of visiting all cities, the genetic algorithm can be run. The fitness function, as noted above, is to evaluate the path costs for each child and then to decide which "cheapest" paths to keep for the next iteration of the algorithm.

Genetic algorithms are used in a wide range of applications. They have also been applied to more complex representations, including *if... then...* production rules, to evolve rule sets adapted to interacting with an environment. An example of this approach is John Holland's (1986) *classifier systems.* A further example, genetic programming, combines and mutates fragments of computer code in an attempt to evolve a program for solving problems, for example, to discover patterns in sets of data. We consider *genetic programming* next.

6.2.2   *Genetic Programming*

Early research in genetic algorithms focused almost exclusively on lower-level representations, such as strings of $\{0, 1, \#\}$. In addition to supporting straightforward use of genetic operators, bit strings and similar lower level representations give genetic algorithms much of the power of other sub-symbolic approaches, such as connectionist networks. There are problems, however, such as the TSP, which have a more natural encoding at more complex representational levels. We can ask further whether genetic operators can be defined for still richer representations, such as pieces of production rules or computer programs. An important aspect of such representations is their ability to combine distinct, higher level pieces of knowledge through rules or function calls to meet the requirements of specific problems.

It is difficult to define genetic operators that capture the structure of rules or program relationships as well as to have effective application of genetic operators that can be used with these representations. The suggestion of translating rules or programs into bit strings and then to use the standard genetic operators of crossover and mutation fails to produce useful results. As an alternative to representing potential solutions as bit strings, we next describe variations in genetic operators that are applied directly to pieces of computer programs.

Koza (1992, 1994) has suggested that a computer program might evolve through successive applications of genetic operators. In genetic programming, the structures adapted are hierarchically organized segments of computer programs. The learning algorithm maintains a population of candidate programs. The fitness of a program is measured by the ability to solve a set of tasks, and programs are modified by applying crossover and mutation to program subcomponents. Genetic programming searches a space of computer programs of varying size and complexity. The search space is the space of all possible computer programs composed of functions and terminal symbols appropriate to the problem domain. As with all genetic learning algorithms, this search is random, largely blind, and yet surprisingly effective.

Genetic programming starts with an initial population of randomly generated programs made up of appropriate program pieces. These pieces, suitable for a problem domain, may consist of standard mathematical functions, as well as logical and domain-specific procedures, and other related programming operations. Program components include data items of the usual types: boolean (true/false), integers, real numbers, vectors, and symbolic expressions.

After initialization, the production of new programs comes with the application of genetic operators. Crossover, mutation, and other operators must be customized for the production of computer programs. The fitness of each new program is then determined by seeing how well it performs in a particular problem environment which will vary according to the problem domain. Any program that does well on this fitness task will survive to help produce the children of the next generation.

To summarize, *genetic programming* includes five components, many very similar to those of genetic algorithms:

1. A set of structures that undergo transformation by genetic operators.
2. A set of initial structures suited to a problem domain.
3. A fitness measure, e.g., problems from the solution domain, to evaluate structures.
4. A set of genetic operators to transform structures.
5. A set of termination conditions.

In the following paragraphs, we address each of these topics. First, genetic programming manipulates hierarchically organized program modules. The Lisp computer language, created in the late 1950s by John McCarthy, one of the organizers of the 1956 AI Dartmouth summer workshop, is *functional,* Sect. 1.3. Lisp program components are *symbol expressions* or *s-expressions*. These symbol expressions have a natural representation as trees, Sect. 4.1, where the function is the root of the tree, and the arguments of the function, either terminating symbols or other functions, descend from the root. Figures 6.2, 6.3, and 6.4 are examples of s-expressions represented as trees. Koza's genetic operators manipulate these s-expressions. In particular, operators map tree structures of s-expressions into new trees or new Lisp program segments. Although s-expression manipulation is the basis for Koza's early work, other researchers have applied genetic programming to different languages and paradigms.

Genetic programming constructs meaningful programs given that the atomic pieces and appropriate functions of the problem area are available. When setting up a domain for creating programs sufficient to address a set of problems, we must first analyze what terminal symbols are required. Then, we select program segments sufficient for producing these terminals. As Koza notes (1992, p. 86) "... the user of

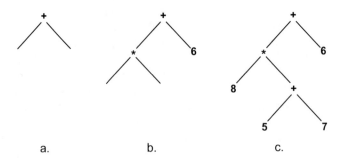

Fig. 6.2 The random generation of a program of Lisp s-expressions. The operator nodes, +, *, are from the set F of Lisp functions. The figure is adapted from Koza (1992)

Fig. 6.3 Two programs, selected for fitness, are randomly chosen for crossover. The "|" represents the point selected for crossover. Figure adapted from Koza (1992)

Fig. 6.4 The child programs produced by the crossover operator are applied to Fig. 6.3. Figure adapted from Koza (1992)

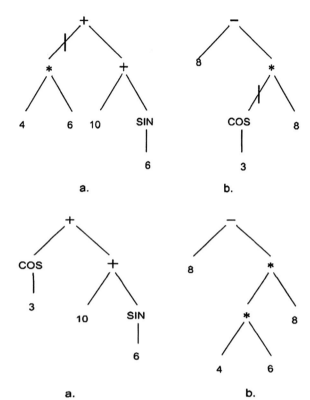

genetic programming should know ... that some composition of the functions and terminals he supplies can yield a solution of the problem."

Thus, to create the structures for use by genetic operators, first create two sets: F, the set of functions, and T, the set of terminal values required for the domain. F can be as simple as $\{+, *, -, /\}$ or may require more complex functions such as sin(X), cos(X), or matrix operations. T may be the integers, real numbers, matrices, or more complex expressions. The symbols in T must include all symbols that the functions defined in F can produce.

Next, a population of initial "programs" is generated by randomly selecting elements from the union of sets F and T. For example, if we begin by selecting an element of T, we have a degenerate tree of a single root node. When we start with an element from F, say +, we get a root node of a tree with two potential children. Suppose the initialization then selects *, with two potential children from F, as the first child, and then terminal 6 from T as the second child. Another random selection might yield terminal 8 and then the function + from F. Assume it concludes by selecting 5 and 7 from T.

The program we have randomly produced is represented in Fig. 6.2. Figure 6.2a gives the tree after the first selection of +, Fig. 6.2b after selecting terminal 6, and Fig. 6.2c the final program. A population of similar programs is created to initialize the genetic programming process. Sets of constraints, such as the maximum depth for programs to evolve, can help control population growth. A more complete description of these constraints, as well as different methods for generating initial populations, may be found in Koza (1992).

The discussion to this point addresses the issues of representation, s-expressions, and the set of tree structures necessary to initialize a situation for program evolution. Next, we require a fitness measure for populations of possible programs. The fitness measure is problem-dependent and usually consists of a set of tasks the evolved programs must be able to solve. The fitness measure itself is a function of how well each program does on these tasks.

One example fitness measure is called *raw fitness*. This score adds the differences between what a program produces and the results that the actual task of the problem required. Thus, raw fitness is the sum of errors across a set of tasks. Other fitness measures are also possible. *Normalized fitness* divides raw fitness by the total sum of possible errors which puts all fitness measures within the range of 0 to 1. Normalization can have an advantage when trying to select from a large population of programs. Fitness measures can also include an adjustment for the size of the program, for example, to reward smaller, more compact programs.

Genetic operators, besides transforming program trees, also include the exchange of structures between trees. Koza (1992) describes the primary transformations as *reproduction* and *crossover*. Reproduction simply selects programs from the present generation and copies them unchanged into the next generation. Crossover exchanges subtrees between the trees representing two programs.

For example, suppose we are working with the two parent programs of Fig. 6.3 and that the random points indicated by ‖ in parents a and b are selected for crossover. The resulting children are shown in Fig. 6.4. Crossover can also be used to transform a single parent by interchanging two subtrees from that parent. Two identical parents can create different children with randomly selected crossover points. The root of a program can also be selected as a crossover point.

There are a number of secondary, less used, genetic transforms of program trees. These include *mutation*, which simply introduces random changes in the structures of a program. For example, replacing a terminal value with another value or a function subtree. The *permutation* transform, similar to the inversion operator on strings, also works on single programs, exchanging terminal symbols, or subtrees.

The state of the solution is reflected by the current generation of programs. There is no record keeping for backtracking or any other method for skipping around the fitness landscape. From this viewpoint, genetic programming is much like a *hill-climbing* algorithm (Pearl 1984), where the "best" children are selected at any time, regardless of what the ultimate best program might be. The genetic programming paradigm parallels nature in that the evolution of new programs is a continuing process. Nonetheless, lacking infinite time and computation, termination conditions are set. These are usually a function of both program fitness and computational resources.

The fact that genetic programming is a technique for the computational generation of computer programs also places it within the *automated programming* research tradition. From the earliest days, AI practitioners have worked to create programs that automatically produce programs and solutions from fragmentary information. We saw this with John von Neumann's research in Sect. 6.1. Genetic programming is another tool in this important research domain.

6.2.3   An Example: Kepler's Third Law of Planetary Motion

John Koza (1992, 1994) describes many applications of genetic programming that solve interesting problems, but most of his examples are rather large and too complex for our present purposes. Melanie Mitchell (1996), however, has created an example that illustrates many of the concepts of genetic programming. Kepler's *Third Law of Planetary Motion* describes the functional relationship between the orbit time period, P, of a planet and its average distance, A, from the sun.

Kepler's Third Law with c, a constant, is:

$$P^2 = cA^3.$$

If we assume that P is expressed in units of earth years, and A in units of earth's average distance from the sun, then $c = 1$. The s-expression of this relationship is:

$$P = \left(\text{sqrt}\left(*A\left(*A\,A\right)\right)\right).$$

Thus, the program we want to evolve for Kepler's third Law is represented by the tree structure of Fig. 6.5. The selection of the set of terminal symbols in this example is simple; it is the single real value given by A. The set of functions could be equally simple, say {+, −, *, /, sq., sqrt}.

We begin with a random population of programs. This population might include:

$$\left(*A\left(-\left(*A\,A\right)\left(\text{sqrt}\,A\right)\right)\right), \text{with fitness} = 1.$$

Fig. 6.5 The target program for relating the orbit P to the period for Kepler's Third Law. A is the average distance of the planet from the sun. Figure adapted from Mitchell (1996)

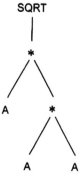

$$\big(/A\big(/\big(/AA\big)\big(/AA\big)\big)\big), \text{with fitness} = 3.$$

$$\big(+A\big(*\big(\text{sqrt}\,A\big)A\big)\big), \text{with fitness} = 0.$$

As noted earlier in this section, the initial population often has a priori limits, both of size and search depth, given knowledge of the problem. These three examples are represented with the program trees of Fig. 6.6.

Next, we determine a suite of tests for the population of programs. Suppose we know some planetary data we want our evolved program to explain. For example, we have the planetary data in Table 6.1, taken from Urey (1982), which gives a set of data points that the evolving programs must explain.

Since the fitness measure is a function of the data points of Table 6.1, we will define fitness as the number of results from running each program that come within 20% of these correct values. We used this definition to create the fitness measures for the three programs of Fig. 6.6. It remains for the reader to create more members of this initial population, to build crossover and mutation operators that can produce further generations of programs, and to determine termination conditions.

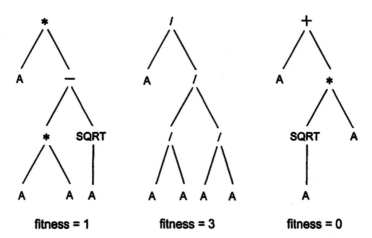

Fig. 6.6 Members of the initial set of random programs generated to solve the orbital/period problem. Figure adapted from Mitchell (1996)

Table 6.1 A set of observed
planetary data, adapted from
Urey (1982), used to
determine the fitness of each
evolved program

Planet	A (input)	P (output)
Venus	0.72	0.61
Earth	1.0	1.0
Mars	1.52	1.87
Jupiter	5.2	11.9
Saturn	9.53	29.4
Uranus	19.1	83.5

A is Earth's semi-major axis of orbit
and P, the length of time for an orbit,
is in units of earth-years

6.3   Artificial Life: The Emergence of Complexity

Section 6.2 presented genetic algorithms and programming, one research direction
that grew out of John von Neumann's 1940s work in cellular automata, Sect. 6.1. A
second major result of von Neumann's effort is *artificial life* or *a-life*.

Artificial life programs demonstrate the emergence of "life forms" changing over
time. The success of these programs is not shaped by a priori fitness functions, as
seen in genetic algorithms and programs, but rather by the simple fact that they can
survive and replicate. There is an inductive bias implicit in the design of the automata that supports a-life programs, but their success is their replication and endurance
over time. On the darker side, we have all experienced the legacy of a-life in computer viruses and worms that are able to work their way into foreign hosts, replicate
themselves, often destroying information in memory, and then move on to infect
other hosts.

The *Game of Life*, often called *Life*, is not to be confused with Milton Bradley's
board game, *The Game of Life*, created and patented in the 1860s. The computational *Game of Life* was originally created by the mathematician John Horton
Conway and introduced to the larger community by Martin Gardner (1970, 1971) in
Scientific American.

In the computational game, the birth, survival, or death of individuals is a function of their own state and the states of their near neighbors. Typically, a small
number of rules, usually three or four, are sufficient to define the game. Despite this
simplicity, experiments with the game have shown it to be capable of evolving structures of extraordinary complexity and ability, including self-replicating, multi-
cellular "organisms" (Poundstone 1985).

The Game of Life is most effectively demonstrated in computational visual simulations (url 6.1) with succeeding generations rapidly changing and evolving on a
screen display. The Game of Life and von Neumann's automata of Sect. 6.1 are
examples of a model of computation called the *finite-state machine* or *cellular
automaton*. Cellular automata exhibit interesting and emergent behaviors through

interactions within a population. We explain these next, but begin with a definition:

A *finite state machine* or *cellular automaton* is a connected graph consisting of three components, sets S and I, and a transition function F:

1. A finite set of states, $S = s_1, s_2, s_3, \ldots s_n$, each part of the connected graph.
2. A finite set of input signals, $I = i_1, i_2, i_3, \ldots i_m$ called the *input alphabet*.
3. F is a state transition function that, for each input signal from the set I, takes a state of S to its next state in the connected graph.

Figure 6.7a presents an example of a simple two-state finite state machine, and Fig. 6.7b describes the transition rules for Fig. 6.7a. The transition rules are given by the rows of Fig. 6.7b. For example, the row to the right of s_0 says, when the present state is s_0 and 0 is the input signal, then s_0 remains as s_0. If 1 is the input, then s_0 transitions to state s_1. Thus any "next state" of the finite state machine of Fig. 6.7 is the result of its present state and the input values for that state.

The cellular automata for artificial life, as we see next in Sect. 6.3.1, can be seen as a two-dimensional grid of states. Each state will receive its input signal at every discrete period of time, and so every state will be acting in parallel. The input to each state is a function of the value of the current state and all its "neighbors." Thus, a state at time $(t + 1)$ is a function of its present state and *the state of its neighbors* at time t. It is through these interactions with neighbors that collections of cellular automata achieve much richer behaviors than simple finite state machines. Because the next state for all states of the system is a function of its neighboring states, we can consider these state machines as examples of society-based adaptation.

For the societies described in this section, there is no explicit evaluation of the fitness of individual members. Survival results from interactions within the population. Fitness is implicit in the survival of individuals from generation to generation. As occurs in natural evolution, adaptation is shaped by the actions of other co-evolving members of the population.

A global or society-oriented viewpoint also supports an important perspective on learning: We no longer need to focus exclusively on the individual as learning but rather can see invariances and regularities emerging from within the society as a whole. This is an important aspect of the Crutchfield and Mitchell research (1995).

Finally, unlike supervised learning, evolution is not teleological or goal oriented. That is, the society of agents needn't be seen as "going somewhere," e.g., to some *omega point* (de Chardin 1955). There is supervised learning when using the explicit fitness measures of genetic algorithms and programs. But as Stephen Jay Gould

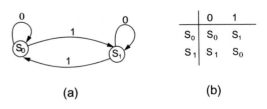

Fig. 6.7 A connected graph representing a finite state machine. (**a**) Is the graph and (**b**) is the transition rules for (**a**)

(1977, 1996) points out, evolution need not be viewed as making things "better," rather it just favors survival. The only success is continued existence, and the patterns that emerge are the patterns of an interacting society.

6.3.1   Artificial Life

Consider the simple, potentially infinite, two-dimensional grid or game board of Fig. 6.8. Here one square, in black, is "alive," having state value 1, with its eight neighbors indicated by gray shading. The four shaded states that share a boundary line with the black, alive state, are the direct neighbors. The board is transformed over time periods, where the state of each square at time $t + 1$ is a function of its own state value and the state values of its neighbors at time t.

Figure 6.9 describes an a-life example of a "blinking light." Three simple rules drive evolution in this example: First, if any square, alive or not, has exactly three of its neighbors alive, it will survive at the next time period. Second, if any square has exactly two of its direct neighbors alive, it will survive in the next time period. Finally, for all other situations, the square will not be alive at the next time period. One interpretation of these rules is that, for each generation, life at any location is a result of its own situation as well as that of its neighbors during the previous generation. Specifically, at any time period, too dense a population of surrounding neighbors, more than three, or too sparse a neighboring population, less than two, will not support life for the next generation.

Consider, as an example, the state of life for Fig. 6.9a. Here, two squares, indicated by an x, have exactly three occupied neighbors. At the next life cycle, Fig. 6.8b will be produced. Here again there are two squares, indicated by y, with exactly three occupied neighbors. It can be seen that the state of the world will cycle back and forth between Fig. 6.9a, and Fig. 6.9b. Using the same transition rules as applied

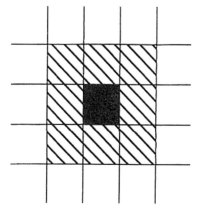

Fig. 6.8 The shaded region indicates the set of neighbors for the dark region in the Game of Life. The four neighbors sharing a boundary are the "direct" neighbors

Fig. 6.9 A set of a-life neighbors that generate the "blinking light"

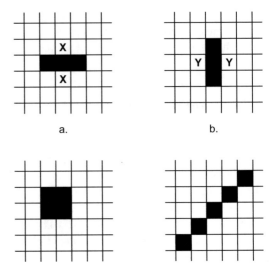

a.

b.

Fig. 6.10 What happens to these a-life patterns at their next state when using the same next state rules as used with the "blinking light" of Fig. 6.9?

a.

b.

in Fig. 6.9, the reader can determine what the next states will be for Figs. 6.10a and b and can examine other possible "world" configurations.

One tool for understanding possible worlds is to simulate and analyze society-based movement and interaction effects. We have several examples of this, including the sequence of time cycles demonstrated in Fig. 6.11 that implements a *glider*. In five time steps, the glider sweeps across the game space as it cycles through a small number of patterns. Its action is simple as it moves to a new location one row further to the right and one row below on the grid.

Because of their ability to produce rich collective behaviors through the interactions of simple cells, cellular automata have proven a powerful tool for studying the mathematics of the emergence of life from simple, inanimate components. *Artificial life* is defined as *life made by human effort rather than by nature*. As can be seen in the examples, artificial life has a strong "bottom-up" flavor; that is, the atoms of a life system are defined and assembled, and their physical interactions "emerge." Regularities of this life form are captured by the rules of the finite state machine.

In the game of life, entities such as the glider persist until interacting with other members of their society. The result can be difficult to understand and predict. For example, in Fig. 6.12, two gliders emerge and engage. After four time periods, the glider moving down and to the left is "consumed" by the other glider. It is interesting to note that our ontological descriptions, our use of terms such as "entity," "blinking light," "glider," "consumed," reflects our own anthropocentric biases on viewing life's forms and interactions, whether artificial or not. It is very human, and expected of us, to give names to regularities that emerge within our social structures, as pointed out by William James (1902) and other pragmatists.

The "Game of Life" is an intuitive, highly descriptive example of cellular automata.

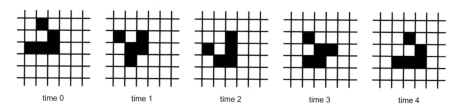

Fig. 6.11 A "glider" moves across the display

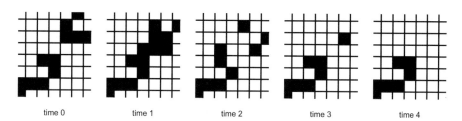

Fig. 6.12 A "glider" is "consumed" by another entity

Although we have presented the fundamentals of this technology, our visualizations of active parallel cellular automata are minimal! Computer-based simulations are best for appreciating the evolution and complexity of a-life forms (url 6.1). We next extend our discussion of cellular automata by discussing alternative perspectives that have grown from the a-life tradition.

6.3.2   Contemporary Approaches to A-Life

To conclude Sect. 6.3, we mention several research domains that use the technology of evolutionary computation to extend our understanding of ourselves and the world. The topics we mention are a small subset of the research in evolutionary computation. The a-life community has regular conferences and journals reflecting this diversity (Langton 1995).

Synthetic Biological Models of Evolution

An important challenge for *artificial life* is to simulate the conditions of biological evolution itself through the interactions of finite state machines, defined by sets of states and transition rules. These automata are able to accept information from outside themselves, in particular from their closest neighbors. Their transition rules include instructions for birth, continuing in life, and dying. When a population of such automata is set loose in a domain and allowed to act as parallel asynchronous cooperating agents, we sometimes witness the evolution of seemingly independent "life forms."

One definition of *synthetic biology* is "An emerging discipline that uses engineering principles to design and assemble biological components" (Wellhausen and Oye 2007). Applications of computational biology include building living cell structures that can perform analog and digital computing (Purcell and Lu 2014). One task for these computers is to control the transcription of synthetic DNA. Another task would be to act as biosensors, able to report the presence of heavy metals or toxins within a living organism. Other tasks for synthetic biology include building gene circuits, designing synthetic proteins, and perhaps even artificial living cells.

On a larger scale, the determined effort of many biologists and engineers is to fill in the gaps in knowledge of our actual evolution; there is continued speculation about rerunning the story of evolution itself. What might have happened if evolution began with different initial conditions? What if there were alternative intervening "accidents" within our physical and biological surroundings? What might have emerged? What would remain constant? The biological path that actually did occur on earth is one of many possible trajectories. These questions might be addressed if we could generate some of the different biological systems that might be possible.

How can a-life constructs be used in biology? For example, the set of living entities provided by nature, as complex and diverse as they may be, are dominated by accident and historical contingency. We trust that there are logical regularities at work in the creation of this set, but there need not be, and it is unlikely that we will discover many of the total possible regularities when we restrict our view to the set of biological entities that nature actually provides. It is critical to explore the full set of possible biological regularities, some of which may have been eliminated by historical or evolutionary accident. We can always wonder what the present world would be like had not the dinosaurs' existence been peremptorily terminated. To have a theory of the actual, it is necessary to understand the limits of the possible.

Artificial Chemistry

A-life technology is not just an artifact of computational or biological domains. Research scientists from areas as diverse as chemistry and pharmacology build synthetic artifacts, many related to the knowledge of actual entities existing in our world. For example, in the field of chemistry, research into the constitution of matter and the many compounds that nature provide has led to the analysis of these compounds, their constituent pieces, and their bonds.

This analysis and recombination have led to the creation of numerous compounds that do not exist naturally. Our knowledge of the building blocks of nature has led us to our own synthetic versions, putting components of reality together in new and different patterns. It is through this careful analysis of natural chemical compounds that we come to some understanding of the set of possible compounds.

In a survey of work in artificial chemistry, Dittrich et al. (2001) describe research activities in three domains: modeling, information processing, and optimization. In modeling, the working hypothesis is that biotic phenomena can be described through the use of complex combinations of many interacting components. From this viewpoint, living organisms have certain properties not because their components have these properties, but their overall functioning emerges through the organization of these constituent components. Local interactions, under simple effective rules, produce global behavior. Dittrich et al. (2001) conjecture that models should lead to an explanation of the growth of evolutionary systems as well as support for the investigation of the theoretical conditions enabling the origin and evolution of life.

In the area of information processing, the computation properties supporting chemical systems are explored. For example, chemical reaction networks support the movement of bacteria. Other chemical properties support neuron growth within the development of the human brain. Actual chemical computing, it is conjectured, supports most aspects of both normal human growth as well as the creation of disease states. In optimization, artificial chemical systems search for solutions in complex problem applications. Optimization search, actualized as artificial chemical systems, employs many of the evolutionary algorithms seen earlier in this chapter.

Other Abstract Machines and Evolutionary Computation

The first and most noteworthy approach to evolutionary computing was John von Neumann's *construction universal* machine, described in Sect. 6.1. von Neumann's machine was created as a theoretical construct and only programmed on a computer in the 1990s. von Neumann's machine was also proven to be able to compute any task that we currently know as computable.

Since von Neumann, a number of computer scientists, anthropologists, chemists, philosophers, and others have continued in this tradition. This is a natural expectation, since, in theory, the process of evolution is not restricted to taking place on earth or with a carbon basis. We briefly describe several of these efforts:

1. **Tierra**. Tom Ray (1991) describes Tierra programming as "virtual computing with a Darwinian operating system." Tierra's architecture is designed so that machine codes are evolvable. The machine code can be mutated, by flipping bits at random, and recombined by swapping segments of code. The operating system tracks the interactions that take place between individuals and maintains a "genebank" of successful, that is, surviving, genomes. Tierra's different genotypes compete for CPU time, their energy resource, and for memory space, their material resource.
2. **Avida**. Chris Adami and Titus Brown (1994) have created a Tierra-inspired artificial life system with local interactions in two-dimensional geometry. Avida is based on mechanisms similar to that of two-dimensional cellular automata. The special geometry is intended to support diversity and thus improve adaptation. Cells are bred with simple computing abilities. This computation supports adaptation's relationships with mutation rate and with population size.
3. **Ulam**. David and Elena Ackley (2016) describe Ulam as a programming language designed to work on hardware where deterministic execution is not guar-

anteed. Ulam's programs are organized less like traditional algorithms and more like living processes using reproduction, swarming, growth, and healing. Ulam's primary task is to provide a framework for envisioning, expressing, and reasoning about physically realizable dynamic behavior.

4. **OOCC.** Inspired by the work of Fontana and Buss (1996) who built an artificial chemistry-based *lambda-calculus*, Lance Williams (2016) demonstrates parallel distributed spatially embedded self-replicating programs that resemble living cells. Williams uses compositional devices borrowed from the field of programming languages as the basis for new artificial chemistry called *Object-Oriented Combinator Chemistry*. From object-oriented programming languages, Williams borrows the idea of association of programs with the data they act on and encapsulation of one object inside another (Paun 1998). From functional programming languages, he borrows the idea of combinators returning monadic types (Wadler 1990). These combinators function as the building blocks of computer programs that mediate the behavior of computational elements. The result produces living processes that are similar to those described by Ackley and Ackley (2016) in Ulam.

Concluding this subsection, we offer several comments on the various forms of a-life presented. First, no evolutionary computation research to date has suggested how life itself might begin. Second, there is no demonstration of how, with increased complexity, new species might emerge. Finally, the question remains whether a-life computation is limited by our current understanding of what is computable.

Psychological and Sociological Foundations for Life and Intelligence

The combination of a distributed, agent-based architecture and the adaptive pressures of natural selection is a powerful model of the origins and operations of the mind. Evolutionary psychologists (Cosmides and Tooby 1992, 1994; Barkow et al. 1992) have provided models of how natural selection has shaped the development of the innate structure and biases in the human mind. The basis of evolutionary psychology is a view of the mind as modular and as a system of interacting, highly specialized agent processors.

There is increasing evidence that human minds are highly modular. Fodor (1983) offers a philosophical argument for the modular structure of the mind. Minsky (1985) explores the ramifications of modular theories for human and artificial intelligence. A modular architecture is important to theories of the evolution of the mind. It would be difficult to imagine how evolution could shape a single system as complex as a mind. It is, however, plausible that evolution, working over millions of years, could successively shape individual, specialized cognitive skills. As evolution of the brain continues, it could also work on combinations of modules, forming the mechanisms that enable modules to interact, to share information, and to cooperate to perform increasingly complex cognitive tasks (Mithen 1996).

Theories of neuronal selection (Edelman 1992) show how these same processes can account for the adaptation of the individual neural system. *Neural Darwinism* models the adaptation of neural systems in Darwinian terms: the strengthening of particular circuits in the brain and the weakening of others is a process of selection in response to the world. Learning requires the extraction of information from training data and using that information to build models of the world. Theories of neuronal selection examine the effect of selective pressures on populations of neurons and their interactions. Edelman (1992, p. 81) states:

> In considering brain science as a science of recognition I am implying that recognition is not an instructive process. No direct information transfer occurs, just as none occurs in evolutionary or immune processes. Instead, recognition is selective.

Collaborative agent components offer models of social cooperation as well. Using such approaches, economists have constructed informative, if not completely predictive, models of economic markets. Agent technologies have an increasing influence on the design of distributed computing systems, the construction of Internet search tools, and the implementation of cooperative work environments.

Modular collaborating processors have also exerted influence on theories of consciousness. For example, Daniel Dennett (1991, 1995, 2006) has based an account of the function and structure of consciousness as an agent-based architecture of mind. He begins by arguing that it is incorrect to ask where consciousness is located in the mind/brain. Instead, his *multiple draft theory of consciousness* focuses on the role of consciousness in the interactions of different components within a distributed mental architecture.

In the course of perception, motor control, problem-solving, learning, and other mental activities, we form coalitions of interacting processes. These coalitions are highly dynamic and change in response to the needs of different situations. Consciousness, for Dennett, serves as a binding mechanism for these coalitions, supporting agent interaction and raising critical coalitions of agents to the foreground of cognitive processing.

This chapter concludes with a discussion of the epistemic constraints of evolutionary computation as well as some summary thoughts on Part II.

6.4 Evolutionary Computation and Intelligence: Epistemic Issues

Genetic and emergent models of computation offer one of the most exciting approaches to understanding both human and artificial intelligence. These systems demonstrate that globally intelligent behavior can arise from the cooperation of large numbers of restricted, independent, and individual agents. Genetic and emergent theories view complex results through the interrelationships of societies of relatively simple structures.

John Holland (1995) offers an example of the emergence of a complex solution. By what mechanisms, Holland asks, is a large city such as New York supplied with bread each day? The fact that the city has adequate quantities of bread demonstrates the fundamental processes underlying the emergence of intelligence in an agent-based system. It is unlikely that anyone could write a centralized planning program that would successfully supply New Yorkers with the rich variety of bread to which they are accustomed. Indeed, several unfortunate experiments with central planning have revealed the limitations of such approaches.

However, without a centralized planning algorithm that keeps New Yorkers supplied with bread, the loosely coordinated efforts of the city's many bakers, truckers, suppliers of raw materials, as well as its retailers and consumers solve the problem quite well. Again, as in all agent-based emergent systems, there is no central plan. No one baker has more than a very limited knowledge of what the city's bread requirements might be. Each baker simply tries to optimize his or her own business opportunities. The solution to the global problem emerges from the collective activities of these independent and local agents.

By demonstrating how highly goal-directed, robust, nearly optimal behaviors can arise from the interactions of local individual agents, these models provide yet another answer to the old philosophical questions of the origins of mind. The central lesson of emergent approaches to intelligence is that full intelligence can and does arise from the interactions of many simple, individual, local, and embodied agent intelligence, as Minsky (1985) suggested in his book *Society of Mind*.

Another major feature of emergent models is their reliance on Darwinian selection as the basic mechanism that shapes the behavior of individuals. In the bakery example, it seems that each individual baker does not behave in a manner that is, in some sense, globally optimal. The source of their optimality is not of a central design; it is the simple fact that bakers who do a poor job of satisfying the needs of their local customers generally fail. It is through the tireless, persistent operations of these selective pressures that individual bakers arrive at the behaviors that lead to their individual survival as well as to a useful emergent collective behavior that, each day, supplies the bread needs of the city.

An important source of the power of evolutionary computation is the *implicit parallelism* inherent in evolutionary operators. In comparison with state-space search and an ordering algorithm for considering next states, search moves in parallel, operating on entire families of potential solutions. By restricting the reproduction of weaker candidates, genetic algorithms may not only eliminate that solution but all of its descendants. For example, the string, 101#0##1, if broken at its midpoint, can parent a whole family of strings of the form 101#____. If the parent is found to be unfit, its elimination can also remove all of these potential offspring and perhaps, the possibility of a solution as well. As seen in Fig. 6.12, two shapes that artificial life created in parallel can then interact and change each other.

Algorithms for evolutionary computation are now widely used in both applied problem-solving and in scientific modeling. There remains, however, interest in understanding their theoretical foundations, the practical implications of their evolving forms, and the limits of their productive possibilities. Several questions that naturally arise include:

1. How are the beginning forms for evolutionary computation created? Where do these entities come from?
2. What does it mean for an evolutionary computational algorithm to perform well or poorly for a fixed problem type? Is there any mathematical or empirical understanding of its strengths and/or constraints?
3. Is there any way to describe the differential effects of different genetic operators: crossover, mutation, inversion, etc., over time?
4. Using finite state machines, what is the relationship between the choices, or inductive biases, implicit in building the automaton and what it is possible for the automaton to produce?
5. Under what circumstances, i.e., what problems and what genetic operators, will genetic algorithms or artificial life technology perform better than traditional symbol-based or connectionist AI search methods? Aren't all these computational tools within the limits of what is currently known to be computable?
6. The inability of emergent computation to produce new species or categorically new skills, such as language use, is a very sober reminder that we have much to learn about the forces of evolution.

Agent-based and emergent approaches to computation have opened up a number of problems that must be solved if their promise is to be realized. As just noted, we have yet to fill in all the steps that have enabled the evolution of higher level cognitive abilities such as language. Like paleontologists' efforts to reconstruct the evolution of species, tracing the development of these higher level skills will take additional detailed work. We must both enumerate the processing modules that underlie the architecture of mind as well as trace their continuing evolution across time.

Another problem for agent-based theories is explaining the interactions between modules. Minds exhibit extensive, highly fluid interactions between cognitive domains: We can talk about things we see, indicating an interaction between visual and linguistic modules. We can construct buildings that enable a specific social purpose, indicating an interaction between technical and social intelligence. Poets can construct tactile metaphors for visual scenes, indicating a fluid interaction between visual and tactile modules. Defining the representations and processes that enable these inter-module interactions is an active area of research (Karmiloff-Smith 1992; Mithen 1996; Lakoff and Johnson 1999).

Practical applications of agent-based technologies are also increasingly important. Using computer simulations, it is possible to model complex systems that have no closed-form mathematical description and were heretofore impossible to study in this detail. Simulation-based techniques have been applied to a range of phenomena, such as the adaptation of the human immune system and the control of complex processes, including particle beam accelerators, Klein et al. (2000) and see Sect. 8.4, the behavior of global currency markets, and the study of weather systems. The representational and computational issues that must be solved to implement such simulations continue to drive research in knowledge representations, algorithms, and even the design of computer hardware.

Further practical problems that agent architectures must deal with include protocols for interagent communication, especially when local agents often have limited knowledge of the problem at large or indeed of what knowledge other agents might already possess. Furthermore, few algorithms exist for the decomposition of larger problems into coherent agent-oriented subproblems, or indeed how limited resources might be distributed among agents.

Perhaps the most exciting aspect of emergent theories of mind is their potential for placing mental activities within a unified model of the emergence of order from chaos. Even the brief overview provided in this section has cited work using emergent theories to model a range of processes, from the evolution of the brain over time, to the forces that enable learning in individuals, and to the construction of economic and social models of behavior.

There is something extraordinarily appealing in the notion that the processes of emergent order, as shaped by forms of Darwinian evolution, can explain intelligent behavior at a variety of resolutions. Evolution has structured the interactions of individual neurons, the shaping of the modular structure of the brain, and the functioning of economic markets and social systems.

6.5   Some Summary Thoughts on Part II: Chaps. 4, 5, and 6

We conclude this chapter, and the middle third of this book, with some general thoughts on the artificial intelligence representations and search strategies just presented. We present two epistemic issues next, the *rationalist's inductive bias* and the *empiricist's dilemma*. These *a priori* assumptions are especially relevant in the context of understanding the program designers' pragmatic goals in building intelligent software.

6.5.1   Inductive Bias: The Rationalist's a priori

The AI community's approaches to intelligence described in the last three chapters reflect the a priori biases of their creators. The problem of inductive bias is that the resulting representations and search strategies offer a medium for encoding an already interpreted world. This bias rarely offers mechanisms for questioning our interpretations, generating new viewpoints, or for backtracking and changing specific perspectives when they prove unproductive. This implicit bias leads to the rationalist epistemological trap of seeing in the world exactly and only what we expect or are conditioned to see.

The role of inductive bias must be made explicit in each learning paradigm. Furthermore, just because no inductive bias is acknowledged, doesn't mean it doesn't exist and critically affect the parameters of learning. In symbol-based learning, the inductive bias is often obvious, for example, using a particular search space for a robot controller or a specific set of rules to do medical diagnosis.

Many aspects of connectionist and genetic learning also assume an inductive bias. For instance, the limitations of perceptron networks led to the introduction of hidden nodes. We may well ask what contribution the structuring of the hidden nodes make in solution generation. One way of understanding the role of hidden nodes is that they add dimensions to the representation space.

As a simple example, we saw in Sect. 5.2 that the data points for the *exclusive-or* problem could not be separated by a straight line in two dimensions. The learned weight on the hidden node provides another dimension to the representation. In three dimensions, the points are separable using a two-dimensional plane. Given the two dimensions of the input space and the hidden node, the output layer of this network can then be seen as an ordinary perceptron that is discovering a plane that separates the points in a three-dimensioned space.

Even the generalizations that produce functions can be seen from many different viewpoints. Statistical techniques, for example, have for a long time been able to discover data correlations. Iterative expansion of the Taylor series can be used to approximate most functions. Polynomial approximation algorithms have been used for over a century to approximate functions for fitting data points.

To summarize, the commitments made within a learning scheme, whether symbol-based, connectionist, emergent, or stochastic, to a very large extent mediate the results we can expect from the problem-solving effort. When we appreciate this synergistic effect in the process of designing computational problem-solvers we can both improve our success as well as interpret our failures more insightfully.

6.5.2 The Empiricist's Dilemma

Current approaches to machine learning, especially supervised learning, also possess a dominant inductive bias. Unsupervised learning, including many of the genetic and evolutionary approaches seen in this chapter, has to grapple with the opposite problem, sometimes called *the empiricist's dilemma*. Predominant themes of these research areas include the beliefs that solutions will emerge, alternatives are evolved, and populations reflect the survival of the fittest. This is powerful stuff, especially situated in the context of parallel and distributed search power. But there is a problem: How can we know we are someplace when we are not sure where we are going? How do we accomplish a task if we are not sure what that task is?

Nonetheless, there remains great excitement about unsupervised and evolutionary models of learning. For example, creating networks based on exemplars or energy minimization can be seen as fixed-point attractors or basins for complex relational invariances. We watch as data points "settle" toward attractors and are tempted to see these new architectures as tools for modeling dynamic phenomena. What, we might ask, are the limits of computation in these paradigms?

What is it then, that supervised, unsupervised, or hybrid learners, whether symbolic, connectionist, genetic, or evolving finite state machines, can offer?

1. One of the most attractive features of connectionist learning is that most models are data- or example-driven. That is, although their architectures are explicitly designed, they learn by example, generalizing from data in a particular problem domain. But the question still arises as to whether the data are sufficient or clean enough not to perturb the solution process. What are the roles of meta-parameters, such as the number and size of hidden layers and the learning constant, in network learning?
2. Genetic algorithms also support a powerful and flexible search of a problem space. Genetic search is driven both by the diversity enforced by mutation and by operators such as crossover and inversion, that preserve important aspects of parental information for succeeding generations. How can the program designer understand this diversity/preservation trade-off?
3. Genetic algorithms and connectionist architectures may be viewed as instances of parallel and asynchronous processing. Do they indeed provide results through parallel asynchronous effort not possible with explicit sequential programming?
4. Although the neural and/or sociological inspiration is not important for many modern practitioners of connectionist and genetic and emergent computation, these techniques do reflect many important aspects of natural evolution and selection. We saw in Chap. 5 models for error reduction learning with perceptron, backpropagation, and Hebbian models.
5. Finally, all learning paradigms are tools for empirical enquiry. As we capture many of the invariants of our world, are our tools sufficiently expressive to ask further questions related to perception, understanding, and learning? How do they address the generalization problem seen in Sect. 4.3.2?

We continue discussing many of these themes in the final chapters.

6.6   In Summary

The focus of this chapter was to present genetic and emergent computational models and algorithms for understanding the world. We considered genetic algorithms and programming, artificial life, and evolutionary programming techniques for representing intelligent behavior. Section 6.5 discussed many of the strengths and limitations of the symbolic, connectionist, and emergent approaches to computation-based problem-solving.

With this chapter, we finish the middle section of the book where we described and gave very simple examples of the symbol-based, connectionist, and emergent models of computation. Our goal with each approach was to demonstrate programs and to discuss the epistemic assumptions that both supported their successes as well as limited their possible uses within the AI agenda. Of necessity, our presentation covered only a limited sample of these technologies.

In the final three chapters, we propose that a constructivist epistemology, coupled with the stochastic experimental methods of modern science, offers the tools and techniques for continuing the exploration of a science of intelligent systems as well as affording us the ability to articulate a foundation for a modern epistemology.

Further Thoughts and Readings   The Bibliography offers full reference information for the following reading suggestions.

There are several introductory readings on genetic algorithms and artificial life:

> Holland (1995), *Hidden Order: How Adaptation Builds Complexity.*
> Mitchell (1996), *An Introduction to Genetic Algorithms.*
> Koza (1994), *Genetic Programming: On the Programming of Computers by Means of Natural Selection.*
> Gardner (1970, 1971), *Mathematical Games.*
> Luger (2009a). *Artificial Intelligence: Structures and Strategies for Complex Problem Solving*, Part IV.

Several classic readings the discussion on the constitution of the human mind:

> Edelman (1992), *Bright Air, Brilliant Fire: On the Matter of the Mind.*
> Fodor (1983), *The Modularity of Mind.*
> Haugeland (1997), *Mind Design: Philosophy, Psychology, Artificial Intelligence.*
> Minsky (1985), *The Society of Mind.*
> Mithen (1996), *The Prehistory of the Mind.*

I am indebted to Prof. Lance Williams for comments on this chapter. The figures exemplifying genetic programming were adapted from Koza (1994). The artificial life examples were adapted from Luger (2009a).

Programming Ideas   The reader was offered several challenges in this chapter. One example is to use a programming language, or by hand, to work through the genetic programming discovery of Kepler's Third Law, described in Sect. 6.2.3.

Follow the chapter's references to obtain freely available computer code exploring many of the topics and algorithms presented. Visualization is critical for appreciating the complexities of evolutionary computation.

Part III
Toward an Active, Pragmatic, Model-Revising Realism

Part III is the raison d'être for this book and also presents the fourth emphasis in current AI technology: probabilistic reasoning and dynamic modeling. In Chap. 7, a philosophical rapprochement is proposed between the different approaches AI has taken, which we describe as following the rationalist, empiricist, and pragmatist philosophical traditions. Based on this constructivist synthesis, the chapter ends with a set of assumptions and follow-on conjectures that offer a basis for both current AI research and modern epistemology.

Chapter 8 presents Bayes' theorem along with a proof in a simple situation. The primary reason for introducing Bayes and the technology of Bayesian belief networks and hidden Markov models is to demonstrate a mathematics-based linkage between the *a priori* knowledge of the human subject and *a posteriori* information perceived at any particular time. We see this cognitive quest for equilibrium as a foundation for a modern epistemology. The final half of Chap. 8 describes a number of programs, supported by the Bayesian tradition, that capture and display these epistemic insights.

Chapter 9 summarizes our project and describes building and adapting models of the world through active exploration in the world. We describe the promising future of AI as it continues to use the scientific tradition to expand its horizons, explore our evolving environment, and build intelligent artifacts. We consider the neo-pragmatist thinking of Wittgenstein, Putnam, Kuhn, and Rorty, and insights from cognitive neuroscience that explore the nature of knowledge, meaning, and truth. We conclude with a critique of postmodern relativism and propose the epistemic stance we call *an active, pragmatic, model-revising realism*.

Chapter 7
A Constructivist Rapprochement and an Epistemic Stance

Theories are like nets: he who casts, captures...
—L. WITTGENSTEIN (quoting the poet Novalis)

The essential quality of a proof is to compel belief
—P. de FERMAT

Contents

Part III has three chapters. In Chap. 7, we propose a synthesis of the empiricist, rationalist, and pragmatist AI worldviews seen in Part II. This synthesis is then reflected in a set of five assumptions that ground an epistemic stance. These assumptions support eight conjectures that together offer the components of a modern epistemology. In Chap. 8, we present Bayes' theorem and probabilistic reasoning as sufficient examples of this synthesis. In Chap. 9, we offer several further AI examples and summarize our project, proposing an epistemology called an *active, pragmatic, model-revising realism*.

7.1 A Response to Empiricist, Rationalist, and Pragmatist AI

Computer programs, including those created by the AI community, are the product of human design. Program builders use computer language skills and a commitment to what is "real" in an application domain. Their goal is to produce programs that are "good enough" to produce the desired solutions. This process often includes continued revision of the program itself as its designers come to better understand the problem.

The computer program itself offers a medium for appreciating this exploratory design challenge. We can critique a program's use of symbols, associations of symbols formed in data structures and networks. We can understand a program's algorithms and its embodiment of, and commitment to, a worldview. Allen Newell and Herbert A. Simon suggests exactly this in their Turing Award Lecture (1976):

> Each new program that is built is an experiment. It poses a question to nature, and its behavior offers clues to an answer. Neither machine nor programs are black boxes; they are artifacts that have been designed, both hardware and software, and we can open them up and look inside. We can relate their structure to their behavior, and we can draw many lessons from a single experiment.

Newell and Simon wrote their Turing Award address as symbol-based artificial intelligence was nearing its time of greatest influence. Throughout Chap. 4, we noted how programs using symbol-based technology are transparent, with their structure clearly related to their behavior. Examples included state-space search, game-playing, planning, and the expert systems technology.

As we noted in Sect. 5.4, researchers building deep learning programs, where neural networks with multiple hidden layers consider image classification, robotics, game playing, and other problem areas, continue to explore issues of transparency. We mentioned in Sect. 5.4 the importance of explanation, trust, and accountability from the human use viewpoint. Also critical from the program designer's perspective is the ability to extend functionality, generalize results, and remove inappropriate outcomes.

As examples of Newell and Simon's structure–behavior relationship, the AlphaGo Zero (Silver et al. 2017) and PRM-RL (Faust et al. 2018) research at Google used a reinforcement learning structure to give transparency to solution path data. Micro-actions became integrated into coherent plans as the network searched the space of possible reward-based actions. Other research groups including Balestriero and Baraniuk (2018) and Wang et al. (2019) use affine spline operators in an attempt to capture the utility of hidden nodes in large networks. Research in networks for image classification explains and optimizes their results (van Noord and Postma 2016). Finally, as noted in Sect. 5.4, Riberio et al. (2016) created the LIME program that offers model-agnostic interpretations of results from any deep learning classifier.

In Chap. 6, we saw how evolutionary algorithms produced results through genetic operators. Each generation of possible solutions and the operators that produced them can be examined. In artificial life, the rules of the finite state machines produced specific observable results. The program's structure–behavior relationship for evolutionary algorithms was specific and observable.

Although the search for more transparency and interpretability in deep learning networks a-life models continues as a research challenge, Newell and Simon's description of the experimental nature of program building remains fundamentally correct. As a result, we can, with confidence, continue to explore the ontological commitments and the epistemic stance of the AI program designers' and builders' world views.

We have found through the deconstruction of running programs that the purer forms of rationalism, although useful for conveying ideas that are indeed "clear and distinct," often fail in situations of imprecision and uncertainty. The rationalists' a priori assumptions are not always sufficient for addressing the complexity of evolving environments. Symbol grounding, or the concern of how abstract symbols can in important ways be "meaningful," is also a challenge.

From the empiricist perspective, the association-based or behaviorist tradition has offered powerful tools for AI research. Example-driven learning can capture and classify relations in data that symbol-based AI programming often miss. But the empiricist perspective is not always appropriate for discovering higher level generalizations and causal relationships between entities. The difficulty in clarification of the effects of an inductive bias implicit in connectionist and emergent computing can complicate their successes. Consequently, results are not always interpretable in the context of the networks that produce them, nor do they always support easy revisions or extensions to new challenges.

A pragmatist viewpoint has been both a major asset and an underlying curse for AI. It is an asset in that it supports finding the "good enough" solution, where the "perfect" might be too costly or not attainable. It allows researchers to move forward in their solution attempts even when there may be little mathematical or psychological justification supporting their efforts. Finding processes that produce sufficiently successful results is a critical supporting philosophy for AI.

The curse of pragmatism is exactly what supports many of its benefits: How, precisely, does the "good enough" solution relate to the "ideal?" Without a mathematical or psychological foundation, how can results be fully interpreted? How can different models be compared if research doesn't have a definitive understanding of where it is heading, or for what "it works" actually implies?

We next motivate and then propose a foundation for a constructivist epistemology. We see this epistemology both as a basis for continuing research and development in artificial intelligence but even more as a sufficient model for our own human exploration, use of, and integration into our environment. In Chaps. 8 and 9 we present probabilistic models and reasoning. These examples demonstrate how actions in the world may be understood as agents, using their current knowledge and disposition, interpret and act on new information within an ever-evolving environment. Finally, we will see in Sect. 9.5 how this epistemic stance addresses the various forms of skepticism noted in Chap. 2.

7.2   The Constructivist Rapprochement

I contend that all human experiences are modulated by an expectation, a model if you will, that mediates between the agent and the so-called real perceived thing. Following Maturana and Verela (1987), human agents have no "direct access" to anything, including their own epistemic dialectic. Descartes' (1637/1969) simple stick-in-the-water example, where a stick standing in clear water and protruding above the water is seen as bent at the water's surface, is one of many examples of *arguments from illusion*. The point of such arguments is that, with active exploration driven by a practical purpose, such perceptions can be understood and interpreted according to their different contexts. Modern vision scientists' analysis of perceptual data also demonstrates illusionary phenomena (Berlin and Kay 1999; Changizi et al. 2008; Brown 2011).

I view a constructivist epistemology as a rapprochement between the empiricist, rationalist, and pragmatist viewpoints. The constructivist hypothesizes that all human understanding is the result of an interaction between energy patterns in the world and mental categories imposed on the world by the perceiving subject. Kant, as discussed in Sect. 2.7, was an early proponent of human understanding being the interaction of mental categories and environment-based perceptions. Modern developmental psychologists also support this view (Piaget 1954, 1970; von Glasersfeld 1978; Gopnik 2011a). Using Piaget's terms, we humans *assimilate* external phenomena according to our current understanding and *accommodate* our understanding to phenomena that do not meet our prior expectations.

Constructivists have used the term *schema* to describe the a priori structure that mediates human's experience of the world. The term schema is taken from the writing of the British psychologist Bartlett (1932), and its philosophical roots go back, as noted in Chap. 2, to Kant (1781/1964). From this viewpoint, observation is not passive and neutral but active and interpretative. There is also a pragmatic component in human perception where, in a critical way, we are biased toward seeing what we need, want, and expect to see: what we are "looking for." There are many current psychologists and philosophers that support and expand this pragmatic and goal-based account of human perception (Glymour 2001; Gopnik et al. 2004; Gopnik 2011a; Kushnir et al. 2010).

Perceived information, Kant's a posteriori knowledge, rarely fits precisely into our preconceived and a priori schemata. From this tension to comprehend and act, the schema-based biases a subject uses to organize experience are strengthened, modified, or replaced. Attempts to *accommodate* in the context of unsuccessful interactions with the environment drive a process of cognitive *equilibration*. The constructivist epistemology is one of cognitive evolution and continuous model refinement. An important consequence of constructivism is that the interpretation of any perception-based situation involves the imposition of the observer's unique concepts and categories on what is perceived. This constitutes an *inductive bias*.

When Piaget first proposed a constructivist approach to a child's understanding of the world, he called it a *genetic epistemology*. When encountering new phenomena, the lack of a comfortable fit of current schemata to the world "as it is" creates a cognitive tension. This tension drives a process of schema revision. Schema revision, Piaget's *accommodation*, is the continued evolution of the agent's understanding towards *equilibration*.

I contend that schema revision and continued movement toward equilibration is a genetic predisposition of an agent for an accommodation to the constraints of self, society, and the world. Schema revision integrates these three forces and represents an embodied predisposition for survival. Schema modification is both an a priori reflection of our genetics and an a posteriori function of society and the world. It reflects the embodiment of a survival-driven agent, of a being in space, time, and society.

There is a blending here of empiricist and rationalist traditions, mediated by the pragmatist requirement of agent survival. Because they are embodied, human agents cannot experience anything except that which first passes through their senses. As accommodating, humans survive through learning the general patterns implicit in sensory data. What is perceived is mediated by what is expected; what is expected is influenced by what is perceived: These two functions can only be understood in terms of each other. A Bayesian model-refinement representation, as presented in Chap. 8, offers an appropriate computational medium for integrating the components of this constructivist and model-revising epistemic stance.

We, as intelligent agents, are seldom consciously aware of the schemata that support our interactions with the world. The sources of bias and prejudice, both in science and in society, are often based on our a priori schemata and expectations. These biases are constitutive of our equilibration with the world and are not usually an acknowledged component of our conscious mental life.

Interestingly enough, David Hume acknowledged this very dilemma in *A Treatise on Human Nature* (1739/1978) where he states:

> All the sciences have a relation, greater or less, to human nature; and ... however wide any of them may seem to run from it, they still return back by one passage or another. Even Mathematics, Natural Philosophy, and Natural Religion, are in some measure dependent on the science of MAN; since they lie under the cognizance of men and are judged of by their powers and faculties.

Further, we can ask why a constructivist epistemology might be useful in addressing the problem of understanding intelligence itself? How can an agent within an environment understand its own understanding of that situation? I believe that a constructivist stance can also address this problem often called *epistemological access.*

For more than 150 years, there has been a struggle in both philosophy and psychology between two factions: the logical positivist who proposes to infer mental phenomena from observable physical behavior and a more phenomenological approach that allows the use of first-person reporting to support understanding of cognitive phenomena. This factionalism exists because both modes of access require some form of model construction and inference.

In comparison to physical objects like chairs and doors, which often, naively, seem to be directly accessible, the mental states and dispositions of an agent seem to be particularly difficult to characterize. We contend that this dichotomy between direct access to physical phenomena and indirect access to mental phenomena is illusory. The constructivist analysis suggests that no experience of the external or the internal world is possible without the use of some model or schema for organizing that experience. In scientific enquiry, as well as in our normal human cognitive experiences, this implies that *all* access to phenomena is through exploration, approximation, and continued expectation refinement.

I see five important components of this expectation-based model refinement. First, it is continuous and teleological or always working toward new goals and syntheses. Both philosophers and psychologists have pointed out the phenomenon of continuous active exploration even in very young children (Glymour 2001; Gopnik et al. 2004; Gopnik 2011a, b). Second, new knowledge of the world is always encoded with the full emotional entailments of the survival-driven agent. Thus, learned knowledge always includes the fears, needs, satisfactions, and all other aspects of a learning agent's survival and maturation.

Third, I contend that a sufficient encoding scheme for representing this complex information in agents are networks of multiple inheritance hierarchies. The inheritance or association with multiple sources reflects how knowledge is embedded in emotion and other human survival energies, as just mentioned. Philosophers, including Hume (1739/1978, 1748/1975), describe how knowledge is characterized as conditioned through experience-driven associations.

As pointed out in Chap. 5, psychologists including Collins and Quillian (1969) and Anderson and Bower (1973) demonstrate how semantic hierarchies are sufficient to account for aspects of human associative memory. Further, AI researchers, especially those involved in human information processing and language understanding (Wilks 1972; Schank and Colby 1973; Stern and Luger 1997), have suggested the use of multiple inheritance hierarchies as sufficient psycho/physical models for encoding knowledge, intention, meaning, and related actions.

The fourth component of expectation-based model refinement is that all knowledge of the world is best represented probabilistically. As just noted, we have no direct access to anything, so our perceptions of phenomena can be best seen as sampling from distributions of phenomena. New probabilistic relations are folded, or interpreted, into the present associational hierarchy described in point 3. As a result, learning is actively creating new probabilistic associations.

Finally, a form of the scientific method drives our understanding. We actively struggle to fit new perceptions into our current worldview, and when these do not fit, we continue our search for better integration. In Piaget's terms, perception, as an accommodation of posterior information, moves the self towards equilibration. This accommodation, although the subject might not be fully aware of its expectation-revision process, is creative energy actively seeking stasis and equilibrium.

7.3   Five Assumptions: A Foundation for an Epistemic Stance

In this section, we motivate the creation of assumptions intended to provide both a foundation and a communication language to support a science of epistemology. An assumption about phenomena is a statement taken without proof but supported by reflection and intuition. An assumption is a statement of "let's assume that this is true."

In science, axioms and postulates are used to construct foundations for mathematical systems. We take Hilbert's (1902) position, where he makes no distinction between axioms and postulates. Hilbert uses the word axiom as a basis for his mathematical systems. Assumptions/axioms/postulates are, above all, pragmatic commitments. They are *about* something: In our case, "assumptions" are about establishing a foundation for further reasoning in the arena of human knowledge.

It can be argued that the first set of assumptions that formed the basis of a mathematical system was that of Euclid. Euclid's five axioms laid a foundation that still endures for traditional geometry, including Descartes' algebraic geometry. It was necessary to revise these assumptions to describe and explain Einstein's energy-configured universe.

Consider Euclid's first axiom/assumption that "it is possible to draw a straight line from any point to any other point." This "draw a straight line" assumption entails some meaning for the notions of "straight," "line," as well as a meaning for "draw," "point," and "any other point." These terms are mutually understood components of purposeful human intention, understanding, communication, and even insight (Lonergan 1957). This action of understanding pragmatically affirms and accepts what is proposed as well as its implicit purpose.

Similarly, consider the first assumption we propose: "Survival is the motivation or driving force of all living agents." It is assumed that "survival," "motivation," "living," and "agent" are all understood and, when asserted together, and affirmed by individuals and society, establish a logical and useful basis for understanding what is real. In this sense, a system of assumptions is not "turtles, or definitions, all the way down" but is founded on the creation of a *useful* set of symbols and relationships with their implied meanings. This act of a committed and purposeful insight or understanding answers the criteriological regress argument of Sextus Empiricus, the Greek skeptic mentioned in Sect. 2.2.

Ancient and medieval geometers questioned whether Euclid's five-axiom set was necessary and sufficient to support all useful extensions of his geometry. Perhaps, they at one time thought, axiom five, the parallel lines axiom, could be deduced from the other four. In the nineteenth century, mathematicians, including Riemann, Gauss, Bolyai, and Lobachevsky, demonstrated that all five axioms were necessary. These mathematicians proposed new and different fifth axioms that, as a result, supported different, not Euclidean, realities.

Two of these geometries are important, the hyperbolic and the elliptic. In a hyperbolic geometry, an infinite number of lines pass through a point off a line l, and are parallel to, or do not cross, that line l. With an elliptic geometry, all lines through a point off line l intersect l. The development of non-Euclidian geometries offered an important medium for representing the new insights in the physics of the early twentieth century. For example, Einstein's general theory of relativity describes space as not flat, or Euclidian, but as elliptically curved, or Riemannian, near areas where energy is present. Thus, Euclid's fifth axiom was shown to be independent and could be purposely altered to capture relationships critical to the understanding of new realities, including modern physics.

Given these revisions of Euclid's original assumptions, it is interesting to question how these assumptions themselves could be considered "wrong?" This very question is misguided, because, in themselves, assumptions or the axioms of science are neither right nor wrong. They are either sufficient or not for describing aspects of a possible world. As we noted, a new formulation of assumptions was necessary to transition from a Newtonian to an Einsteinian understanding of the physical world.

A new language was also required to reflect the insights of Heisenberg's (2000) probabilistic universe. The question to be asked about sets of assumptions is whether or not they are *useful* constructs as a language supporting the understanding of the phenomenal world. Finally, our set of assumptions suggests eight follow-on conjectures that extend to an epistemic vision created for active consideration and possible affirmation.

7.4   A Foundation for a Modern Epistemology

We now present the five assumptions, or suppositions, that support a worldview consistent with contemporary artificial intelligence technology and offer a basis for a modern epistemology.

Assumption 1 *Survival is the motivation or driving force of all living humans.*

The first assumption suggests that survival, either directly or indirectly, motivates, underlies, and supports all individual human behavior. Individual humans may not always be aware of their source of motivation and continue their course of survival regardless of what they might "think" their motivations are. Behaviors such as eating and sex obviously support Assumption 1, and even leisure activities are an important component of a surviving ecosystem. Self-destructive behaviors, such as suicide, are the actions of unsuccessfully calibrated humans. We discuss this topic further in Sect. 9.5.

An alternative statement of Assumption 1 might replace *survival* with descriptions supporting *free energy* or of *entropy minimization* (Friston 2009). Regardless of how survival is characterized, Assumption 1 offers a motivating epistemic force for each living human.

Assumption 2 *Survival of society is essential for individual human survival.*

Individuals and groups of cooperating agents both directly and indirectly underlie and support society's survival. Individuals within societies need not be explicitly aware of their roles in this survival. This individual–society synergism is demonstrated by, among many things, the fact that the normal human requires a lengthy time to reach maturity—about 25 years for full cortical growth. Thus, the presence and cooperation of other agents are essential. Obviously, agents need other agents to produce progeny.

Assumption 3 *Perception is the coupling of a perceiving human and a perceived stimulus.*

The perceptual coupling phenomenon is not decomposable into constituent components. In particular, for agent perception, there is no internal/external separation. There is simply the act of coupling itself. The notion of an internal or external "world," and what these two different worlds might be, including the reification of *qualia*, is an arbitrary abstraction from the experience of perception. Assumption 3 does not explain how the act of perception encodes signals in cortex. There are several excellent theories on this including *predictive coding*, the *free energy principle*, and Bayesian models for brain function (von Helmholtz 1925; Rao and Ballard 1999; Feldman and Friston 2010).

The act of perception, or agent-stimulus coupling, perturbs both the state of the agent and only approximates the perceived entity. As Heisenberg states in *Physics and Philosophy* (2000), "We have to remember that what we observe is not nature itself, but nature exposed to our method of questioning." Thus, neither does the agent remain invariant across the act of perceptive coupling nor is the perceived stimulus a full reflection of the entity (see also Maturana and Varela 1987). There is no direct access to the *essence*, the being, of anything. For this and other reasons, we propose that the perception relationship is best described, measured, and understood probabilistically. See Knill and Pouget (2004) *The Bayesian Brain: The Role of Uncertainty in Neural Coding and Computation.*

Assumption 4 *Individual and collaborating humans create symbols/tokens to represent associated clusters of perceptions.*

Eleanor Rosch (1978) claims that "Since no organism can cope with infinite diversity, one of the most basic functions of all organisms is the cutting up of the environment into classifications by which non-identical stimuli can be treated as equivalent…" Thus, agents make a purpose-driven commitment to specific symbol–perception relations, e.g., denoting a class of perceived energy patterns as "red."

This commitment to symbolic names is a function of the needs and goals of the agent and society. The "commitment to names" is an example of a pragmatist epistemic stance (James 1981, p. 114). The naming process also, and necessarily, leaves aspects of the perceived "object" unaccounted for. This "leftover" is called the *empirical residue* and often necessitates model revision, Conjecture 8.

There have been several interesting research projects from the cognitive and neuroscience traditions that conjecture how stimulus patterns are transduced to nerve and muscle activations within the human response system. These include McClelland and Rumelhart (1981), Rao and Ballard (1999), Hinton (2007), and Friston (2009).

Assumption 5 *Assumption 4 is generalized when patterns of societies' named perceptions are further associated with symbols and patterns of symbols. These systems are called models.*

Assumption 5 is an extension and not independent of Assumption 4, where, recursively, symbols/tokens can be assigned to other sets of symbols. Thus, again, agents and society make purposeful commitments to relationships among sets of perception-linked symbols. The names of the relationships between symbols are often arbitrary, but the relationships are always utilitarian and purposeful, for example, "creating" the set of integers or the square root of 2.

Given the imprecise relationships among perceptions, symbols, and sets of symbols, or models, these are all best understood probabilistically. Bayes (1763), Pearl (2000), Knill and Pouget (2004), and others propose algebras, or languages, that reason with probabilistic relationships, see Conjecture 6 and Chaps. 8 and 9.

These five assumptions offer a foundation for understanding agents' perceptions and the purposeful creation of symbols and structures of symbols or models. These assumptions also offer support for the following eight conjectures that make explicit a perspective on how intelligent agents perceive stimuli and interact in an ever-evolving world.

Conjecture 1 *All perception is purposeful.*

Agent perception is a component of agent survival. Even agent dreams, reflection, and meditation are the attempted integration of perceptual information into long term, or more permanent memories to assist in the accommodation of new perceptions and survival; see also Clark (2015) and Friston (2009).

Conjecture 2 *Symbols are created for practical use and thus are inherently purposeful.*

The crux of Assumption 4 is that individuals and collaborating agents create symbols. Conjecture 1 asserts that all perception is purposeful, and therefore symbols are purposeful. Symbols need not be verbal tokens. They can be written, gestures, or even a pile of stones representing a number. Conjecture 2 asserts that, for agents, "things" represent "other things," including and especially perceptions; see Clark (2013).

Conjecture 3 *Systems of symbols, or models, reflect an agent's commitment to perceptions as well as to patterns and relationships between perceptions.*

Conjecture 3 is supported by Conjecture 2 that symbols are created for purposeful use and by Assumptions 4 and 5. Symbol systems, or models, do not exist independent of use-based and agent-oriented interpretive contexts. Symbol systems are fundamentally *about* whatever aspects of reality they were designed to represent. This view is an important consequence of pragmatist thinking (James 1981). A problem with many modern computer-based representational systems is that they view symbols in the abstract and not for the purposes intended in their creation.

Conjecture 4 *Both individuals and society commit themselves or have a survival-based linkage to perception-based symbols and to symbol systems or models. The name for this commitment is for symbols and symbol systems to have "meaning" or to be "grounded."*

Conjecture 4 is supported by Assumptions 2 and 5 as well as by Conjecture 3. Symbol systems are both individually and socially grounded, built by agreement, and used with a shared commitment. As a result, these systems form a communicative medium, a language (Heisenberg 2000). This language is reflects the efforts of different communities sharing a common purpose, e.g., a particular science or religion. Thus, symbol systems are said to have meaning and be grounded both individually and socially. This society-wide utilitarian focus does not change the fact that individual names for symbols and symbol systems are often arbitrary.

Conjecture 4 also suggests that there are many symbols that are only understood within the context of a particular knowledge system; these symbols include *energy*, *entropy*, *correlation*, *causality*, and *diddy wa diddy*, to name but a few. Agent commitment to specific symbol systems and their associated purposes is called having *knowledge* of that system.

Conjecture 5 *Both individual symbol–perception associations and symbol systems reflecting abstract relationships among symbols, or "knowledge," are best characterized probabilistically.*

Conjecture 5 is supported by the fact that both individual symbol perception attributions, "this fire engine is red," as well as patterns perceived in associations of perceptions, "the sun will rise tomorrow," are best represented probabilistically as asserted by Assumption 3. Just as symbols are assigned to acts of perceptual coupling, Assumption 4, systems of symbols may be assigned to perceived relationships/associations between symbols, Assumption 5.

Mathematical systems, it can be conjectured, are born from regularities found within perceptual coupling-based symbol systems. For example, *category theory* is the study of mappings of abstract structured relationships with further abstract relationships (Awodey 2010). Mathematical systems generalize properties from the world of perception-based symbols and suggest how these systems might be interpreted. An example is the creation of non-Euclidian geometries long before Einstein showed how an elliptical geometry best captures the regularities of a curved space–time–energy continuum.

Conjecture 6 *Both agents and groups of agents make survival-based commitments to the symbols or knowledge systems of other agents or societies. The symbol describing this commitment of agents' symbol or knowledge systems to another symbol or knowledge system is called an attribution of truth.*

Conjecture 6 is supported by Assumptions 1 and 2, namely, that agent's and society's energies are focused on survival. The acknowledgment of energy related to an agent or society's commitment to the utility of a particular symbol or a system of symbols supports the attribution of *truth*.

Truth represents a commitment to the ascribed relationship between different symbols and knowledge systems: These relationships can be between agent–agent, agent–society, or society–society symbol/knowledge systems. This affirmation of symbol correspondence can be as simple as agreeing that "this fire engine is red" or "this ice cream tastes good." Of course, the correspondence can be as complex as agreeing with the values and relationships of a country's constitution or with the tenets of a religion's set of values.

Individual agents and societies do not always share agreement on the meanings of perception-based symbols and/or symbol systems. Thus *truth* is the relationship between an agent's commitment to knowledge and another agent or society's commitment to that same piece of knowledge. Although all individual agent's commitments to creating knowledge are important, still each agent is ultimately represented within the distribution of a society's commitment to that same knowledge.

Pilot said, "What is truth?" Well, truth is utilitarian, what an individual or a society *needs* to make itself function. Is pi the ratio between the circumference and the diameter of a circle? The answer is "yes," particularly for those needing this relationship to function as engineers or mathematicians. Humans, both individuals and groups, are willing to die for what they believe as *truth,* for example, the survival of their children or their society. Is there some "objective truth" beyond this? Perhaps none that we can know independently of our concepts and their relationships. There is further discussion of this neopragmatist notion of truth in Sect. 9.5.

Conjecture 7   *Knowledge structures serve as fixed stochastic models when they are employed for purpose-based interpretations at any particular point in time.*

Assumption 4 and Conjectures 2 and 3 support Conjecture 7. Knowledge systems are a collection of perception-related symbols and relationships. They can be seen as fixed for any particular point in time when they serve as a constituent of an interpretive context. By Assumption 4 and Conjecture 5, the "fixed" interpretive system is best understood probabilistically. Finally, and as already noted, knowledge systems are primarily purposeful/utilitarian, and they can only be understood when deployed as a component of the act of interpretation.

The most important result of Conjecture 7 is that the agent and society use fixed probabilistic systems that mediate interpretation. When these interpretative schemas occasionally fail to produce useful results, they must be revised. We discussed the Kantian and Piagetian modes of interpretation leading to equilibration in previous sections. We present more computational demonstrations of this phenomenon in Chaps. 8 and 9. The continuing movement of knowledge systems towards equilibration suggests a final conjecture.

Conjecture 8   *Agents' and societies' knowledge systems are revised and reformulated through a consistent and continuing model revision process.*

Assumption 3, describing perceptual coupling, and Conjecture 1, that perception is purposive, both support Conjecture 8. The act of perception is never exhaustive, and there will always be aspects of the phenomena that are not captured in the act. As mentioned earlier, this remaining component of interpretation is called the *empirical residue.* Further, as agent's and society's purposes and needs change or are clarified, the currently used symbol systems are either reinforced or revised.

In physics, for example, when it was noticed that the mass of a particle increased as it was subjected to extreme acceleration, the symbol system afforded by Newtonian mechanics was no longer a sufficient model for explanation. Similarly, the measurement indeterminism observed by Heisenberg, required a revision of the Einsteinian interpretative context. Both of these situations forced model revision and the creation of revised language structures to support these new and necessary purpose-driven interpretations (Einstein 1940; Heisenberg 2000).

Conjecture 8 also suggests that intelligent agents can reason about the entire process of creating symbol systems. For example, Gödel (1930) demonstrated that any system of first-order logic plus Peano's axioms is incomplete. Thus, there are statements that can be formulated in that system that cannot be shown to be either true or false. Turing showed with the *halting problem*, Sect. 1.2, that statements could be *undecidable* using his machine. It may always be necessary to expand and revise formal systems and models for new interpretative contexts. For example, Bertrand Russell revised his first-order logic system and expanded it to include axioms for a meta-language of self-reference.

Finally, as seen through these last examples, the scientific method offers both a medium and method for model reformulation. When a purpose-driven explanation fails to satisfy its designers' expectations, the methods of science offer suggestions for its revision. We see examples of this in the concluding chapters.

7.5 In Summary

This chapter proposed a constructivist rapprochement to address the shortcomings found in the rationalist, empiricist, and pragmatist traditions. It was argued that a survival-based tension exists between the expectations of the perceiving agent and perceived information. The agent's expectations can be characterized by Kant's, Bartlett's, or Piaget's schemas that are either reinforced or recalibrated as new information is perceived. Friston (2009) refers to this phenomenon as *free energy minimization*; Piaget (1970) describes it as continuing to move towards a state of *equilibration*.

A set of five assumptions and 8 follow-on conjectures were proposed to capture this active subject perception dialectic. The set of conjectures included characterizing the meta-concepts of *knowledge, meaning*, and *truth*.

In Chap. 8, we consider Bayes' theorem and see how our constructivist synthesis is reflected in a number of AI programs. In Chap. 9, we conclude with further examples of model calibration and refinement.

Further Thoughts and Readings This chapter sets the basis for a modern epistemology. We suggest supporting readings; full references are in the Bibliography.

For a philosophical approach to constructivism:

Bartlett (1932), *Remembering*.
Piaget (1970), *Structuralism*.
Glymour (2001), *The Mind's Arrows: Bayes Nets and Graphical Causal Models in Psychology*.

For children and developmental learning:

Piaget (1954), *The Construction of Reality in the Child.*
Gopnik et al. (2004), "A Theory of Causal Learning in Children: Causal Maps and Bayes Nets."
Gopnik, A. (2011b), "Probabilistic Models as Theories of Children's Minds."

An important case study of a physicist's explanations of the language-based paradigm shifts necessary to understand the modern world:

Heisenberg (2000), *Physics and Philosophy.*

There are computer models, especially from the cognitive science community, that attempt to capture aspects of a constructivist worldview. Several of these were described in Sect. 3.5 and more a represented in Sect. 9.3.

Chapter 8
Bayesian-Based Constructivist Computational Models

God does not play dice…
—ALBERT EINSTEIN (His response to the conjectures of Quantum Theory)

God not only plays dice, but he sometimes throws them where they can't be seen…

—STEPHEN HAWKING

Contents

In this chapter, we introduce the fourth, and since the 1990s, arguably one of the most important components of AI research. This is called the *probabilistic*, or often the *stochastic*, approach to understanding our world. It is used in applications across the AI spectrum including understanding, generating, and translating human languages; it is used for machine learning, vision systems, and the control of robots and other complex processes.

This chapter has three parts. First, we present Bayes' theorem and demonstrate how it works for the situation of a single hypothesis and a single piece of evidence. Although this is not a full proof of the theorem, it helps build an intuition and understanding of what probabilistic reasoning is about. Second, we offer Bayes' formula with several extensions, including *Bayesian belief networks* (*BBNs*), as mathematics-based models sufficient to account for many aspects of the perception, reasoning, and diagnostic skills found in intelligent humans. Finally, we demonstrate the use of probabilistic models for diagnosing complex situations, including a program for the monitoring and control of nuclear power generation. The goal of this chapter

© Springer Nature Switzerland AG 2021
G. F. Luger, *Knowing our World*, https://doi.org/10.1007/978-3-030-71873-2_8

is to offer computational accountability and epistemic sufficiency for the constructivist rapprochement and epistemic conjectures proposed in Chap. 7.

8.1 The Derivation of a Bayesian Stance

Probabilistic modeling tools have supported significant components of AI research since the 1950s. Researchers at Bell Labs built a speech system that could recognize any of the ten digits spoken by a single speaker with accuracy in the high 90% range (Davis et al. 1952). Shortly after this Bledsoe and Browning (1959), built a probabilistic letter recognition system that used a large dictionary to serve as the corpus for recognizing hand-written characters, given the likelihood of character sequences and particular characters. Later research addressed authorship attribution by looking at the word patterns in anonymous literature and comparing these to similar patterns of known authors (Mosteller and Wallace 1963).

By the early 1990s, much of computation-based language understanding and generation in AI was accomplished using probabilistic techniques, including parsing, part-of-speech tagging, reference resolution, and discourse processing. These techniques often used tools like *greatest likelihood* measures (Jurafsky and Martin 2020) that we will describe in detail. Other areas of artificial intelligence, especially machine learning, became more Bayesian-based (Russell and Norvig 2010; Luger 2009a). In many ways, these uses of stochastic technology for pattern recognition and learning were another instantiation of the constructivist tradition, as collected sets of patterns were used to condition the recognition of new patterns. We begin by asking how an epistemologist might build a model of a constructivist worldview.

Historically, an important response to David Hume's skepticism was that of the English cleric, Thomas Bayes (1763). Bayes was challenged to defend the gospel and other believers' accounts of Christ's miracles in the light of Hume's claims that such "accounts" could not attain the credibility of a "proof." Bayes response, published posthumously in the *Transactions of the Royal Society*, was a mathematics-based demonstration of how an agent's prior expectations can be related to their current perceptions. Bayes' approach, although not supporting the creditability of miracles, has had an important effect on the design of probabilistic models. We develop Bayes' insight next and then conjecture, using several examples, how Bayes' theorem can support a computational model of epistemological access.

Suppose a medical doctor is examining the symptoms of a patient to determine a possible infecting organism. In this example, there is a single symptom, evidence **e**, and a single hypothesized infecting agent, **h**. The doctor wishes to determine how the perception of a patient's bad headache, for example, can indicate the presence of meningitis infection.

In Fig. 8.1, there are two sets: One set, **e**, contains all the people who have bad headaches, and the second set, **h**, contains all people that have the meningitis infection. We want to determine the probability that a person who has a bad headache also has meningitis. We call this **p(h|e)**, or "the probability **p** that a person has the disease **h**, given that he/she suffers headaches **e**, the evidence."

To determine **p(h|e)**, we need to determine the number of people having both the symptom and the disease and divide this number by the total number of people having the symptom. We call this the *posterior probability*, or the probability that the new information the diagnostician obtains is indicative of the disease. Since each of the sets of people in the example of Fig. 8.1 may be divided by the total number of people considered, we represent each number as a probability. Thus, to represent the probability of the disease **h** given the symptom **e** as **p(h|e)**:

$$p(h \mid e) = \left| h \cap e \right| / \left| e \right| = p(h \cap e) / p(e),$$

where "|" surrounding symbols, e.g., | **e** |, indicates the number of people in that set.

Similarly, we wish to determine the *prior probability*, or expectations of the diagnostician, given this situation. This prior information reflects the knowledge the diagnostician has accumulated in medical training and during past diagnostic experiences. In this example, the probability that people with meningitis also have headaches, or the probability of evidence **e**, given the disease **h**, is **p(e|h)**. As previously argued:

$$p(e \mid h) = \left| e \cap h \right| / \left| h \right| = p(e \cap h) / p(h).$$

The value of **p(e ∩h)** can now be determined by multiplying by **p(h)**:

$$p(e \mid h) p(h) = p(e \cap h).$$

Finally, we can determine a measure for the probability of the hypothesized disease, **h**, given the evidence, **e**, in terms of the probability of the evidence given the hypothesized disease:

$$p(h \mid e) = p(e \cap h) / p(e) = p(e \mid h) p(h) / p(e).$$

This last formula is Bayes' law for one piece of evidence and one disease.

Let's review what Bayes' formula accomplishes. It creates a relationship between the posterior probability of the disease given the symptom, **p(h|e)**, and the prior

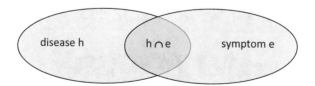

Fig. 8.1 A representation of the numbers of people having a symptom, **e**, and a disease, **h**. We want to measure the probability of a person having the disease given that he/she suffers the symptom, i.e., the number of people in both sets **e** and **h**, or **e ∩ h**. We then divide this number by the total number of people in set **e**

knowledge of the symptom given the disease, **p(e|h)**. In this example, the medical doctor's experience over time supplies the prior knowledge of what should be expected when a new situation—the patient with a symptom—is encountered. The probability of the new person with symptom **e** having the hypothesized disease **h** is represented in terms of the collected knowledge obtained from previous situations, where the diagnosing doctor has seen that a diseased person had a symptom, **p(e|h)**, and how often the disease itself occurs, **p(h)**.

Consider the more general case with the same set-theoretic argument of the probability of a person having a possible disease given two symptoms, say of having meningitis while suffering from both a bad headache and a high fever. The probability of meningitis given these two symptoms is a function of the prior knowledge of having the two symptoms at the same time as the disease and the probability of the disease itself.

We present the general form of Bayes' rule for a particular hypothesis, h_i, given a set of possibly multiple pieces of evidence, **E**:

$$p(h_i \mid E) = p(E \mid h_i)p(h_i)/p(E)p(h_i \mid E)$$

is the probability a particular hypothesis, h_i, is true given evidence **E**.

$$p(h_i) \text{ is the probability that } h_i \text{ can happen.}$$

$$p(E \mid h_i) \text{ is the probability of observing evidence } E \text{ when hypothesis } h_i \text{ is true.}$$

$$p(E) \text{ is the probability of the evidence being true in the population.}$$

When extending Bayes rule from one to multiple pieces of evidence, the right-hand side of the rule reflects the situation where a number of pieces of evidence co-occur with each hypothesis h_i. We make two assumptions on this evidence. First, for each hypothesis h_i, the pieces of evidence are independent. Second, the sum, or set union, of all the individual pieces of the evidence, e_i, make up the full set of evidence, **E**, as seen in Fig. 8.2.

Given these assumptions about the evidence occurring with each hypothesis, it is possible to directly calculate, when required in Bayes' theorem, the probability of that evidence, given an hypothesis, $p(E|h_i)$:

$$p(E \mid h_i) = p(e_1, e_2, \dots, e_n \mid h_i) = p(e_1 \mid h_i) \times p(e_2 \mid h_i) \times \dots \times p(e_n \mid h_i).$$

Fig. 8.2 The set of all possible evidence, **E**, is assumed to be partitioned by the individual pieces of evidence, e_i, for each hypothesis h_i

Under the independence assumption, the denominator of Bayes', **p(E)**, is then:

$$\mathbf{p(E)} = \Sigma_i \, \mathbf{p(E \mid h_i)} \times \mathbf{p(h_i)}$$

In most realistic diagnostic situations, the assumed independence of the evidence, given an hypothesis, is not supported. Some pieces of evidence may not be unrelated to others, such as the presence of individual words in a sentence. This violates the independence assumption for calculating **p(E|h_i)**. Making this independence of evidence assumption, even when it is not justified, is called *naive Bayes*.

The general form of Bayes' theorem offers a computational model for the probability of a particular situation happening, given a set of evidence clues. The right-hand side of Bayes' equation represents a schema describing how prior accumulated knowledge of phenomena can relate to the interpretation of a new situation, described by the left-hand side of the equation. This theorem itself can be seen as an example of Piaget's *assimilation*, where new information is interpreted using the patterns created from prior experiences.

There are limitations to proposing Bayes' theorem, as just presented, as an epistemic description of interpreting new data in the context of prior knowledge. First, the fact is that the epistemic subject is not a calculating machine. We simply do not have all the prior numerical values for calculating the hypotheses/evidence relations. In a complex situation such as medicine, where there can be hundreds of hypothesized diseases and thousands of symptoms, this calculation is impossible.

One response to the "requirement of extensive mathematics" criticism is that a Hebbian (1949) like conditioning occurs across time and expectations to the point where new posterior information triggers an already constituted expectation-based interpretation. This would be particularly true for the trained expert, such as a doctor, working within her own area of expertise. Hume's (1748/1975) suggestion that associations are built up over time from accumulated perceptual experience also describes this interpretation.

Further, in many applications, the probability of the occurrence of evidence across all hypotheses, **p(E)**, the right-hand-side denominator of Bayes' equation, is simply a normalizing factor, supporting the calculation of a probability measure in the range of 0 to 1. The same normalizing factor is utilized in determining the actual probability of each of the **h_i**, given the evidence, and thus it can be ignored. When the denominator is simply ignored, the result is described as a determination of the *most likely explanation*, or *greatest likelihood measure* for any hypothesis **h_i**, given the accumulation of evidence.

For example, if we wish to determine which of all the **h_i** has the most support at any particular time, we can consider the largest p(E|h_i) p(h_i) and call this the **argmax(h_i)** for the hypothesis **h_i**. As just noted, this number is not a probability.

$$\mathbf{argmax(h_i)} \, \text{of} \, \mathbf{p(E \mid h_i)} \, \mathbf{p(h_i)}, \text{for each} \, \mathbf{h_i}.$$

In a dynamic interpretation, as pieces of evidence change across time, we will call this *argmax* of hypotheses given a set of evidence at a particular time the *greatest likelihood of that hypothesis at that time.* We show this relationship, an extension of the Bayesian *maximum a posteriori* (*MAP*) estimate, as a dynamic measure of time **t**:

$$\mathbf{gl}\left(\mathbf{h_i} \mid \mathbf{E_t}\right) = \mathbf{argmax}\left(\mathbf{h_i}\right) \text{of } \mathbf{p}\left(\mathbf{E_t} \mid \mathbf{h_i}\right)\mathbf{p}\left(\mathbf{h_i}\right), \text{for each } \mathbf{h_i}.$$

When there are multiple pieces of evidence at time **t**, that is $\mathbf{E_t} = \mathbf{e^1_t, e^2_t, ..., e^n_t}$, the *naive Bayes* independence assumption means that:

$$\mathbf{p}\left(\mathbf{E_t} \mid \mathbf{h_i}\right) = \mathbf{p}\left(\mathbf{e^1_t, e^2_t, ... e^n_t} \mid \mathbf{h_i}\right) = \mathbf{p}\left(\mathbf{e^1_t} \mid \mathbf{h_i}\right) \times \mathbf{p}\left(\mathbf{e^2_t} \mid \mathbf{h_i}\right) \times \cdots \times \mathbf{p}\left(\mathbf{e^n_t} \mid \mathbf{h_i}\right).$$

This model is both intuitive and simple: the most likely interpretation of $\mathbf{h_i}$, given evidence **E,** at time **t,** is a function of which interpretation is most likely to produce that evidence at the time **t** and the probability of that interpretation itself occurring.

We can now ask how the argmax specification can produce a computational epistemic model of phenomena. First, we see that the argmax relationship offers a falsifiable approach to explanation. If more data turns up at a particular time, an alternative hypothesis can attain a higher argmax value. Furthermore, when some data suggest an hypothesis, $\mathbf{h_i}$, it is usually only a subset of the full set of data that can support that hypothesis. Going back to our medical hypothesis, a bad headache can be suggestive of meningitis, but there is much more evidence gathered over time that is even more suggestive of this hypothesis, for example, fever, nausea, and the results of certain blood tests. As other data become available, it might also decrease the likelihood of a diagnosis of meningitis.

We view the evolving greatest likelihood relationship as a continuing tension between a set of possible hypotheses and the accumulating evidence collected across time. The presence of changing data supports the continuing revision of the greatest likelihood hypothesis, and, because data sets are not always complete, the possibility of a particular hypothesis motivates the search for data that can either support or falsify it. Thus, the greatest likelihood measure represents a dynamic equilibrium, evolving across time, of hypotheses suggesting supporting data as well as the presence of data supporting particular hypotheses. Piaget (1983) refers to this perception/response processing as finding *equilibration.*

When a data/hypothesis relationship is not "sufficiently strong" over any time period $\mathbf{t_i}$, and/or no particular data/hypothesis relationship seems to dominate, as measured by the values of **argmax($\mathbf{h_i}$)** of **p($\mathbf{E_t}$|$\mathbf{h_i}$) p($\mathbf{h_i}$)**, the search for better explanations, based on revised models, becomes important. Two approaches often help in this task: First, to search for new relationships among the already known data/hypothesis relationships—perhaps some important component of the possibility space is overlooked. For example, when the amount of energy required to accelerate a particle increases, as well as the mass of the particle, at extreme accelerations, Newton's laws needed to be revised.

A second approach to model revision is to actively intervene in the data/hypothesis relationships of the model. "Is there a new diagnosis if the patient's headache goes away?" "What has changed if a fever spikes?" "How should a parent respond when their 2-year-old throws food on the floor?" How evidence changes over time can suggest new hypotheses. These two techniques support *model induction*, the creation of new models to explain data. *Model induction* is an important component of current research in machine learning (Tian and Pearl 2001; Sakhanenko et al. 2008; Rammohan 2010). This type of agent-based model revision demonstrates Piaget's notion of *accommodation* and will be discussed further in Sect. 9.3.

In Sect. 8.2, we present *Bayesian belief networks* and show how these can, in a form called *dynamic Bayesian networks,* model changes in hypotheses, given the perception of new data across time. In Sect. 8.3, we discuss model revision and the use of contrapositive, or *what if*, reasoning as an epistemic tool for understanding complex tasks in a changing world.

8.2 Bayesian Belief Networks, Perception, and Diagnosis

Data collection is often a limiting factor for using full Bayesian inference for diagnoses in complex environments. To use Bayes' theorem to calculate probabilities in medicine, for example, where there can be hundreds of possible diagnoses, and thousands of possible symptoms, the data collection problem becomes impossible (Luger 2009a, p. 185). As a result, for complex environments, the ability to perform full Bayesian inference can lose plausibility as an epistemic model.

The *Bayesian belief network* or *BBN* (Pearl 1988, 2000) is a graph whose links are conditional probabilities. The graph is *acyclic*, in that there are no link sequences from a node back to itself. It is also *directed*, in that links are conditioned probabilities that are intended to represent causal relationships between the nodes. With these assumptions, it can be shown that BBN's nodes are independent of all their non-descendants, nodes that they are not directly or indirectly linked to, given knowledge of their parents, that is, nodes linking to them.

Judea Pearl proposed the use of Bayesian belief networks, making the assumption that their links reflected causal relationships. With the demonstrated independence of states from their non-descendants, given knowledge of their parents, the use of Bayesian technology came to entirely new importance. First, the assumption of these networks being directed graphs that disallowed cycles was an improvement to the computational costs of reasoning with traditional Bayes (Luger 2009a, Sect. 9.3).

More importantly, the independence assumption that splits, or *factors*, the reasoning space into independent components makes the BBN a transparent representational model and captures causal relationships in a computationally useful format. We demonstrate, in our next examples, how the BBN supports both transparency and efficient reasoning.

We next illustrate the BBN diagnosing failures in discrete component semiconductors (Stern and Luger 1997; Chakrabarti et al. 2005). The semiconductor failure model determines the greatest likelihood for hypotheses, given sets of data. Consider the situation of Fig. 8.3 showing two different types of semiconductor failure.

The examples of Fig. 8.3 show a failure type called *open*, or the break in a wire connecting components to other parts of the system. For the diagnostic expert, the perceptual aspects of a break support a number of alternative hypotheses of how the break occurred. The search for the most likely explanation for an open failure broadens the evidence search: How large is the break? Is there any discoloration related to the break? Were there any sounds or odors when it happened? What are the resulting conditions of the other components of the system?

Driven by the data search supporting multiple possible hypotheses that can explain the open, or break, the expert notes the *bambooing* effect in the disconnected wire in Fig. 8.3a. This suggests the greatest likelihood hypothesis that the open was created by metal crystallization and likely caused by a sequence of low-frequency, high-current pulses. The greatest likely hypothesis for the wire break of Fig. 8.3b, where the wire's end is seen as *balled*, is melting due to excessive current. Both of these diagnostic scenarios have been implemented by an expert system-like search through an hypothesis space (Stern and Luger 1997) as well as reflected in a Bayesian belief net (Chakrabarti et al. 2005). Figure 8.4 presents the Bayesian belief net (BBN) capturing these and other related diagnostic situations for discrete component semiconductor failures.

The BBN, before new data are presented, represents the a priori state of the experts' knowledge of this application domain, including the likelihood of the failures of the individual components. These networks of causal relationships are usually carefully crafted through many hours of working with human experts' analysis of components and their known failures. As a result, the BBN captures the a priori expert knowledge implicit in a domain of interest. When new data are given to the BBN, e.g., the wire is "bambooed" or the color of the copper wire is normal, the belief network "infers" the most likely explanation for the break using its a priori model and given this new information.

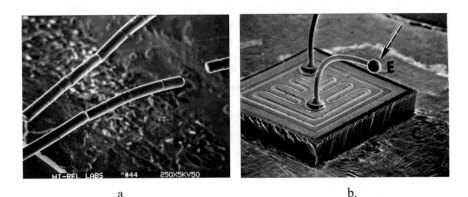

a.   b.

Fig. 8.3 Two examples of discrete component semiconductors, each exhibiting the "open" failure (Luger et al. 2002; Chakrabarti et al. 2005)

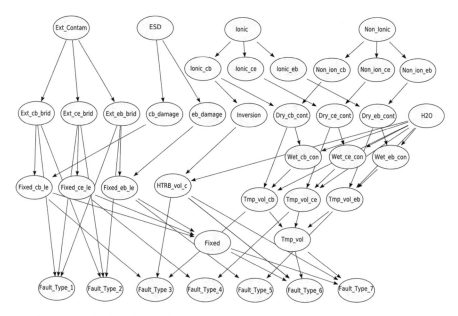

Fig. 8.4 A Bayesian belief network representing the causal relationships and data points implicit in the discrete component semiconductor domain. As data are discovered and presented to the BBN, probabilistic hypotheses change. Figure adapted from (Luger et al. 2002)

There are several BBN reasoning rules available for arriving at this best explanation, including *loopy belief propagation* (Pearl 1988), discussed later. An important result of using the BBN technology is that as one hypothesis achieves its greatest likelihood, other related hypotheses are "explained away," i.e., their likelihood measures decrease within the BBN. We will see further demonstrations of this phenomenon in our next example.

Finally, the BBN semiconductor example supports both Conjectures 7 and 8 of Sect. 7.4. Conjecture 7 states that a priori knowledge, data known at a particular time, supports purpose-driven diagnoses. Conjecture 8 claims that world knowledge is continuously reformulated through a model revision process. We next demonstrate how, as data changes across time, different hypotheses can offer best explanations. For this, our model must change its probabilities over time as new data is encountered.

A *dynamic Bayesian network*, or *DBN*, is a sequence of identical Bayesian networks whose network nodes are linked in the directed dimension of time. This representation extends BBNs into multidimensional environments and preserves the same tractability in reasoning toward best explanations. With the factoring of the search space and the ability to address complexity issues, the dynamic Bayesian network becomes a potential model for exploring diagnostic situations across both changes of data and time. We next demonstrate the BBN and the DBN.

Figure 8.5 shows a BBN model for a typical traveling situation. Suppose you are driving your car in a familiar area where you are aware of the likelihood of traffic slowdowns, road construction, and accidents. You are also aware that flashing lights often indicate emergency vehicles at an accident site and that orange traffic control barrels indicate construction work on the roadway. (Weighted orange barrels are often used in the United States to control traffic flow for road projects). We will name these situations T, C, A, L, and B, as seen in Fig. 8.5. The likelihoods, for the purpose of this example, are reflected in the partial probability table of Fig. 8.5, where the top row indicates that the probability of both construction, C, and bad traffic, T, being true, t, is 0.3.

For full Bayesian inference, this problem would require a 32-row probability table of 5 variables, each either true or false. In the separation, or *factoring*, that BBN reasoning supports (Pearl 2000), this becomes a 20-row table, where **Flashing Lights** is independent of **Construction**, **Orange Barrels** is independent of **Accident**, and **Construction** and **Accident** are also independent (Luger 2009a, Sect. 9.3). We present part of this table in Fig. 8.5.

Suppose that, as you drive along and without any observable reasons, the traffic begins to slow down; now **Bad Traffic, T**, becomes true, t. This new fact means that the probabilities of Fig. 8.5, **Bad Traffic**, is no longer false. The sum of the probabilities for the first and third lines of the table in Fig. 8.5 goes from t = 0.4 to t = 1.0. This new higher probability is then distributed proportionately across the probabilities for **Construction** and **Accident** and, as a result, both situations become more likely.

Now suppose you drive along farther and notice **Orange Barrels, B**, along the road that blocks a lane of traffic. This means that on another probability table, not shown here, B is true, and in making its probabilities sum to 1.0, the probability of **Construction, C**, gets much higher, approaching 0.95. As the probability of **Construction** gets higher, with the absence of **Flashing Lights, L**, the probability of an **Accident** decreases. The most likely explanation for what you now experience is road **Construction**. The likelihood of an **Accident** goes down and is said to be *explained away*. The calculation of these higher probabilities as new data are encountered is called *marginalization* and, while not shown here, may be found in Luger and Chakrabarti (2008).

Figure 8.6 represents the changing dynamic Bayesian network for the driving example just described. The perceived information changes over the three time periods: driving normally, cars slowing down, and seeing orange traffic control barrels. At each new time with new information, the values reflecting the probabilities for

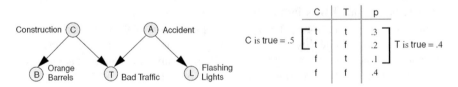

Fig. 8.5 A Bayesian belief network (BBN) for the driving example and a partial table giving sample probability values for **Construction, C**, and **Bad Traffic, T**

that time and situation change. These probability changes reflect the best explanations for each new piece of information the diver perceives at each time period.

Finally, in Fig. 8.6, consider the state of the diagnostic expert at the point where Time = 2. Once traffic has slowed, the diagnostician may begin an active search for Orange Barrels or Flashing Lights, to try to determine, before Time = 3, what might be the most likely explanation for the traffic slowdown. In this situation, the driver's expectations motivate his/her active search for supporting information. These changing situations and their explanations support Conjecture 8 of Sect. 7.4.

In another example of using dynamic Bayesian networks, Chakrabarti et al. (2007) analyze a continuous data stream from a set of distributed sensors. These sensors reflect the running "health" of the transmission of a US Navy helicopter rotor system. These data consist of temperature, vibration, pressure, and other measurements reflecting the state of the various components of the helicopter's transmission. In the top portion of Fig. 8.7, the continuous data stream is broken into discrete and partial time slices.

Chakrabarti et al. (2007) used a Fourier transform to translate these signals into the frequency domain as shown on the left side of the second row of Fig. 8.7. These frequency readings were then compared across time periods to diagnose the health of the rotor system. The diagnostic model used for this analysis is the *auto-regressive hidden Markov model* (AR-HMM) of Fig. 8.8. The internal states S_t of the system are made up of the sequences of the segmented signals in the frequency domain. The observable states, O_t, are the health states of the helicopter rotor system at time t. The "health" recommendations, that the transmission is safe, unsafe, or faulty, are shown in Fig. 8.7, lower right.

The hidden Markov model (HMM) is an important probabilistic technique that can be seen as a variant of the dynamic BBN. In the HMM, we attribute values to states of the network that are themselves not directly observable; in this case, we cannot directly "see" the "health state" of the transmission. There are instruments in the helicopter for directly observing temperature, vibration, oil pressure, and other data of the running system. But there is no instrument that can directly tell the pilot the health of the system. The pilot, given all the other information, must make an estimate of this health value. Producing this health information is the task of the HMM.

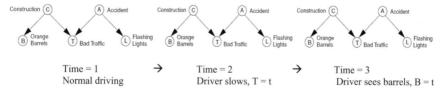

Fig. 8.6 An example of a dynamic Bayesian network where at each time period the driver perceives new information and the DBN's probabilities change, as described in the text, to reflect these changes

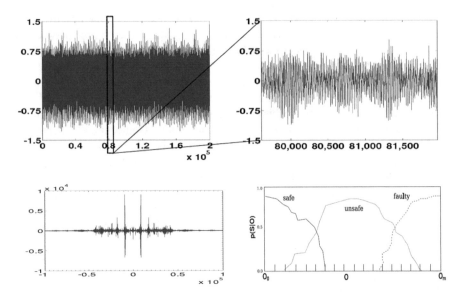

Fig. 8.7 Real-time data from the transmission system of a helicopter's rotor system. The top component of the figure presents the original data stream, left, and an enlarged time slice, right. The lower left figure is the result of Fourier analysis of the time slice data transformed into the frequency domain. The lower right figure represents the "hidden" states of the rotor system (Chakrabarti et al. 2005, 2007)

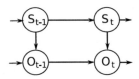

Fig. 8.8 The data of Fig. 8.7 are processed using an auto-regressive hidden Markov model. States O_t represent the observable values at time t; these are {safe, unsafe, faulty}. The S_t states capture the processed signals from the rotor system at time t (Chakrabarti et al. 2007)

In the helicopter example, the US Navy supplied data for model training purposes. Data from a normally running transmission conditioned the model. Other sets of data containing faults, such as a transmission running after metal fatigue had broken the cogs of a gear assembly, were also used to train the model. After the model was conditioned on these tagged data sets, new untagged data, where the testers did not know whether the data was from a sound or faulty transmission, were tested. The model was asked to determine the health state of the rotor system, and if the data were from a faulty system, to determine when the unsafe state occurred. The HMM was able to successfully accomplish these tasks.

In Fig. 8.8, the processing states S_t of the A-RHMM capture the fused data from the transmission system and combine these to produce the most likely hypothesis, O_t, of the state of the system. This output is the observed state O_t at any time t.

Because the HMM is *auto-regressive*, the value of the output state O_t is also a probabilistic function of the output state at the previous time, O_{t-1}.

The helicopter transmission model is not a "knowledge-based" program in the traditional sense of Chap. 4. In the knowledge-based system, specific rules relate the parameters of the model to each other, for example, "if a cog is broken in a gear then the vibration of the transmission increases" or "if the oil temperature increases then the oil circulation component has failed." There are no such rules in this model, but rather the fusion of multiple perceptual sensor readings whose changes over time are indicative of the "health" of the overall system. Thus, the program can conclude "there is a problem here" without having any idea of exactly what the problem is. This is an important example of a complex perceptual system interpreting "danger" or "time to take action" without specific knowledge of why that action is necessary.

It bears repeating that the families of Bayesian network models we have demonstrated in this section are *data-driven*, in the sense that the a priori knowledge of the network's designers is reflected in the model itself. When training data are presented, the combination of data and model adjusts to produce the most likely interpretation for each new piece of data. In many situations, probabilistic models can also ask for further information, given several possible explanations. Finally, when critical information is missing, perhaps from a sensor that is damaged, the network can also suggest that sensor's most likely value, given the current state of the model and the perceived data (Pless and Luger 2003). We see further examples of this in Sect. 8.4.

This movement of Bayesian belief networks toward a steady state where sets of data are linked to their most likely explanations is similar to Piaget's notion of equilibration seen in Sect. 7.2. For further details on algorithms that implement Bayesian belief networks, see Pearl (2000) and Chakrabarti et al. (2007). A Bayesian belief net interpreter, based on Pearl's *loopy belief net propagation* algorithm, is available at url 8.2.

8.3 Bayesian-Based Speech and Conversation Modeling

An area where the HMM technique is widely used is the computational analysis of human speech. To determine the most likely word that is spoken, given a stream of acoustic signals, the computer compares these signals to a collection, called a *corpus*, where signal patterns and their associated words are stored. We humans have our own version of the HMM. We interpret other people's words according to the sound patterns we hear, the gestures we see, and our current social context. Since we have no direct access to what is going on within another person's head, we must make our best interpretation of what they are intending, given the observed expressions. This is an ideal task for a hidden Markov model and is precisely what Piaget's theory of interpretation suggests is happening.

One intuition we often have is that speech recognition software systems must translate sound patterns into words for the speaker's intentions to be understood. Paul De Palma (2010) and De Palma et al. (2012) made a different assumption and produced a program that, given human speech, converted these sound waves to patterns of syllables. De Palma then determined, using the greatest likelihood measure, how syllable patterns can indicate the most likely *concept* intended by the speaker. In De Palma's research, there was no transduction of sounds into words but rather the program interpreted voice patterns directly to the most likely concepts of the speaker, given the patterns of sounds produced.

Earlier we saw the maximum likelihood equation used to determine which hypothesis $\mathbf{h_i}$ was most likely, given evidence at a particular time, $\mathbf{E_t}$.

$$\mathbf{gl}\left(\mathbf{h_i} \mid \mathbf{E_t}\right) = \mathbf{argmax}\left(\mathbf{h_i}\right) \text{for each } \mathbf{h_i} \text{ as the maximum value of } \mathbf{p}\left(\mathbf{E_t} \mid \mathbf{h_i}\right)\mathbf{p}\left(\mathbf{h_i}\right).$$

This equation can be modified to determine which concept, $\mathbf{con_i}$, of a set of concepts is most likely, given a particular syllable, $\mathbf{syl_t^1}$, or set of syllables, $\mathbf{syl_t^1}$, $\mathbf{syl_t^2}$, ..., $\mathbf{syl_t^n}$, at time $\mathbf{t}$. We assume the naive Bayes independence of evidence:

$$\mathbf{gl}\left(\mathbf{con_i} \mid \mathbf{syl_t^1}, \mathbf{syl_t^2}, \ldots, \mathbf{syl_t^n}\right)$$
$$= \mathbf{argmax}\left(\mathbf{con_i}\right) \text{for each } \mathbf{con_i} \text{ as the maximum value}$$
$$\text{of } \mathbf{p}\left(\mathbf{syl_t^1} \mid \mathbf{con_i} \times \mathbf{syl_t^2} \mid \mathbf{con_i} \times \cdots \times \mathbf{syl_t^n} \mid \mathbf{con_i}\right)\mathbf{p}\left(\mathbf{con_i}\right).$$

The De Palma (2010) and De Palma et al. (2012) research used standard language software available from the SONIC group at the University of Colorado and a syllabifier from the National Institute of Standards and Technology to transduce voiced speech into a stream of syllables. Then, a corpus of acoustic data, where known syllable patterns were linked to concepts, was used to train the syllable language model.

This corpus was taken from human users talking to human agents from a major airline call center. Most users were attempting to purchase tickets for air travel. A typical request might be: "I want to fly from Seattle to San Francisco" or "I need to get to Seattle." Human agents created the tagged corpus where syllable patterns were linked to concepts. For example, the syllables of "want to fly to," "travel to," "get to," and "buy a ticket to" were grouped into concepts, such as "customer"... travel to... "airport" Similarly, syllable patterns describing a city are clustered into an airport's name.

There are a number of interesting aspects to the De Palma (2010) and De Palma et al. (2012) research. First, the number of words in the English language is much larger than the number of syllables. Therefore, it was predicted, and it turned out to be true, that the syllable error rate was much smaller than the word error rate in the sound decoding process. Second, in the context of people working with airline service staff, it was straightforward to determine concepts, given syllable strings, e.g., "fly" has a specific intended meaning. Finally, it seems entirely reasonable that a human's sound patterns should be at least as indicative of their intentions as are their words.

We next consider programs that are intended to communicate with humans. In the simplest case, many computer programs answer questions, for example, Amazon's Alexa, Apple's Siri, or even IBM's Watson. In more demanding situations, programs are intended to have a dialogue, i.e., a more complete and goal-directed conversation with the human user. Typical examples of this task might be when a human goes on-line to change a password or, more interestingly, to get financial, insurance, medical, or hardware troubleshooting advice.

In these more complex situations, the responding program must have some notion of teleology or the implicit end purposes of the conversation. Chakrabarti and Luger (2015) have created such a system where probabilistic finite state machines, such as in Fig. 8.9, monitor whether the human agent's implied goal is met by the computational dialogue system. Meanwhile, at each step in the communication, a data structure, called a goal-fulfillment map, Fig. 8.10, contains the knowledge necessary to answer particular questions.

This dialog management software demonstrates a method for combining knowledge of the problem domain with the pragmatic constraints of a conversation. A good conversation depends on both a goal-directed underlying process and conversation grounding in a set of facts about the knowledge supporting the task at hand. Chakrabarti's approach combines content semantics, a knowledge-based system,

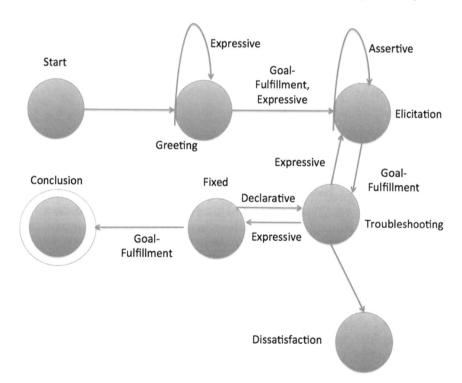

Fig. 8.9 A probabilistic finite-state automaton for conversations used in the troubleshooting domain, from Chakrabarti and Luger (2015)

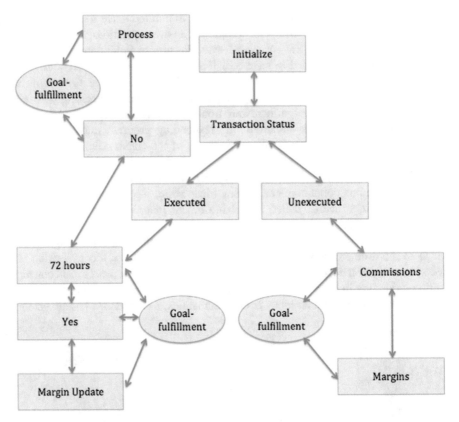

Fig. 8.10 A goal-fulfillment map that supports discussion of a financial transaction, from Chakrabarti and Luger (2015)

with pragmatic semantics, in the form of a conversation engine that generates and monitors the conversation.

The knowledge engine employs specifically designed goal-fulfillment maps that encode the background knowledge needed to drive conversations. The conversation engine uses probabilistic finite state machines that model the different types of conversations. Chakrabarti and Luger (2015) used a form of the Turing test to validate the success of the resulting conversations. Grice's (1981) maxims were used as measures of the conversation quality. Transcripts of computer-generated conversations and human-to-human dialogues in the same domain were judged by humans as roughly (~86%) equivalent, with the computational dialogue significantly (<0.05) more focused on the task or goal of the conversation.

To summarize, the probability-based schemas that represent the knowledge of particular problem domains are driven by the goal-fulfillment state machines in an attempt to both determine and satisfy the concerns of the customer that initiated the conversation. It is important to note that the schema knowledge is *about* understanding and solving customer problems, and in this example, support Conjectures 4 and

5 from Sect. 7.4. Conversations are seen as speech actions (Searle 1969) focused on finding solutions.

The stochastic examples presented in this chapter are intended to demonstrate how the human agent can interpret perception-based patterns. Over time, experience in a world of perception-coupled intentions conditions the expectations of the human agent. Whether the conditioning model is Hebbian, Bayesian, or otherwise, the epistemic issue is that the human agent's expectations are conditioned by these experiences over time. In our examples, we have attempted to demonstrate that probabilistic models are sufficient for capturing aspects of the phenomena of human interpretation.

The final section considers two probabilistic monitoring and diagnostic models in complex problem-solving applications.

8.4   Diagnostic Reasoning in Complex Environments

We next describe two programs that use combinations of different AI software tools, including knowledge rules, neural networks, and dynamic Bayes, to address complex problem situations. These examples demonstrate how constructing and training a program to "learn" about its world can then enable it to react appropriately in novel situations.

The first example of model learning comes from the domain of particle accelerator beam tuning. A particle beam accelerator is a device that is used to transport highly charged particles from a source to a target. The beamline consists of a number of devices designed to either change the beam's characteristics, its direction, size, or shape, or to monitor these characteristics.

The purpose of the particle accelerator is to steer, focus, and otherwise modify the beam of sub-atomic particles. The beam must be transported through a "pipe" to a specified location all the while maintaining desired characteristics of strength and focus. This final beam should reach the target with a set of characteristics determined by the task of the physicists employing the beam. Figure 8.11 shows a simple accelerator beamline, which includes trim magnets for steering, quadrupole magnets for focusing, Faraday cups and stripline detectors for measuring current, and profile and popup monitors for measuring the size and position of the beam (Klein et al. 1999, 2000).

Accelerator beamlines are designed by placing these various components along the beampipe to produce specific effects. A good design will minimize the number of components necessary to maintain acceptable beam conditions while still allowing freedom of control to achieve a range of target conditions. Unfortunately, actual systems rarely work exactly as designed. Problems arise from imperfect beam production, remnant magnetic fields, poorly modeled beam behavior, misplaced or flawed control elements, and changes to the design and use of the beam facility once it has been built. Even with built-in diagnostic tools, the uncertainties of each situation can make beamline control difficult.

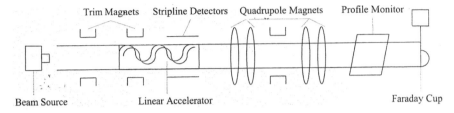

Trim Magnets   Stripline Detectors   Quadrupole Magnets   Profile Monitor

Beam Source   Linear Accelerator   Faraday Cup

Fig. 8.11 A graphic representation (Klein et al. 1999) of an accelerator beam or stripline. The magnets steer and focus the beam by guiding and changing the direction of the particles. Monitors, such as the Faraday cup, measure the beam's strength and profile

Klein and his colleagues (1999, 2000) built an object-oriented control system that utilized AI tools, including connectionist networks, fuzzy reasoning, and *teleo-reactive*, or goal-oriented, planning (Nilsson 1994). With this approach, they were able to successfully model and control particle beam environments at Brookhaven and Argonne National Laboratories. One of their major achievements shows the power of their modeling tools. The task was to discover the location of a trim magnet at the Argonne ATLAS facility.

Because of time, use, and the changing conditions of the Argonne facility itself, the precise location of the magnet was unknown. The fact that the exact location of a multi-hundred-pound magnet could not be determined is not as impossible as it might seem. Many of these magnets are not physically accessible, buried under the facility where, with earth movements and temperature variations, they can change their location, power, and field strength over time.

Klein et al.'s model refinement algorithm was able to re-establish the location and power parameters of the magnet. The model-based approach simply asked, over repeated trials on the beamline, what model or organization of components was most likely to account for the observed behavior. What is even more interesting to consider is that Klein and his colleagues may not have found the exact location of the magnet at all! But for all the practical purposes required by the experiments involved, the imputed location was a good enough fit. This is an important issue from an epistemic viewpoint: What is really "out there," and in what sense can/do we know and use "it?"

Finally, one of Klein's colleagues, Stern (Stern and Lee 2001), extended this model refinement approach. While working at the Stanford Linear Accelerator Center, SLAC, doing what they describe as *model calibration*, the research team was able to improve their understanding of and their models for the accelerator. They did this through the processes of using the accelerators' current supposed models to get a more precise fit of these models to the actual accelerator hardware. Better calibration of the accelerator model itself makes it conform more closely to the physicists' needs and expectations.

Our final example comes from the domain of building computational models to monitor potential problems in producing electric power using a sodium-cooled nuclear reactor. Nuclear accidents are rare, but their effects are extremely harmful to people, the environment, and the economy. Jones et al. (2016) and Darling et al. (2018) have designed a computational monitoring system based on dynamic Bayesian networks to support the observations and knowledge of the human monitors. There are several reasons for employing the DBN technology in this challenging environment.

First, the Bayesian network is composed of nodes and links that reflect expert human knowledge and judgment in the field of reactor physics. This fact is important as the day-to-day monitors are usually not as skilled as the experts that designed the system. The probabilities of the DBN also reflect the results of multiple tests on individual components of the power system, such as sensors, as well as on simulations of the full working environment. Thus, the resulting model contains both explicit human physics and engineering knowledge as well as a probabilistic account of the reactor's running health.

Second, in the very complex environment of nuclear power generation, the DBN is able to produce faster than real-time analytic and diagnostic results. Kevin Murphy (2002) has described the transparent and tractable reasoning powers of DBN-based technology. As a result the human monitor is able to understand events as soon as, and often before, they actually happen. The monitor also receives from the model itself recommendations for remediating potential problems.

Figure 8.12 presents a schematic for a sodium-cooled nuclear reactor that produces electric power. The reactor system, and its model, have multiple sensors monitoring the states of the pumps, the temperatures of the various vessels, the positions of the control rods, and the turbine speeds. The ten monitors of the state of the power generation system are represented by the rectangular boxes of Fig. 8.13. The circles of Fig. 8.13 represent the nodes of the DBN and the cylinders extending off the circles represent the values of each circle changing over time.

Training the dynamic Bayesian network takes place as the power generation system runs across multiple scenarios and time cycles. Training on near-normal data establishes a state of equilibrium of the DBN model. The DBN model, in a near-normal running situation, can also provide approximate values for missing sensor data from the system. The values proposed for missing information or damaged sensors are what the model determines, using the expectation maximization algorithm to be most likely, given the current state of the running system (Pless and Luger 2001, 2003). The algorithm used to determine these most likely values is Baum - Welch, a variant of expectation maximization (Dempster et al. 1977, Luger 2009a, Sect. 13.2).

Once the DBN model was trained, the research group generated multiple accident sequences using their simulation system. In each scenario, for example, having differential pressures within the plants cooling system or performing control rod insertion, the model captured the state of the system as the "accident" evolved. This allowed visualization of all parameters related to each situation as well as presented options for remediation. The fact that these options could be realized faster than real time supported the human operators' steps toward remediation.

An important component of the Darling et al. (2018) DBN nuclear power generation modeling project was that it supported what Pearl (2000) calls *counterfactual reasoning*. What this means is that the system can reason about situations that are not currently happening in the reactor. For example, in a danger situation, the DBN

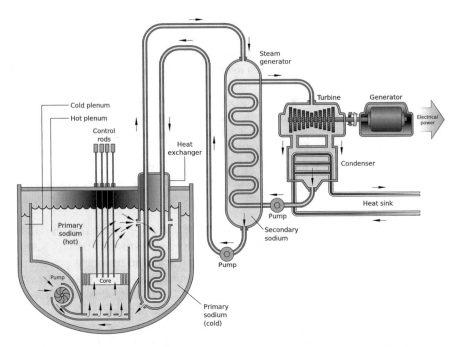

Fig. 8.12 The schematic of a sodium-cooled nuclear power generation system (Darling et al. 2018). The various reservoirs, pumps, control rods, turbine, etc. have sensors reporting their states to the DBN, as seen in Fig. 8.13

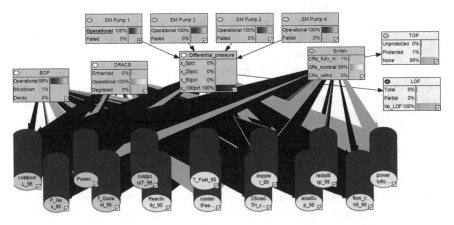

Fig. 8.13 The dynamic Bayesian network model of the sodium-cooled nuclear reactor of Fig. 8.12. The ten rectangular boxes represent the monitors collecting sensor data from the reactor. The circles represent the nodes of the DBN, lines from the rectangles to the circles represent the connectivity of the network, and the cylinders emanating from the nodes represent the nodes as they change over time

model can be asked "What would be the result of inserting the control rods further into the sodium?" Similarly, when the coolant temperature is getting dangerously high, the monitor could ask "What if I added supplementary coolant to the current state of the system?" The result of such queries is that the model moves forward into future time predicting what the state of the system would be if these actions were actually taken. This prognostic information can be critical in determining an optimal outcome, given a current danger state of the reactor.

This hypothetical reasoning is supported by the fact that the computational model offers an accurate reflection of the power-producing reactor. The knowledge-based and probabilistic model allows monitors to try out different control strategies and get almost immediate feedback on what would happen, as well as the time sequence for it to occur. Examining these possible responses can direct the reactor monitors to make the most informed decisions at appropriate times. This trained computational model captures the human-like reasoning that an informed diagnostic expert would offer in similar situations.

The research projects of this chapter are presented at a rather high level of detail, and further information may be found in the references for each project. As noted earlier, the reason for presenting these examples is to both demonstrate their sufficiency as models of human perception, understanding, and decision-making in complex situations and also to offer concrete examples of the epistemic conjectures presented in Sect. 7.4.

8.5   In Summary

Chapter 8 first considered Bayes' theorem, its extensions, and several of its epistemic implications. In offering a demonstration of how Bayes works in simple situations, we develop the intuition of its importance: new information, the *a posteriori*, is interpreted in the context of already understood, the *a priori*, knowledge of a situation. This *a priori* knowledge can be understood as a form of Kant's (1781/1964), Bartlett's (1932), or Piaget's (1970) schemata used in problem resolution.

We presented a number of research projects in the second, third, and fourth sections of the chapter. The goal of presenting these problem scenarios was to show how Bayesian systems are sufficient for characterizing important aspects of human perception and reasoning. The final example, monitoring sodium-cooled nuclear power generation, used a dynamic Bayesian network to show "what would happen if …" scenarios. Visualizing possible alternatives was a direct way to address potential problems. Many aspects of the program examples of this chapter reflect the conjectures supporting a modern epistemology presented in Sect. 7.4.

We begin the final chapter with a brief summary of the task of this monograph. We ask how, through active exploration, an agent can come to understand its environment. We next question what happens when the state of the world no longer matches an agent's expectations. As an example, we propose a Bayesian belief net explanation for the changes in the stages of early childhood development described by Piaget (1983), Bower (1977), and others (Gopnik 2011a, b). We then make the case for the overall health, excitement, and promise of continuing research in artificial intelligence. We conclude by describing again our human-centric epistemic stance called an *active, pragmatic, model-revising realism*.

Further Thoughts and Readings   Pearl's books have introduced probabilistic reasoning and the Bayesian belief network technology to modern AI (see the Bibliography for full reference details):

> Judea Pearl (1988), *Probabilistic Reasoning in Intelligent Systems: Networks of Plausible Inference.*
> Judea Pearl (2000), *Causality.*

To understand the importance of probabilistic techniques in modern AI, here are several relevant textbook resources:

> Jurafsky and Martin (2020), *Speech and Language Processing*, third ed.
> Luger (2009a), *Artificial Intelligence: Structures and Strategies for Complex Problem Solving.*
> Nilsson (1997), *Artificial Intelligence: A New Synthesis.*
> Russell and Norvig, (2010), *Artificial Intelligence: A Modern Approach*, third ed.

See also *Bayesian Epistemology* in the Stanford Encyclopedia of Philosophy, at url 8.1. Although based on Bayesian assumptions, it differs from what we propose.

Dr. Dan Pless created the BBN traffic example of Sect. 8.2. Many of my other PhD graduates, especially Dr. Chayan Chakrabarti, Dr. Michael Darling, Dr. Thomas Jones, Prof. Paul De Palma, and Dr. Roshan Rammohan, are responsible for building many of the probabilistic models for the applications presented in this chapter.

Figures 8.7 and 8.8 were developed for SBIR research sponsored by the US Navy. We thank Karger Publications, Basel, for permission to use Figs. 8.3, 8.4, and 8.8. These appeared in Luger et al. (2002). Figures 8.9 and 8.10 are from the PhD dissertation at UNM of Dr. Chayan Chakrabarti. Figure 8.11 was developed for the US Dept of Energy, as part of an SBIR contract. We thank Sandia National Laboratories (DOE) for creating Figs. 8.12 and 8.13 as part of our research contract for monitoring sodium-cooled nuclear reactors. I created all other figures in this chapter to support my teaching needs at UNM.

Programming Support   There are a number of Bayesian belief net and hidden Markov model software products available on the internet. A probabilistic interpreter, called *Generalized Loopy Logic*, created by Dr. Daniel Pless as part of his PhD thesis can be found at url 8.2.

Chapter 9
Toward an Active, Pragmatic, Model-Revising Realism

Contents

Chapter 9 brings into focus the task of this book, using insights from the histories of philosophy and artificial intelligence as the foundation for a science of understanding ourselves and the world. Section 9.1 briefly reviews the story to this point. Section 9.2 discusses model building through exploring the environment, and Sect. 9.3 suggests several methods for the adaptation of models in light of new discoveries. Section 9.4 makes conjectures about the future of AI, and Sect. 9.5 offers thoughts on the construction of a modern epistemology. With an analysis of category errors in computation, we see humans, with our life, intelligence, and responsibilities as aessentially different than machines.

9.1   A Summary of the Project

The first chapter addressed the notion of what it means to compute, presenting the Turing machine, the Post production system, and the Church-Turing thesis. We described an important limitation of computation with Turing's undecidability proof. We also addressed the epistemic components of programming. For most AI technicians, programming is an interactive and iterative refinement process, where each new piece of computer code is an experiment in discovery. If that code is successful, it is integrated into the larger program, and if it fails to express the programmer's intentions, it is revised and retested.

This iterative refinement process was initially made possible through the expressive powers of high-level computer languages including Lisp, Prolog, Logo, Smalltalk, ML, OCaml, and Scheme. In fact most modern languages support this active exploratory process. Above all, iterative refinement is an epistemic commitment that supports the programmer as she continues to approximate her desired goals: revising her thoughts and code as she explores its use-based implications.

Chapter 2 offered a review of the philosophical traditions that led to the creation of the digital computer and our present understanding of the world. There were two important themes in Chap. 2. The first theme is skepticism that asks whether the world is actually knowable. Another view of this skepticism is the contention that what we think we know about ourselves and the world may never be proven to be correct. The second theme of Chap. 2 is the use of the scientific method as a strategy for understanding the natural world. Whether one thinks that reality is a form of water, or whether it is earth, air, fire, and water, or fashioned from some atomic substrate, these ideas are proposed as conjectures that can be refuted. In this refutation, there is always the promise of a new synthesis, which again can be questioned.

Chapter 3 included the early history of AI and the Dartmouth College Summer Workshop of 1956. This workshop gathered together the current AI practitioners, adopted the name artificial intelligence, and proposed topics suitable for ongoing research. As the discipline evolved, many philosophical issues, including the idea of trying to better understand how humans solved problems, came into play.

Part II, Chaps. 4 through 6, explored the main representational paradigms of research and development in artificial intelligence. We focused on early examples from each of the symbolic, connectionist, and evolutionary approaches to AI. The goal of these chapters was to represent each approach with examples of early successes as well as to describe their recent products. At the end of each chapter, we summarized the strengths and limitations of that approach to artificial intelligence problem-solving. We also noted the effects on artificial intelligence projects of the rationalist, empiricist, and pragmatist philosophical traditions.

In Chap. 7, we proposed a constructivist epistemology as a synthesis of the philosophical positions of empiricism, rationalism, and pragmatism. After presenting arguments to support this position, we offered five assumptions that give a basis for a modern epistemological science and eight follow-on conjectures that support understanding ourselves and our environment.

In Chap. 8, we presented Bayes' rule and gave a suggestive proof using a single disease and symptom. The critical issue with Bayes' formulation is to see a coherent mathematics-supported relationship between *a priori* knowledge, that is, what an agent already knows, and *a posteriori* information, new data currently perceived. This mathematical relationship can be computationally interpreted, especially as it is used across periods of time. The formula for Bayes' rule can be seen as an interpreter for the schemas of Kant, Bartlett, Piaget as well as many AI practitioners. Section 8.2 described several AI programs that implemented this constructivist epistemic stance.

This final chapter concludes with optimistic support for the future of artificial intelligence research and development. Further, with an analysis of category errors in computation, we see humans, with our life, intelligence, and responsibilities as essentially different from machines. We conclude that AI can raise to, or even surpass, many aspects of human intelligence but that human intelligence and decision-making are *different*.

Through insights gained from our philosophical tradition and the AI endeavor, we suggest that humans are best served by adopting an epistemic stance based on pragmatism, relativism, and an unconditioned commitment to the scientific method that supports progressively comprehending and utilizing our ever-evolving life-environment.

9.2   Model Building Through Exploration

We have described at length the AI program designer's use of computer code to explore their world. An important contribution of the AI community is to have built automata that, through exploration, come to know and use their environments. We saw this happen virtually when, in Sect. 6.3, artificial life designers created entities able to survive, procreate, interact in communities, and explore their environments. The robotics community has designed and built many physical entities able to accomplish similar goals.

Early robots, similar to the tripods created by Aeschylus' Hephaestus to serve the Olympian gods, were designed to perform specific tasks. These early robots have been so successful in tasks including production line assembly, automated welding, directing delicate surgeries, and controlling deep-space vehicles that most are no longer even considered to be a component of AI technology.

Shakey was the first mobile robot to be able to sense and reason about its surroundings. Built in the late 1960s by the Stanford Research Institute, now SRI International, Shakey could follow commands that required making plans for movement and performing simple tasks, such as rearranging objects. The Shakey project was funded by DARPA and Charles Rosen was the lead designer.

Shakey's planning program was STRIPS, the STanford Research Institute Problem Solver (Fikes and Nilsson 1971, see Luger 2009a, Sect. 8.4.2). I first saw Shakey in action at the Third International Joint Conference on Artificial Intelligence at Stanford University in 1973 where I presented my first AI paper in a symposium organized for graduate students to present their PhD research.

After Shakey, many different AI groups entered the robotics domain. The more famous include soccer-playing robots that formed the ROBO Cup annual soccer team competitions that began in 1996 (see url: 9.1). Also important are the groups at NASA that created the Mars rover Opportunity that traveled more than 28 miles on the surface of Mars before its demise in 2018. These efforts continue to this day with the design of autonomous vehicles.

For our story, however, we next take a slightly different tack and describe several early robotic programs that come to understand their world by actively exploring it. More than 30 years ago at MIT, Rodney Brooks and colleagues (1986, 1991) designed a robot explorer. Brooks' goal was to search through and accomplish tasks in an environment without any prior knowledge or planning in that space. Brooks approach actually questioned the need for *any* centralized representational scheme. Brooks employed a *subsumption architecture*, see Fig. 9.1, to show how a general intelligent mechanism might evolve from lower supporting forms of intelligence.

Brooks suggests, and gives examples through his robotic creations, that intelligent behavior does not come from disembodied theorem-prover-based planning systems like STRIPS, nor does it require a global memory and control. Intelligence, Brooks claims, is the product of the interaction between an appropriately designed system and its environment. Furthermore, Brooks espouses the view that intelligent behavior *emerges* from the interactions of architectures of organized simpler behaviors.

Figure 9.1 presents a three-layered subsumption architecture, where each layer is composed of finite-state machines, simple sets of *condition* → *action* production rules, run asynchronously. There is no central locus of control. Rather, each machine is data-driven by the information it perceives. The arrival of a message or the expiration of a time period causes the various machines to change state.

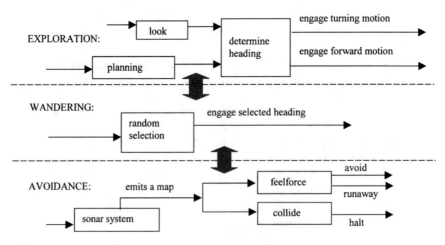

Fig. 9.1 A three-layered subsumption architecture adapted from Brooks (1991). The three levels are defined by their EXPLORE, WANDER, and AVOID behaviors

Brooks' robot had a ring of 12 sonar sensors around it. Every second, these sensors gave radial depth measurements. The lowest level layer of the subsumption architecture, AVOID, implements a behavior that keeps the robot from hitting objects, whether these are static or moving. The machine labeled sonar system emits an instantaneous signal that is passed on to collide and feel force, which in turn can generate halt messages for the finite-state machine in charge of running the robot forward. When feelforce is activated, it is able to generate either runaway or avoid instructions.

Brooks approach to robots learning about their environments was an important first step. AI researchers want robots to be able to enter new and possibly dangerous situations, to be able to explore them, and to draw some conclusions, such as "there is an injured human here." However, as Brooks' robot does not build a model of its world as it discovers new obstacles or passageways, it cannot take that next step. How would it know an "injured human?" How would it even recognize a place that it had previously explored? How can it learn anything? Finally, how could such a robot ever operate in a truly complex environment, e.g., having the knowledge that a taxi, Uber, or other driver needs to navigate a city such as London?

The following generations of robots began to overcome these issues by adding more memory and present state information to their exploring strategies. For example, Lewis and Luger (2000) created a robot that, building on an architecture adopted from Hofstadter's (1995) work, was able to map and remember wall and navigation pathways as it explored its environment as shown in Fig. 9.2.

Lewis's robot maps possible wall structures using signals from adjacent sonar sensors. In Fig. 9.3, Lewis's robot is able to recognize and travel a pathway through object structures in attempting to achieve a goal. The Brooks and Lewis examples are early attempts for robots to discover and cope with their environment by exploring and building ever-improving models of that environment.

As we saw in Sect. 5.3.2, the Google Brain community (Faust et al. 2018) created a much more modern and powerful solution to this get-to-know-your-world--through-exploration research. The robot system called PRM-RL used deep neural net learning coupled with reinforcement learning to discover goal-focused path components. The PRM-RL robot can then apply this "knowledge" to discover solution paths in entirely new environments.

The goal of this section was to demonstrate several AI problem solvers that used active search to build computational models that approximate the world that they explore. Brooks' subsumption approach used a hierarchy of finite-state machines to explore its environment but had no memory to record its achievements. Lewis and his colleagues added limited memory structures to learn invariants of the explored world, including solid obstacles and passageways, and to reuse these discoveries later in their search. Finally, Faust and her colleagues used a probabilistic planning algorithm, along with reinforcement learning, to train a robot to discover new paths in previously unexplored territory.

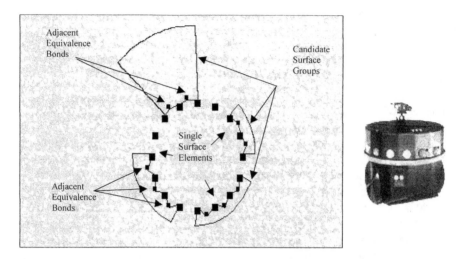

Fig. 9.2 Lewis (2001) created representational structures for barrier discovery and location. Feedback from the robot's sonar sensors indicates the presence or absence of barriers

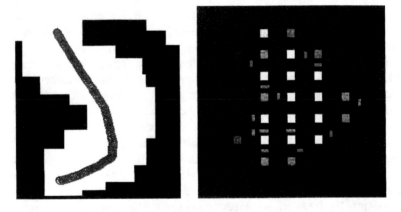

Fig. 9.3 The robot's path, left, and map or model, right, for barriers and passageways learned from the use of its sonar sensors. Figure adapted from Lewis (2001)

9.3   Model Revision and Adaptation

In Sect. 3.5, based on the modeling traditions of the cognitive science community, we presented several programs that demonstrated the assimilation of new information into appropriately conditioned cognitive systems. These programs presented mechanisms sufficient to describe many of the conservation tasks in children's learning behavior described by Jean Piaget (1983) and other developmental psychologists.

At the Artificial Intelligence Department of the University of Edinburgh, Young (1976), using production rules, demonstrated children's seriation skills. In seriation tasks, children are asked to organize blocks by their sizes, which requires under-standing the relationship of partial and total orderings (Young 1976).

Also, at Edinburgh, Luger (1981) and Luger et al. (1983) created a production system accounting for object permanence in children, based on behaviors originally noted by the child psychologist T.G.R. Bower (1977). An object's permanence is its continued existence across time despite being out of immediate sight. As mentioned in Sect. 3.4, Drescher's (1991) program at MIT also demonstrated infants' responses during the stages of object permanence. Finally, Wallace et al. (1987) developed the BAIRN program at Carnegie Mellon that used production rules to demonstrate number conservation.

The programs just mentioned described children *within* their different stages of development. There has been little accounting, however, for how children moved between these stages as they matured. Section 9.3 discusses the issue of *model revision*. What can be done when perception-based data cannot be interpreted by the present system's a priori worldview? This is a difficult problem: how to make "adjustments" when new data cannot be interpreted, given the viewer's current expectations for that data.

Figure 9.4 presents an overview of this. On the top row, a cognitive model either offers an interpretation of new data or it does not. Piaget has described these situations as instances of *assimilation* and *accommodation*. First, through assimilation, data fit expectations, possibly requiring adjusting its probabilistic measures. Otherwise, through accommodation, the model must reconfigure itself, possibly adding new components. The lower part of Fig. 9.4 presents the COSMOS architecture (Sakhanenko et al. 2008) created to address both these tasks.

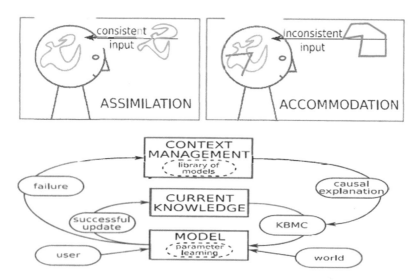

Fig. 9.4 Cognitive model use and failure, above; a model-calibration algorithm, below, for assimilation and accommodation of new data. Adapted from (Sakhanenko et al. 2008)

The COSMOS (Sakhanenko et al. 2008) model selection and model calibration algorithm was tested in complex environments including the flow of liquids through pumps, pipes, and filters. The model interprets real-time pressure measures, pipe flows, filter clogging, vibrations, and alignments. When new data arrive, the program must decide if it fits within its current model of the world or whether it needs to select another model, such as adapting to a clogged filter, from its library of models.

Let's consider a simple example of the model selection and calibration problem. Suppose we are building a program to monitor home burglar alarms. The probabilistic home burglar monitoring program is deployed in a specific location to be trained and tested in realistic situations. In particular, it monitors alarms for false-positive predictions, where the alarm indicates a problem when no problem exists.

As this system is trained successfully during the winter months, the probabilistic values of the alarm reports are learned. The day-to-day deployment has produced data that conditions the system. After the training period, the data are assimilated into the model and the resulting trained program successfully monitors both false alarms and actual home break-ins.

Next, suppose that in the Spring months of the year, there are multiple fierce desiccating winds that shake the alarm sensors mounted on doors and windows and dry out their connections. As a result, when the monitoring program presents many more false alarms, it is necessary to readjust the probabilities of the model and to add new model parameters to reflect the Spring weather conditions. The result will be a new extended system that supports alarm monitoring in the Spring.

Further, when the alarm systems are then sold in a new city, it will be necessary to determine which models will best fit that situation. There may be other important disturbances, such as small earthquake tremors; as a result, more variables will need to be represented. Although the problem of model induction in general is intractable, in most situations, useful new models can be created. A search to discover new causal relationships among a models' constraints can often be sufficient for this task.

The problem of *model induction* is an important component of current research in the development of probabilistic models. A description of this task says that, given new data, what is the most likely model that can explain that data? Judea Pearl and others (Pearl 2000; Tian and Pearl 2001), began this research. There are many exciting challenges for the use of model induction. These include, given fMRI data related to certain mental disorders, find the most likely set of cortical connections that can explain this data (Burge et al. 2007). Rammohan (2010) and Oyen (2013) created algorithms for investigating variables and its possible relationships in this structure search environment.

Deep learning coupled with reinforcement learning also offers technology for model building. We saw the DeepMind and Alpha Zero programs described in Sect. 5.2. In these programs, the legal moves of the problem were used to search through the problem space to discover and reinforce partial solutions. The Faust et al. (2018) robotics project was also, using reinforcement learning, able to create successful paths for the robot to travel by discovering and linking smaller successful components of paths. These examples of reinforcement learning showed how searching and assembling partial components of solutions can lead to successful models of a situation.

Our next example of model-revising search is taken from children's cognitive development. In Piaget's (1965) *conservation* experiments, children aged 4–7 mistakenly confuse the amount of liquid that a glass contains with the height of the glass that contains that liquid. As the child matures and watches her ideas fail in the practical world, i.e., there actually isn't more juice in the taller, thinner glass, she revises her model of volume. New variables, such as the circumference or diameter of the container, expand her understanding of volume. Children come to understand that the quantity of a liquid is constant regardless of the shape of its container.

Figure 9.5 presents the experimental situation where a child sees two containers of liquid, each holding a similar amount. The liquid of one container is then poured into a taller container and the child is asked which container holds the most liquid. The non-conserving child indicates that the taller, thinner glass holds more.

A simple Bayesian belief network is sufficient to model the stages of conservation behavior across time. In Fig. 9.6a, a number of perceptual values are associated with the child observing the vessel containing liquid. These perceptions capture height, thickness, color, and so on.

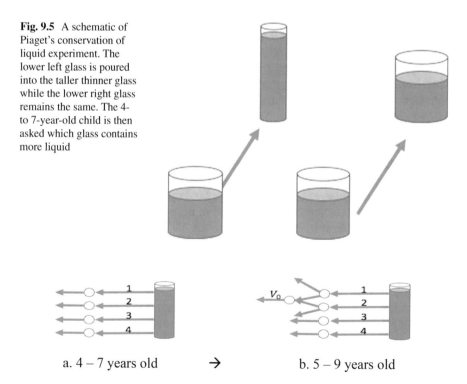

Fig. 9.5 A schematic of Piaget's conservation of liquid experiment. The lower left glass is poured into the taller thinner glass while the lower right glass remains the same. The 4- to 7-year-old child is then asked which glass contains more liquid

a. 4 – 7 years old   →   b. 5 – 9 years old

Fig. 9.6 (**a**) presents a Bayesian network representing a child seeing perceptual cues. 1 indicates the height of the container, 2 indicates width or diameter, 3 and 4 could be the color of the liquid, etc. In (**b**), the child associates the container's height and width to create a measure for volume

Figure 9.6b represents the BBN where the perceptual cues for height and width or diameter of the container are combined. The child is able to unite these two perceptual cues when a teacher or parent points out that both the height and the width of the container are necessary for measuring the amount or volume of the liquid. Alternatively, the bright child might learn this association by herself, through experiment, or perhaps by asking how much liquid an even taller and thinner container held.

Later, as the maturing child approaches the *formal operational* developmental stage, ages 12–16, she realizes that a formula can capture the volume measure precisely. For cylindrical containers, it is the height multiplied by the diameter of the container multiplied by π. The movement through these stages of volume conservation is usually driven by pragmatic concerns, such as "I want to get the most possible juice" or "My teacher told me I didn't understand volume."

The many empirical studies that have identified stages in early human cognitive development, including (Piaget 1954, 1983; Bower 1977; Young 1976; Gopnik et al. 2004; Gopnik 2011a), shed light on the mediating processes through which humans understand and use their environment. These developmental stages suggest a progressive approximation toward a complex equilibration. In many of these situations, dynamic Bayesian models, such as our Piagetian conservation example, can offer a sufficient characterization of the phenomena involved. Even non-human primates seem to go through similar developmental stages as they learn to organize objects by size and shape (McGonigle and Chalmers 2002).

Major advances in the natural sciences can also be viewed as discovering new invariances through questioning the assumptions of older, previously learned, relationships. The insights of Darwin, Eisenstein, Heisenberg, and Hawking can each be analyzed from this perspective. These insights are captured in new models, which will, in time, again be revised. These models are not the "discovery" of divine truths, as Descartes or Leibniz have suggested, but rather discovering new and useful accommodations within the environment. These discoveries can be expressed as new models and, as Heisenberg (2000) suggests, usually produce new language constructs. These represent concepts developed through experimentation and extend both current understanding and practical uses of the environment.

Model calibration, extension, and revision remain important research areas for artificial intelligence. When new puzzling situations develop, how can these be best understood and interpreted in the contexts of what the AI model or human subject already knows? What are the best explanations for how we humans learn new relationships? How do practical needs influence the understanding of new phenomena? Our cognitive and computational research communities are challenged to continue addressing these questions.

> *What we have to learn to do, we learn by doing...*
> —*ARISTOTLE, Ethics.*
>
> *Where is the knowledge we have lost in information?*
> —*T.S. ELIOT, Choruses from the Rock.*

9.4   What Is the Project of the AI Practitioner?

There is no question whether the AI enterprise will continue to be successful. Across the full spectrum of computer-based problem-solving, there are few areas that artificial intelligence techniques have not touched. What some call "first-generation AI" and we prefer "symbol-based AI" is a critical component of that success story. As noted in Chap. 4, applications including controllers for deep-space travel, the Mars rover, guidance systems for complex surgeries, advice systems for medical care, and language communication programs that assist in product sales, are all parts of this early success story. In fact, many components of the symbol-based AI technology are so integrated into commonly used software applications that their AI origins are no longer remembered.

As noted in Sects. 4.3 and 6.5, the successes of symbol-based AI have also led to better understanding of its limitations. The iterative refinement process, so important in creating successful software, also sheds light on the inadequacy of particular approaches. The (rationalist) task of abstraction necessary to create symbols, symbol structures, and logic-like control algorithms constrains the designs of programs intended to capture the patterns in ever-changing environments. Symbols too inflexible and algorithms too rigid for many tasks have led the AI community to new approaches. There should not be an admission of failure here but rather an acknowledgment that responsible use of the methods of science has led the AI community to new insights, technologies, and successes.

An important response to several of the limitations of symbol-based AI is the connectionist or neural network approach to problem-solving. The creation of the Boltzmann machine and backpropagation algorithms in the 1985 time period overcame the limitations of the older perceptron. With added access to server farms and vector-based processors, deep learning technology added to the neural network approach by adding multiple hidden layers. This new approach greatly improved many areas of problem-solving including image classification, facial recognition, language translation, text classifiers, and learning expert skills in new games, given only the rules of the game.

Successes with deep learning and association-based (empiricist) problem solvers have again suggested their limitations. As noted in Sects. 5.4 and 6.5, research continues in making deep-learning systems more transparent and better able to explain their decisions. This transparency is important in areas where a program makes personal, privacy, medical, or financial recommendations. Research also continues to focus on the meta-parameters of deep learning networks to better understand which learning rates, network sizes, and architectures are most appropriate for particular problem situations.

In Chap. 7, we presented the genetic and emergent approaches to AI. Although the successes of this approach are not as obvious as those of the symbolic or connectionist, they do offer a radically different perspective. Genetic algorithms and programming are able to evolve new perspective solutions using only reproduction operators and fitness functions.

The artificial life algorithms produce new generations of both individuals and societies. There remains hope that areas including artificial chemistry, physics, and biology can produce useful new life forms. These technologies may be critical for better understanding complex systems, including the human genome and the development of antibody therapies. There also remains the challenge for the artificial life community to shed some insight on the origins of life itself and the processes for producing new species within the a-life world. Section 6.4 discusses the strengths and limitations of emergent approaches to AI.

In Part III, we presented stochastic approaches to building AI solutions. We began Part III proposing a compromise, a synthesis, among philosophical positions. This compromise recognized the role that the current, *a priori*, knowledge of an agent has for integrating newly perceived, *a posteriori*, data. This Bayesian-based methodology echoed the expectations, or schemas, proposed by Kant, Bartlett, Piaget, and others in Chaps. 2–4.

Perhaps the most important contribution to the Bayesian approach was the insights of Judea Pearl. The Bayesian belief networks (Pearl 1988, 2000) allowed Bayesian representations to be viewed as causal relationships that, when factored, become more tractable, i.e., their solution algorithms were realistically computable. We presented in Chap. 8 a number of examples of Bayesian solutions, including the use of dynamic Bayes.

One singularly important accomplishment of the AI and the cognitive science communities has been to offer an answer to the dualism or the mind–body problem described in Sect. 2.4. Since the days of Descartes, philosophers have asked for an explanation of the interactions and integration of intelligent responses through the human mind, consciousness, and a physical body. Philosophers have offered every possible response, from total materialism to subjective and objective idealism and the denial of material existence. Several thinkers even proposed the supporting intervention of a benign god. Artificial intelligence and cognitive science research reject Cartesian dualism in favor of a material explanation of intelligence.

The Oxford philosopher Gilbert Ryle (1949) described Descartes' dualism as the presence of a "ghost in the machine." Ryle, following the then-current tradition in psychology, suggests eliminating this ghost through the assumptions of behaviorism. Artificial intelligence has taken an alternative approach to eliminate Ryle's ghost. AI and cognitive science practitioners hypothesize that intelligence, including human intelligence, is based on the physical implementation, or instantiation, of representations in a processing system. Algorithms manipulate these representations in the process of solving problems. The continuing successes of the AI research project are an indication of the validity of this hypothesis.

With AI, Ryle's ghost is removed or "cashed-out" from the problem solver and replaced by representations and algorithms that support decision-making. The best-first search algorithm (Sect. 4.1.2), for example, gives an estimated "best judgment" for selecting a next move in a search situation. In deep learning, conditioned micro-decisions developed in a reinforcement structure can control a robot in a new environment. We have seen multiple examples of reckoning-based judgments and appropriate actions over recent chapters.

One reason for the continuing successes of the AI enterprise is the influx of bright, young, and excited researchers to the field. These new collaborators are also a very diverse group that includes linguists, psychologists, computer scientists, physicists, sociologists, medical doctors, and contributors from other fields. As pointed out in Sect. 3.3, it is important not to attempt to limit what it means to be an AI practitioner. When challenges seem unlimited, energy and commitment are important, with the only requirement to remain within the constraints and promise of the scientific method.

There are, of course, *AI winters*, a term used several times over the last 60 plus years by the AI community to indicate deep changes in financial support for particular projects. Most of the research funding in artificial intelligence has been afforded by government agencies, and predominantly in the US by the National Science Foundation and the Department of Defense. As different AI projects show their promise or, over time, their lack thereof, funding goals change. The AI community's goals can also change: is funding important for human language understanding, for foreign language translation, or for autonomous vehicles? Are projects that are part of the physical symbol system hypothesis important? Why is there not more support for deep learning neural networks? AI's practitioners have also, at different times, been guilty of overpromising results. When these results are disappointing, lack of interest and funding often follows.

A number of consequential challenges remain for building intelligent systems. We propose three questions that need to be addressed as we continue to build more intelligence into mechanical devices:

1. **What is the role of embodiment and culture in intelligence?** One of the main assumptions of the computational hypothesis is that the particular instantiation of a symbol or network system is irrelevant; all that matters is material representations and algorithms. This viewpoint has been challenged by a number of thinkers (Searle 1980; Johnson 1987; Agre and Chapman 1987; Varela et al. 1993) who essentially argue that intelligent action in the world requires a physical and social embodiment that allows the agent to be integrated into that world.

   The architecture of modern computers does not support this degree of situatedness, requiring that an artificial intelligence agent interacts with its world through the extremely limited window of contemporary input/output devices. If this challenge is correct, then, although some forms of machine intelligence may be possible, full intelligence, as we humans experience it, will require a very different machine, as Searle suggests (1980), than that afforded by contemporary computers.

   Further, as we argued in Chap. 7, knowledge must be regarded as a social as well as an individual construct. In a *meme-based* theory of intelligence (Edelman 1992), society itself carries essential components of knowledge. It is possible that an understanding of the social context of knowledge and human behavior is as important to a theory of intelligence as is an understanding of the dynamics of the individual mind/brain.

2. **What is the nature of interpretation, or how does AI address the *grounding* problem?** Most computational models in traditional AI operate within an already interpreted domain. With this approach, there is an implicit and *a priori* commitment by the system's designers to a set of "meanings" for the program. Once this commitment is made, there is very little flexibility for shifting contexts, goals, or representations as the problem-solving situation evolves.

   One AI approach to semantic meaning is the *possible worlds* of Alfred Tarski (1944, 1956). The Tarskian approach of mapping between sets of symbols and objects in a domain is sufficient to explain *truth values* for reasoning rules. It is insufficient, however, for explaining how one response may have different interpretations in the light of specific practical goals.

   Linguists have tried to remedy semantic limitations by adding theories of pragmatics (Austin 1962). Discourse analysis, with its fundamental dependence on symbol use in context, has also dealt with these issues in the recent years. The problem, however, is broader in that it deals with the failure of referential tools in general (Lave 1988).

   The pragmatist tradition started by Peirce (1958) and James (1981), and continued by Eco (1976), Grice (1981), Seboek (1985), and others, takes a more radical approach to language and intelligence. It places symbolic expressions within the wider context of signs and interpretation. As Peirce (1958, p. 45) indicates "… we come down to what is tangible and practical, as the root to every real distinction of thought, no matter how subtle it may be; and there is no difference of meaning so fine as to consist of anything but a possible difference of practice."

   This *meaning as expression of practical purpose* suggests that a symbol can only be understood in the context of its role as *interpretant*, that is, in the context of purposeful interaction with its environment. There is in the current AI research community an insufficient understanding of the process by which humans and societies create meaning and change interpretations. We visit these issues again with discussion of neopragmatism in Sect. 9.5.

3. **Can the AI and cognitive science communities design computational models that are falsifiable?** Popper (1959) and others have argued that scientific theories must be falsifiable. This means that there must exist circumstances under which the model is *not* a successful approximation of the phenomenon. The obvious reason for this is that *any* number of confirming experimental instances is not sufficient for confirmation of a model. Even more importantly, new research is created in a direct response to the failure of existing theories or models.

   The general nature of most computational models may make them difficult to falsify, and, as a result, of limited use *as science*. Some AI data structures, for example, the semantic or connectionist networks, are so general that they can model almost anything. Like the universal Turing machine, they can describe any computable function. When an artificial intelligence or cognitive science researcher is asked under what conditions his or her characterization of intelligent behavior will *not* work, the answer can be difficult.

Finally, it must be noted that most AI research projects are not focused on building *artificial general intelligence* or *AGI*. The possibility of an AGI seems to be the boogeyman of many popular culture warriors. Even projects trying to win the annual *Turing Competition* (url 9.2) are not pretending to create an AGI. What would this AGI look like? Would it be equivalent to human intelligence, see Sect. 9.5? AI funders, and most all AI researchers, are not interested in this AGI. Research is more committed to expanding our current limited knowledge for solving important problems for both individuals and society.

The most exciting aspect of work in artificial intelligence is that to be coherent and contribute to the endeavor we must address these concerns. To understand problem-solving, learning, and language, we must comprehend the philosophical levels of representations and knowledge. We are asked to resolve Aristotle's tension between *theoria* and *praxis*, to fashion a union of understanding and practice, of the theoretical and practical, to live between science and art.

Researchers in AI, as practitioners and toolmakers who make representations, algorithms, and languages, enable the design and building of mechanisms that exhibit intelligent behavior. Through experimenting, we test both their computational adequacy for solving problems and our own understanding of intelligent phenomena.

There is a tradition for this: Descartes, Leibniz, Bacon, Pascal, Hobbes, Boole, Babbage, Turing, and the others whose contributions were presented in Chap. 2. Engineering, science, and philosophy; the nature of ideas, knowledge, and skill; the power and limitations of formalism and mechanism; these are the expectations and tensions through which the AI vision continues to thrive, and from which we continue our explorations.

> We are just an advanced breed of monkeys on a minor planet of
> a very average star. But we can understand the universe. That
> makes us something very special.
> —STEPHEN HAWKING.

9.5 Meaning, Truth, and a Foundation for a Modern Epistemology

There are four topics in this final section. First, we introduce neo-pragmatism, the continuation of the philosophical traditions introduced in Sect. 2.8. Second, we discuss the computer scientist's notion of *categories*: the division of entities into independent irreducible groupings. Third, we consider findings of the neuroscience community that support our current understanding of human perception and performance. Finally, we conclude with a proposal for a modern epistemology and thoughts on being human, addressing relativism, and the use of the scientific method.

9.5.1 Neopragmatism, Kuhn, Rorty, and the Scientific Method

A number of commentators on the AI tradition, including Winograd and Flores (1986), Searle (1980, 1990), and Weizenbaum (1976), claim that the most important aspects of intelligence are not, and in principle cannot be, modeled with any computational representation. These areas include learning, understanding human language, and the production of meaningful speech acts.

These skeptical concerns have deep roots in our Western philosophical tradition. Winograd and Flores's criticisms, for example, are based on issues raised in phenomenology and postmodern skepticism by Husserl (1970), Derrida (1976), and others. This poststructuralist viewpoint questions the very foundations and growth of our modern intellectual traditions and asks whether *any* truth can be established. Poststructural skepticism questions the possibility of accumulating knowledge, historical processes, and the cultural progress of humanism and the enlightenment.

Heidegger (1962) represents an alternative approach to understanding knowledge and progress. For Heidegger, reflective awareness is found in a world of embodied experience, a life-world. This position, shared by Winograd and Flores, Searle, Dreyfus, and others, argues that a person's understanding of things is rooted in the practical activity of *using* them for coping with the everyday world. This world is essentially a context of socially organized roles and purposes.

In the early twentieth century, the pragmatist position was an important component of the philosophical world view. The pragmatist maxim that the meanings of hypotheses are verified by tracing their practical consequences and implications in specific situations. As noted in Sect. 2.8, William James, Charles Sanders Peirce, and John Dewey were among the primary proponents of this pragmatist position.

As the twentieth century progressed, the logical positivist or "scientific philosophy" tradition emerged, and with it, modern artificial intelligence. Most of the technical assumptions and tools of modern AI can trace their roots through the logical positivist positions of Carnap, Frege, Russell, Tarski, and Turing through Kant, Leibniz, Hobbes, Locke, and Hume, back to Plato and Aristotle. This tradition argues that intelligent processes conform to quantifiable laws and are, in principle, understandable.

But the pragmatist worldview has certainly not ended with the logical positivist. Its revival, often called *neopragmatism*, included the positions of Hilary Putnam, W.V.O. Quine, Ludwig Wittgenstein, Thomas Kuhn, and Richard Rorty. Neopragmatism, with a primary focus on language and meaning, turned from talking about "mind" and "ideas" to considering language use. The neopragmatists felt that analyzing the role of language could bring new understanding to the notions of meaning, objectivity, and truth.

Putnam, in *Words and Life* (1994, p. 152), advocates *fallibilism*, a theory that claims that doubts can be raised about any belief. Putnam claims that philosophical skepticism requires as much justification as any other philosophical position. He also claims that there are no philosophical guarantees against the need to revise a belief and that active involvement in the world is primary in philosophy, echoing the Husserl/Heidegger world views.

Wittgenstein presents his *language game* in *Philosophical Investigations* (2009), revising several of his earlier positions described in the *Tractatus Logico-Philosophicus* (1922). Wittgenstein (2009, p. 23) sees language use as, primarily, for accomplishing tasks within a societal context, and he contends:

> It is not only agreement in definitions, but also (odd as it may sound) agreement in judgements that is required for communication by means of language…
>
> The word "language-*game*" is used here to emphasize the fact that the *speaking* of language is part of an activity, or a form of life.
>
> Consider the variety of language games in the following examples, and in others:
> Giving orders and acting on them—
> Describing an object by its appearance or by its measurements—
> Constructing an object from a description (a drawing)—
> Reporting an event—
> Speculating about an event—
> …
> Translating from one language into another—
> Requesting, thanking, cursing, greeting, praying.

Because of this language game, and as reflected in the "conjectures" of Chap. 7, different social groups can have specific rules governing their communications and circumscribing objects to which their language can refer. As a result, there are often strict limits on communication with other communities. Werner Heisenberg (2000) describes this language incompatibility in his analysis of the evolution of physics.

Quine in *Word and Object* (2013) argues for *ontological relativism*, claiming that language will never support a non-subjective description of reality. Further, ontological relativism claims that things people believe exist are totally dependent on, and delimited by, the subjective mental language used to describe them. Similar to Wittgenstein (2009), and as a strict behaviorist, Quine (2013) contends that a specific language produces words that map concepts to objects in the world. Also, like Wittgenstein, Quine argues that there is no objective method for mapping communications between the languages of different communities.

In *The Structure of Scientific Revolutions*, Kuhn (1962) also appropriates the language game by arguing that our descriptions representing reality are only acceptable if they are sufficient to produce observations and related experiments that expand our knowledge. Kuhn describes these languages as *paradigms*, where "normal" science operates to better understand the constraints within that paradigm. The important step for Kuhn is when a generally accepted paradigm is thrown over by a new world view, with a revised language that supports new sets of relationships and experiments.

Kuhn's (1962) writings suggest that the model must not be confused with the phenomenon being modeled. Models allow humans to capture useful attributes of phenomena: there will, of necessity, always be a "residue" that is not empirically explained. A model is used to explore, predict, and confirm; and when a model can mediate these goals, it is successful. Further, different models may explain different aspects of one phenomenon, such as the wave and particle theories of light.

We contend, contrary to what Husserl and modern phenomenologists might propose, that when anyone suggests that aspects of intelligent phenomena are outside the scope and methods of the scientific tradition, this statement can only be verified by using that method and tradition. The scientific method is the only tool we have for explaining in what sense issues may still be outside our current understanding. Every viewpoint, even from the phenomenological tradition, if it is to have any meaning, must relate to our current notions of explanation, even to be coherent about the extent to which that phenomenon cannot be explained.

Kuhn, as an example, would see a neutrino as a language construct that can be used by physicists to better explain the tensions between matter and antimatter and why there exists a physical reality at all. In a much simpler sense, an electron or π are also useful mental constructs and are therefore meaningful only as a component of a particular explanation or paradigm.

Kuhn does not see successive paradigms as moving toward some absolute TRUTH, as Leibniz or Descartes did, or as the modern French philosopher De Chardin (1955) conjectures. Rather, Kuhn understands revised paradigms as simply creating new viewpoints, incommensurable with their predecessors, that describe the world in new ways. All scientific paradigms, according to Kuhn, should be assumed to be both useful as they currently support science, but possibly false, as ever newer paradigms emerge to supersede them.

Richard Rorty is seen by many as the primary spokesperson for the neopragmatist worldview. In *Philosophy as the Mirror of Nature*, Rorty (1979) argues that the primary problem with modern epistemology is that the human mind is seen as attempting to accurately represent, or mirror, external reality. Since this reality-world is viewed as independent of the mind, this approach must be seen as misguided. As an anti-foundationalist, Rorty argues that there is no *given* in sensory perception or self-evident premises that can act as a fixed foundation for a modern epistemology.

In *Contingency, Irony, and Solidarity*, Rorty (1989) contends that *meaning* is a product of socio-linguistic agreement and *truth* only relates to descriptions of things. Rorty states:

> Truth cannot be out there—cannot exist independently of the human mind—because sentences cannot so exist or be out there. The world is out there but descriptions of the world are not. Only descriptions of the world can be true or false. The world on its own, unaided by the describing activities of humans, cannot.

This notion of truth led Rorty to be considered a postmodern and deconstructionist philosopher. When the utterances of a language are limited to the *describing activities of humans*, many of traditional philosophy's assumptions are undermined. An example of this relativistic viewpoint is Rorty's statement in *Contingency, Irony, and Solidarity* (1989) that "anything can be made to look good or bad by being re-described."

Near the end of his life, Rorty added a more human dimension to many of his earlier positions, writing on the importance of a quality of life that is supported by democratic traditions and a liberal worldview. In an essay entitled "The Fire of Life" (2007), Rorty speaks of cultures with richer vocabularies and of being human: "I now wish I had spent somewhat more of my life with verse. ... men and women are more fully human when their memories are amply stocked with verses." Rorty gives an interesting perspective on his neopragmatist worldview in url: 9.3.

If there is a philosophical tradition supporting the AI enterprise, just as logical positivism seems to support AI's tool-making requirements, I would contend that it is neopragmatism. There is truth in the "small," a representation that captures the important parameters of a particular situation, e.g., the model that supports decision making for the sodium-cooled nuclear reactor seen in Sect. 8.4. There are no absolute truths on the agenda. An AI program is "successful" if it performs according to its specifications. There is no requirement that a program must generalize its results, transfer to related situations, or unless required by its specifications, be transparent to its human users.

Further, the AI community of program designers and builders relies on the scientific method as articulated by Thomas Kuhn (1962). This tradition examines data, constructs models, runs experiments, and evaluates results. Experiments lead to refining models for further experiments. This scientific method has brought an important level of understanding, explanation, and the ability to predict to artificial intelligence as well as to many other human endeavors.

9.5.2 A Category Error

An important trope of modern computer science is that things, including important abstractions such as π and the truth values of *true* and *false,* belong to different categories. Further examples of different categories include the sets of integers and strings of characters or multidimensional arrays and control instructions. This category difference is truly a pragmatic distinction because these different "things" cannot be combined: added, subtracted, or integrated without a category change. For example, *casting* can make a truth value into a 1 or 0 so that it can then be added to an integer. These changes are fundamentally pragmatic: making category changes for some utilitarian purpose.

We contend, and acknowledging a critical category distinction, that humans and machines are fundamentally different. Humans and machines are members of independent categories that are not reducible one to the other. Certainly, humans and machines share properties; as rocks and automobiles can share hardness, or birds and airplanes can both fly. But like the different elements on the periodic table, humans and machines belong in separate irreducible categories, changed only by some pragmatic purpose, for example, to determine their combined weights in kilograms. One property that humans and properly programmed computers do share is the possession of skills and responses that the informed observer can call intelligent.

To point out the differences that categories entail, consider again the assumptions and suppositions of Sect. 7.4. These assumptions and suppositions support the fact that meaning for humans is achieved through a commitment. We *create the real* through an existential affirmation that a perceived symbol or model is good enough for addressing some of our practical needs and purposes. Searle (1969) contends as much with his notion of speech phenomena as human *acts* having intention and purpose. To support the point of different *categories*, consider the grounding problem for computation. Symbol grounding is an AI challenge we have repeatedly discussed: how, specifically, do symbols and systems of symbols have *meaning* within a computational environment?

Grounding or creating meaning for humans is both individual and societal. As a result, meanings may differ across individuals and across groups in society. These differences are often resolved pragmatically, by discovering which meaning commitment leads to more satisfactory results. But the fact of having divergent meanings is not the critical issue here: it is the phenomenon of meaning itself.

The *grounding* issue is but one reason why computers have fundamental problems with expressions of intelligence, including their ability to understand human language and to learn. What disposition might a computer be given that supports appropriate and flexible purposes and goals? Although some (Dennett 1991) may impute grounding to a computer solving problems requiring and using "intelligence," the lack of *sufficient* grounding is easily seen in the computer's simplifications, brittleness, and often limited appreciation of evolving contexts.

The use and grounding of symbols by animate agents implies even more. The particular nature of our human embodiment and social contexts mediate our interactions with the world. Our auditory and visual systems are sensitive to a particular bandwidth. We view the world as erect bipeds. We have arms, legs, and hands. We are part of a world with weather, seasons, sun, and darkness. We are individuals that are born, reproduce, and die. We operate within a society that itself has evolving goals and purposes. All these attributes are critical components supporting metaphors of understanding, learning, and language and they mediate our comprehension of art, life, and love, as we note again in our final section.

To conclude, humans and computers simply "live" and "make decisions" in alternative search spaces: the many components that make up complex decisions are, simply put, different. Aristotle himself noted in his *Essay on Rational Action*, "Why is it that I don't feel compelled to perform that which is entailed?" For humans, sound reasoning is only one part of mature judgments. We must conclude that there are many human activities that play an essential role in responsible human interactions, behaviors, and judgments; these responsibilities cannot be reproduced by or abrogated to machines.

9.5.3 The Cognitive Neurosciences: Insights on Human Processing

Section 3.5 introduced many early studies in the cognitive science research domain. Even a weak interpretation of the physical symbol system hypothesis, that representations and search offer a *sufficient* model for intelligent behavior, has produced many powerful and useful results in cognitive science and psychology. Although much early research was inspired by the physical symbol system hypothesis, various associative and connectionist representations have proven valuable for computational modeling of human language, perception, and performance.

Although current research in psychology and neuroscience offers many possible explanations, or models, for aspects of human processing, there remain many more open and interesting questions. Consider the cortical response system, shaped and conditioned by its social and survival needs. In cortex, for example, the amygdala and limbic systems, connected to every aspect of human perception and understanding, are responsible for emotional reactions, survival instincts, and memories.

Research in cognitive neuroscience (Gazzaniga 2014) has added considerably to our understanding of the components of cortex involved in intellectual activity. A brief summary of open research issues in the cognitive neurosciences include:

1. In the area of perception, attention, and memory formation, there is the *binding problem*. Perceptual representations depend on distributed neural codes for relating parts and properties of objects to each other. What mechanisms are needed to "bind" the various components of information related to each perceived object and to distinguish that object from others?
2. In the area of visual search, what neural mechanisms support the perception of objects embedded in large complex scenes? Experiments show that suppression of information from irrelevant objects plays a role in the selection of a visual focus (Luck 1998).
3. In considering the plasticity of perception, Gilbert (1998), Maturana and Varela (1987), and others contend that what we see is not strictly a reflection of the physical characteristics of a scene. Rather, perception is highly dependent on the processes by which our brain interprets that scene.
4. How does the cortical system represent and index time-related sequences of information, including the interpretation of perceptions and the production of motor activity?
5. Finally, in memory studies, stress hormones, released during emotionally charged situations, modulate memory processes (Cahill and McGaugh 1998). This relates to the *grounding* problem: by what physical processes are thoughts, words, and perceptions, along with their emotional entailments, meaningful to a person?

We see human processing also through the writings of the philosopher Immanuel Kant (1781) and the psychologist Fredrick Bartlett (1932). Kant proposed the notion of a priori knowledge, represented as a schema, that mediated new perceptions and understandings of the world. Bartlett, in his work on human memory, proposed similar ideas. Piaget's genetic epistemology (1965, 1983), with constructs of assimilation and accommodation leading to system equilibration, demonstrated this approach through numerous studies of children moving through the different stages of their development.

Modern philosophers and psychologists have augmented the ideas of Bartlett and Piaget with the notion that humans develop through their continuing and purposive exploration of their environment (Glymour 2001; Gopnik et al. 2004; Gopnik 2011a, b). Complementing this viewpoint must be a serious dose of pragmatism: Human actions are *about something*, and every task has an often-implicit meaning and emotional valence. We have proposed the integration of these philosophical and psychological traditions into a computational modeling medium sufficient to capture important aspects of human problem-solving behavior.

9.5.4   On Being Human: A Modern Epistemic Stance

Section 7.4 offered a set of five assumptions and eight follow-on conjectures that offer a foundation for a modern epistemology. This epistemic stance positions a survival-driven human agent in an ever-evolving context. The scope of this context is societal, in that all individuals not only need a society to survive but that we fashion our reality together. Acts of mutual interaction create symbols and patterns and networks of symbols that we use to both decode our environments and to thrive within them. Together we are the medium for knowledge, meaning, and truth.

We introduced Bayes' theorem, hidden Markov models, Bayesian networks, and dynamic Bayesian networks to offer sufficient modeling tools for understanding how information can be encoded both in the individual and in society. The different probabilistic techniques and examples presented demonstrate how Bayesian technology can support conditioned responses, perceptual learning, as well as the assimilation, integration, and use of knowledge.

The information patterns that are learned and reinforced over time in probabilistic networks are very much in the empiricist tradition, following the insights of David Hume (1748/1975). The general principles and associations encoded in the network reflect the rationalist tradition (Leibniz 1887). Finally, pragmatic requirements of survival are reflected in the network's search for satisfactory conditions of equilibrium or what Piaget calls *equilibration*.

We suggest that sets of integrated dynamic Bayesian networks can be interpreted as *sufficient* models for aspects of human perception, knowledge, and performance. These networks integrate different perceptual modalities, link perception with amygdala-based emotional responses and the cognitive components of the human system. They also control the focusing mechanisms of the prefrontal cortex.

Bayesian-like responses are ubiquitous in humans, for example, in tactile aspects of human perception. How is the human able to withdraw a hand from a hot stove faster than the signal "too hot" can travel from the finger to cortex, generate a "move it" decision, and return that decision back to the hand? The human hand itself is a conditioned response system. The dynamic aspects of these Bayesian networks integrate perception, emotion, and intelligence across time.

The interplay of components of the dynamic Bayesian network actively seeks "missing" information that can lead to system equilibration. We see this in developmental psychology and Piaget's simple conservation experiments. Finding equilibria also drove the more complex scenario of fault detection, remediation, and contrafactual reasoning seen in the sodium-cooled reactor example of Sect. 8.4. In diagnostic situations, the drive for equilibration within a dynamic Bayesian network supports both the search processes that discover and integrate missing data and provide explanations that justify these searches and results.

AI research into model building, refinement, and revision is still active. Although probabilistic models do, by design, seek equilibria, discovering techniques for the identification and integration of new parameters to a model remains a challenge. Hebbian-type conditioning can strengthen components of a model. Connectionist networks that include reinforcement learning attempt to identify and integrate micro-pieces of a solution that can lead to the discovery of larger solutions. Finding methods for refining and extending models, as humans do when facing model failure, remains an open research issue. Answers may emerge from a better understanding of human agents' skills and the purposive exploration of their environments.

The assumptions and conjectures presented in Sect. 7.4 offer a foundation for a modern epistemology. There are multiple conjectures for how the five assumptions might be physiologically enabled within the human subject. The British neuroscientist Karl Friston's (2009) *free energy minimization* theory, for example, can be seen as equivalent to our "survival" assumption. Free energy minimization also offers an explanation for how humans integrate a priori expectations with related sensory input, Piaget's *accommodation*.

Karl Friston (2009) and Geoffrey Hinton (2007) also provide insights on how symbols and patterns of network activations might be integrated into the human processing system. Knill and Pouget (2004) describe the Bayesian brain and neural coding support for addressing uncertainty. Although these researchers describe possible implementation details for components of a human-centric epistemic stance, they do not extend their ideas to building a foundation for a modern epistemology.

There were three goals for creating this book, each inspired by insights gained from research progress made by the artificial intelligence and cognitive science communities. The first goal was to consider and critique the foundational assumptions of AI technology. The second goal was to suggest several data structures, networks, and search algorithms created by the AI community as sufficient models for capturing important components of human perception, understanding, and problem-focused behavior.

The third and most important goal in writing this book was to propose a foundation for a modern epistemology. This goal was described in Chap. 7, with the presentation of five assumptions and a small set of follow-on conjectures. The five assumptions affirm the survival of the individual, and equally that of society, as the motivation for all behavior. Survival mediates the creation of symbols and models.

The subsequent conjectures are intended to capture the essence of how we humans survive, understand, and flourish in our world. These symbol systems have meaning because the humans using them hold a common agreement and commitment as to what the symbols *mean* and *how they are to be used*. As suggested in Conjectures 3 and 5, individuals and society collaborate in creating and giving meaning to symbols and adopting systems of symbols to represent the knowledge and science that supports humans' common purposes.

Only the extreme solipsist, or the mentally challenged, can deny the reality of an extra-subject world. But what is this so-called "real world?" Besides being a complex combination of hard things and soft things, as Putnam (1987) notes there are: "… tables and chairs and ice cubes. There are also electrons and space time regions and prime numbers and people who are a menace to world peace." We would also add that there are systems of atoms, molecules, quarks, gravity, relativity, indeterminacy, cells, DNA, and perhaps even superstrings. All these explanatory constructs are just exploratory models driven by the pragmatic requirements of equilibration-driven humans. These exploratory models are not just about an "external" world. Rather, they capture the dynamic equilibrating tensions of the intelligent and social agent and of a material intelligence evolving and continually calibrating itself within the continuums of space and time.

The assumptions and conjectures of Sect. 7.4 are but a rationalist approximation to, and a beginning understanding of ourselves operating in an evolving and survival-driven world. The full dynamic integration of the human experience is found through actively interacting within our environment, of creating ourselves through our social interactions, of *being there*.

We can also discover important expressions of human maturity through our artistic and literary traditions. Perhaps Richard Rorty is right in suggesting that literature is the new epistemology, that meaning is coming to terms with ourselves and society, and that our artists have the important project of helping us appreciate this relationship. In introducing their songs, the epic poets, including Homer, Virgil, Dante, and Milton, all invoked the Muses of history, wisdom, and poetry. Albert Camus (1946), in *The Stranger* suggests that "Fiction is the lie through which we tell the truth." Joan Didion (1979), in *The White Album* proposes that "We tell ourselves stories in order to live…"

Three examples from my own literary background express this human intellectual and emotional support/requirement. First, after the destruction by the Greeks of his much-loved Troy, Virgil's Aeneas arrives at Carthage. On entering Dido's palace, he sees a mural depicting battles of the Trojan war and the deaths of his fellow countrymen. Aeneas is saddened by the scene and says, "… sunt lacrimae rerum et mentem mortalia tangent." Or "… there are tears at the heart of things and mortality moves the soul…" What integration of human vision, memory, understanding, and emotion can enable a simple mural to evoke such a response?

As a second example, consider lines from Shakespeare's Sonnet XVIII:

> Shall I compare thee to a summer's day?
> Thou art more lovely and more temperate:
> Rough winds do shake the darling buds of May,

And summer's lease hath all too short a date...

These lines capture several complex human emotions. Shakespeare questions comparing his lover to a summer day, and immediately qualifies his comparison by saying she is "more lovely and more temperate." What does this comparison and contrast of a lover to a summer day imply in describing a human relationship? Further, what are the limits of love, emotion, and mortality that permeate the last lines: "Rough winds do shake the darling buds of May, and summer's lease hath all too short a date?"

As a final example of the human condition mediating interpretation, consider Dylan Thomas's plea to his dying father, a verse that speaks to all:

Do not go gentle into that good night.
Rage, rage against the dying of the light.

Meaning is a human-created artifact. It is a derivative of the human agent's need to survive both individually and as a community. And *truth* is a human-created societal norm. Truth is the alignment of a person's or a group of people's meanings with the goal-related meanings of another individual or of a society. Different societies, indeed, different components of the same society, will have different meanings and truths, as is often seen among religious, political, and cultural groups. Examples of societies' different sets of truths can be seen in a science journal articles, beliefs concerning the roles of men and women, or in the declared positions of a political party. The question of *whose truth* can cause multiple conflicts that are often only reconciled through the pragmatic outcomes of their use.

Although truth may be relative to particular sets of meanings established by individuals and societies, all relativism is confined within the limits of self, society, and science for the measure of what is real. Individuals assume a responsible assimilation of knowledge and a measured commitment to truths. Societies provide their methods for conditioning individual members, including schools, jails, mental institutions, and all too often, wars. There is always the dangerous possibility that fears, beliefs, and unrealistic hopes can create an unsustainable "reality," such as that found in some commonly accepted cultures, myths, political stances, and religions.

We conjecture that, as an agent's needs and maturity require and even demand, this "relativist" stance will continue to evolve (Piaget 1983; Heisenberg 2000; Hawking and Mlodinow 2010). As suggested in Conjecture 8, the individual, society, and science are continually recreating and recalibrating models as well as the language for expressing what is knowable. This scientific methodology is the best guarantor of not just surviving in our world but also for coming to understand and enjoy it.

Exploration-driven relativism may appear as a threat to many. But the response to the criticism of total relativism is centered in the responsibility humans take, both individually and collectively, when creating their symbols, sets of symbols, beliefs, truths, and judgments. Our description of human maturity is of a person and of a society that is open and humble before a world that is never fully understood.

This person and society are ready to learn, always open to new appreciation of what an evolving reality portends, and above all, ready to acknowledge both ignorance and error. The person is other-oriented, finding full maturity as a component of its social context. This mature person sees all individuals as seekers similar to themselves and sees in society a medium for finding, expressing, and enjoying a common responsibility.

I contend that using the heuristic and pragmatic constraints of humility, self-awareness, and self-preservation to come to know ourselves, science, and society, we can both appreciate and embody the epistemic stance of an *active, pragmatic, model-revising realism.*

Further Reading The writings of the philosophers Russell Goodman and Clark Glymour, as well as the insights of the developmental psychologist Allison Gopnik, inspired many aspects of this final chapter. Our developmental psychologists have shown that the understanding of how humans learn as they mature support insights into how more mature humans experience, explore, and revise their understandings as they come to appreciate and enjoy their world.

Glymour, C. (2001). *The Mind's Arrows: Bayes Nets and Graphical Causal Models in Psychology.*

Gopnik et al. (2004). *A Theory of Causal Learning in Children: Causal Maps and Bayes Nets.*

Gopnik, A. (2011a). *A Unified Account of Abstract Structure and Conceptual Change: Probabilistic Models and Early Learning Mechanisms.*

Gopnik, A. (2011b). *Probabilistic Models as Theories of Children's Minds.*

I thank my talented graduate students Drs. Joseph Lewis and Nikita Sakhanenko for designing projects in this chapter and my friend Professor Lydia Tapia for introducing me to the PRM-RL robot project at google. Thanks also to Professor Russell Goodman for his comments on this chapter. I recommend Goodman's books:

Goodman (1995). *Pragmatism: A Contemporary Reader.*
Goodman (2002). *Wittgenstein and William James.*
Goodman (2015). *American Philosophy Before Pragmatism.*

We thank Karger Publications, Basel, for permission to use Fig. 9.1. This figure appeared in Luger et al. (2002). Figures 9.2 and 9.3 came from the PhD dissertation in Computer Science at UNM of Dr. Joseph Lewis. Figure 9.4 came from the PhD dissertation in Computer Science at UNM of Dr. Nikita Sakhenenko.

Bibliography

Ackley, D.H. and Ackley E.S. 2016. The *ulam* programming language for artificial life. Artificial Life 22:431-450. Cambridge, MA: The MIT Press.

Adami, C., & Brown, C.T. 1994. Evolutionary learning in the 2D artificial life system "Avida" Adaptation, noise, and self-organizing systems. Report No. MAP-173, Cornell, Cornell University.

Adleman, L. M. 1994. Molecular computation of solutions to combinatorial problems. Science 266 (5187): 1021–1024.

Agre, P. and Chapman, D. 1987. Pengi: An implementation of a theory of activity. Proceedings of the sixth national conference on artificial intelligence, pp. 268–272. CA: Morgan Kaufmann.

Anderson, J.R. and Bower, G.H. 1973. Human associative memory. Hillsdale, NJ: Erlbaum.

Arbib, M. 1966. Simple self-reproducing universal automata. Information and Control 9: 177–189.

Arulkumaran, K., Antoine, C., & Togelius, J. 2020 AlphaStar: An evolutionary computation perspective. *Proceedings of the genetic and evolutionary computation conference companion.*

Austin, J.L. 1962. How to do things with words. Cambridge, MA: Harvard University Press.

Awodey, S. 2010. Category theory, Oxford Logic Guides 49. London: Oxford University Press.

Bacon, F. 1620. Novum organum. Londini: Apud (Bonham Norton and) Joannem Billium.

Baker, Stephen 2011. Final jeopardy: Man vs. machine and the quest to know everything. Boston, New York: Houghton Mifflin Harcourt.

Balestriero, R. and Baraniuk, R.G. 2018. A spline theory of deep networks. Proceedings of the 35th International Conference on Machine Learning, vol. 80 pp. 383-392.

Barkow, J.H., Cosmides, L., and Tooby, J. 1992. The adapted mind. New York: Oxford University Press.

Bartlett, F., 1932. Remembering. London: Cambridge University Press.

Bayes, T. 1763. Essay towards solving a problem in the doctrine of chances. Philosophical Transactions of the Royal Society of London. London: The Royal Society, pp. 370-418.

Ben-Amram, A.M. 2005.The Church-Turing thesis and its look-alikes. SIGART News, 36(3): 113-116.

Bender, E.M and Koller, A. 2020. Climbing towards NLU: On meaning, form, and understanding in the age of data. Proceedings of the 58th Meeting of the Association for Computational Linguistics. ACL: 5185-5198.

Bengio, Y., Ducharme, R., and Vincent, P. 2003. A neural probabilistic language model. Journal of Machine Learning Research 3 pp. 1137-1155.

Berlin, B. and Kay, P. 1999. Basic color terms: Their universality and evolution, 2nd Ed. Stanford: CSLI Publications.

Bishop, C.M. 2006. Pattern recognition and machine learning. Springer, New York.

Black, M. 1946. Critical thinking, New York: Prentice-Hall.

© Springer Nature Switzerland AG 2021

G. F. Luger, *Knowing our World*, https://doi.org/10.1007/978-3-030-71873-2

Blackburn, S. 2008. The Oxford dictionary of philosophy, 15th edn. London: Oxford University Press.

Bledsoe, W.W. and Browning, I. 1959. Pattern recognition and reading by Machine Proceedings of the eastern joint computer conference. New York: IEEE Computer Society.

Boole, G. 1847. The mathematical analysis of logic. Cambridge: MacMillan, Barclay & MacMillan.

Boole, G. 1854. An investigation of the laws of thought. London: Walton & Maberly.

Boden, M. 2006. Mind as machine: A history of cognitive science. Oxford University Press.

Bower, T.G.R. 1977. A primer of infant development. San Francisco: W.H. Freeman.

Brachman, R.J. and Levesque, H. J. 1985. Readings in knowledge representation. Los Altos, CA: Morgan Kaufmann.

Bradshaw, G. L., Langley, P., & Simon, H. A. 1983. Studying scientific discovery by computer simulation. Science, 222, 971-975.

Brooks, R.A. 1986. A robust layered control system for a mobile robot. IEEE Journal of Robotics and Automation. 4:14–23.

Brooks, R.A. 1991. Intelligence without representation. Proceedings of IJCAI–91, pp. 569–595. San Mateo, CA: Morgan Kaufmann.

Brooks, R.A. 1997. The cog project, *Journal of the Robotics Society of Japan, Special Issue (Mini) on Humanoid*, Vol. 15(7) T. Matsui, (Ed).

Brown, P. 2011. Color me bitter: Crossmodal compounding in Tzeltal perception words. The Senses and Society, 6(1). 106-116.

Brown, T.B. et al. (31 co-authors). 2020. *Language models are few-shot learners.* https://arxiv.org/abs/2005.14165.

Bruner, J.S., Goodnow, J., and Austin, G.A 1956. A study of thinking, New York: Wiley.

Buchanan, B.G. and Shortliffe, E.H. eds. 1984. Rule-based expert systems: The MYCIN experiments of the Stanford heuristic programming project. Reading, MA: Addison-Wesley.

Bundy, A. 1983. Computer modelling of mathematical reasoning. New York: Academic Press.

Bundy, A., Byrd, L., Luger, G., Mellish, C., Milne, R., and Palmer, M. 1979. Solving mechanics problems using meta-level inference. *Proceedings of IJCAI-1979*, pp. 1017–1027.

Burge, J., Lane, T., Link, H., Qiu, S., and Clark, V. P. 2007. Discrete dynamic Bayesian network analysis of fMRI data. Human Brain Mapping 30(1), pp 122–137.

Burks, A.W. 1971. Essays on cellular automata. University of Illinois Press. Illinois

Cahill, L. and McGaugh, J.L. Modulation of memory storage. In Squire and Kosslyn 1998.

Camus, A. 1946. The stranger. New York: Vantage Books.

Carlson, N.R. 2010. Physiology of behavior, 10th edn. Needham Heights, MA: Allyn Bacon.

Carnap, R. 1928. Der Logische Aufbau der Welt (The Logical Structure of the World). Leipzig: Felix Meiner Verlag.

Castro, F.M., Marin-Jimenez, M.J., Guil, N., Schmid, C., & Alahari, K., 2018. *End-to-end incremental learning.* https://doi.org/arXiv:1807.09536v2.

Ceccato, S. 1961. Linguistic analysis and programming for mechanical translation. New York: Gordon & Breach.

Chakrabarti, C. and Luger, G.F. 2015, Artificial conversations for customer service chatter bots: Architecture, algorithms, and evaluation metrics. Expert Systems with Applications 42(20), 6878–6897.

Chakrabarti, C., Pless, D. J., Rammohan, R., and Luger, G. F. 2005. A first-order stochastic prognostic system for the diagnosis of helicopter rotor systems for the US navy, In Proceedings of the FLAIRS-05, Menlo Park, CA: AAAI Press.

Chakrabarti, C., Pless, D. J., Rammohan, R., & Luger, G. F. 2007, Diagnosis using a first-order stochastic language that learns, Expert systems with applications. Amsterdam: Elsevier Press. 32: 3.

Changizi, M.A., Hseih, A., Nijhawan, R., Kanai, R. and Shimojo, S. 2008. Preceiving the present and a systematization of illusions. Cognitive Science, 32(3): 459-503.

Chen, L. and Lu, X., 2018. Making deep learning models transparent. Journal of Medical AI, 1:5.

Chomsky N. 1959. A review of B.F. Skinner's verbal behavior. Language 35 (1): 26-58.

Church, A. 1935. Abstract No. 204. Bull. Amer. Math. Soc. 41: 332-333.

Church, A. 1941. The calculi of lambda-conversion. Annals of mathematical studies. Vol. 6. Princeton, NJ: Princeton University Press.

Clark, A., 2013. Whatever next? Predictive brains, situated agents, and the future of cognitive science. The Behavioral and Brain Sciences, 36 (3), 181-204.

Clark, A., 2015. Radical predictive processing. The Southern Journal of Philosophy, 53 S1.

Codd, E.F. 1968. Cellular automata. New York: Academic Press.

Codd, E.F. 1992. Private communication to J. R. Koza. In Koza.

Collins A. and Quillian, M.R. 1969. Retrieval time from semantic memory. Journal of Verbal Learning and Verbal Behavior, 8: 240–247.

Cosmides, L., & Tooby, J. . 1992 *Cognitive adaptations for social exchange*. In Barkow et al.

Cosmides, L., & Tooby, J. 1994 *Origins of domain specificity: The evolution of functional organization*. In Hirschfeld and Gelman.

Crutchfield, J.P., & Mitchell, M. 1995. The evolution of emergent computation. *Working Paper 94-03-012*. Santa Fe Institute.

D'Amour, A. et al. (40 co-authors) 2020. *Underspecification presents challenges for credibility in modern machine learning*. https://arxiv.org/abs/2011.03395.

Darling, M.C., Luger, G.F., Jones, T.B., Denman, M.R., & Groth, K.M. (2018). Intelligent monitoring for nuclear power plant accident management. *Int. J. of AI Tools*. World Scientific Pub.

Darwin, C. 1859. On the origin of species. New York: P.F. Collier & Son.

Davis, M. (ed.) 1965. The undecidable, basic papers on undecidable propositions, unsolvable problems and computable functions. New York: Raven Press.

Davis, L. 1985. Applying adaptive algorithms to epistatic domains. Proceedings of the International Joint Conference on Artificial Intelligence, 1985: 162-164.

Davis, K.H., Biddulph, R., & Balashek, S. 1952. Automatic recognition of spoken digits. Journal of the Acoustical Society of America, 24(6), 637-642.

Dawkins, R. 1976. The selfish gene. Oxford: The University Press.

De Chardin, P.T. 1955. The phenomenon of man. New York: Harper and Brothers.

De Palma, P. 2010. *Syllables and Concepts in Large Vocabulary Speech Recognition.* PhD Thesis University of New Mexico, Department of Linguistics.

De Palma, P., Luger, G.F., Smith, C., & Wooters, C. 2012. Bypassing words in automatic speech recognition. MAICS-2012.

Dechter, R. 1986. Learning while searching in constraint-satisfaction problems. Proc. of the 5th National conference on artificial intelligence. AAAI Press, New York.

Deerwester, S., Dumais, S.T., Furnas, G.W., Landauer, T.K., and Harshman, R. 1990. Indexing by latent semantic analysis. Journal of the American Society for Information Science 41 (6): 391-407.

Dempster, A.P., Laird, N.M., and Rubin, D.B. 1977. Maximum Likelihood from Incomplete Data via the EM Algorithm. Journal of the Royal Statistical Society, B, 39, p 1-38.

Dennett, D.C. 1991. Consciousness explained. Boston: Little, Brown.

Dennett, D.C. 1995. Darwin's dangerous idea: Evolution and the meanings of life. New York: Simon & Schuster.

Dennett, D.C. 2006. Sweet dreams: Philosophical obstacles to a science of consciousness. Cambridge: MIT Press.

Derrida, J. 1976. Of grammatology, Baltimore, MD: Johns Hopkins University Press.

Descartes, R. 1637/1969. Discourse on method: Meditations on the first philosophy. New York: Duton.

Descartes, R. 1680. Six metaphysical meditations, wherein it is proved that there is a God and that man's mind is really distinct from his body. W. Moltneux, translator. London: Printed for B. Tooke.

Devlin, J., Chen, M., Lee, K., & Toutanova, K. (2019). *BERT: Pre-training of deep bidirectional transformers for language understanding*. https://arxiv.org/abs/1810.04805.

Dewey, J. 1916. Democracy and education. New York: Macmillan.

Didion, J. 1979. The white album. New York: Simon and Schuster.

Dittrich, P., Ziegler, J, and Banzhaf, W. 2001. Artificial Chemistries - A Review. Artificial Life 7: p. 225-275 Cambridge: MIT Press.

Drescher, G.J., 1991. Made-up minds. Cambridge, MA: MIT Press.

Dreyfus, H., 1972. What computers can't do: The limits of artificial intelligence. New York: Harper and Row.

Dreyfus, H., 1992. What computers still can't do: A critique of artificial reason. Cambridge MA: Mit Press.

Duda, R.O., Hart, P.E., Konolige, K. and Reboh, R 1979. A computer based consultant for mineral exploration, Palo Alto, CA: SRI International.

Eco, U. 1976. A theory of semiotics. Bloomington, Indiana: University of Indiana Press.

Edelman, G.M. 1992. Bright air, brilliant fire: On the matter of the mind. New York: Basic Books.

Einstein, A. 1940. On science and religion, Nature. Edinburgh: Macmillan Publishers Group 146 (3706): 605–607.

Elman, J.L., Bates, E.A., Johnson, M.A., Karmiloff-Smith, A., Parisi, D., and Plunkett, K. 1998. Rethinking innateness: A connectionist perspective on development. Cambridge, MA: MIT Press.

Euler, L. 1735. *The seven bridges of Konigsberg*. In Newman (1956).

Faust, A., Ramirez, O., Fiser, M., Oslund, K., Francis, A., Davidson, J., & Tapia, L. (2018). PRM-RL: Long-range robotic navigation by combining reinforcement learning with sampling-based planning. *Proceedings of ICRA-18*.

Feigenbaum, E.A. and Feldman, J., eds. 1963. Computers and thought. New York: McGraw-Hill.

Feldman, H. and Friston, K., 2010. Attention, uncertainty, and free-energy. Frontiers in Human Neuroscience 4, 215.

Ferrucci, D., Brown, E., Chu-Carroll, J., Fan, J., Gondek, D., Kalyanpur, A.A., Lally, A., Murdock, J.W., Nyberg, E., Prager, J., Schlaefer, N., and Welty, C. 2010. Building WATSON: An overview of the DeepQA project. AI Magazine 31: 3.

Ferrucci, D., Levas, A., Bagchi, S., Gondek, D., and Mueller, E.T. 2013. Watson: Beyond Jeopardy!. Artificial Intelligence 199: 93–105.

Feynman, R. P. 1982. Simulating physics with computers (PDF). International Journal of Theoretical Physics 21 (6): 467–488.

Fikes, R.E. and Nilsson, N.J. 1971. STRIPS: A new approach to the application of theorem proving to artificial intelligence. Artificial Intelligence, 1: 2.

Finn, C., Abbeel, P., & Levine, S. (2017). *Model-agnostic meta-learning for fast adaptation of deep networks*. https://arxiv.org/abs/1703.03400.

Fillmore, C.J. 1968. The Case for Case. In Bach, E. and Harms, R. (eds.) Universals of Linguistic Theory, New York: Holt, Rinehart, and Winston.

Fillmore, C.J. 1985. Frames and the Semantics of Understanding. Quaderni di Semantica, 6, p.222-254.

Fodor, J.A. 1983. The modularity of mind. Cambridge, MA: MIT Press.

Fontana, W., & Buss, L. W. 1996. The barrier of objects: From dynamical systems to bounded organizations. *International Institute for Applied Systems Analysis*.

Freeman, C., Merriman, J., Beaver, I., and Mueen, A. 2019. Experimental comparison of online anomaly detection algorithms, Proceedings of the 32nd International flairs conference, Palo Alto: AAAI Press.

Frege, G. 1879. Begriffsschrift, eine der arithmetischen nachgebildete Formelsprache des reinen Denkens. Halle: L. Niebert.

Frege, G. 1884. Die Grundlagen der Arithmetic. Breslau: W. Koeber.

Friston, K., 2009. The free-energy principle: A rough guide to the brain. Trends in Cognitive Sciences, 13 (7), 293-301.

Fukushima, K. 1980. Neocognitron: A self-organizing neural network model for a mechanism of pattern recognition unaffected by shift or position. Biological Cybernetics (Springer-Verlag) 36, pp. 193-202.

Gardner, M. 1970. Mathematical games. *Scientific American* (October 1970).

Gardner, M. 1971. Mathematical games. *Scientific American* (February 1971).

Gazzaniga, M.S. ed. 2014. The new cognitive neurosciences (4th edn). Cambridge: MIT Press.

Gazzaniga, M.S., Ivry, R.B., and Mangun, G.R. 2018, Cognitive neuroscience 5th edn. New York: W.W. Norton and Co.

Gelernter, H. 1959. Realization of a geometry-theorem proving machine. Proceedings of the International Conference on Information Processing. Paris: UNESCO House.

Gelernter, H. and Rochester N. 1958. Intelligent behavior in problem-solving machines. IBM Journal of Research and Development, 2(4):336-345.

Gilbert, C.D. 1998. Plasticity in visual perception and physiology. In Squire and Kosslyn (1998).

Gilpin, L.H., Bau, D., Yuan, B.Z., Bajwa, A., Specter, M., & Kagal, L. (2019). *Explaining explanations: An approach to evaluating interpretability of machine learning.*https://arxiv.org/abs/1806.00069.

Glymour, C. 2001. The mind's arrows: Bayes nets and graphical causal models in psychology. Cambridge: MIT Press.

Goddard, C. 2011. Semantic analysis: A practical introduction. Oxford, UK: The University Press.

Gödel, K. 1930. Die Vollstandigkeit der Axiome des Logischen Funktionenkalkuls. Monatshefte fur Mathematick und Physik, 37: 349-360.

Goldberg, A., & Kay, A. 1976. Smalltalk-72 instruction manuel. Xerox Palo Alto Research Center, CA: Palo Alto.

Goldin, G.A. and Luger G.F. 1975. Problem structure and problem solving behavior. Proceedings of IJCAI-75. Cambridge, MA: MIT-AI Press.

Goodfellow, I., Pouget-Abadie, J., Mirza, M., Xu, B., Warde-Farley, D., Ozair, S., Courville, A., & Benjio, Y. 2014. Generative adversarial nets. Advances in Neural Information Processing Systems, 2014: pp. 2672-2680.

Goodman, R.A. 1995. Pragmatism: A contemporary reader. New York: Routledge.

Goodman, R.A. 2002. Wittgenstein and William James. New York: Cambridge University Press.

Goodman, R.A. 2015. American philosophy before pragmatism. Oxford, UK: The University Press.

Gopnik, A. 2011a. A unified account of abstract structure and conceptual change: Probabilistic models and early learning mechanisms. Commentary on Susan Carey "The Origin of Concepts" Behavioral and Brain Sciences 34 (3):126-129.

Gopnik, A. 2011b. Probabilistic models as theories of children's minds. Behavioral and Brain Sciences 34(4):200-201.

Gopnik, A., Glymour, C., Sobel, D.M., Schulz, L.E., Kushnir, T. and Danks, D., 2004. A theory of causal learning in children: Causal maps and Bayes nets. Psychological Review, 111(1): 3-32.

Gotlieb, A. 2000. The dream of reason: A history of western philosophy from the greeks to the renaissance. New York: W.W. Norton and Company.

Gotlieb, A. 2016. The dream of enlightenment: The rise of modern philosophy. New York: W.W. Norton and Company.

Gould, S.J. 1977. Ontogeny and Phylogeny. Cambridge MA: Belknap Press.

Gould, S.J., 1996. Full House: The Spread of Excellence from Plato to Darwin. NY: Harmony Books.

Grice, H.P. 1981. Presupposition and conversational implicature, in P. Cole (ed.), Radical pragmatics, Academic Press, New York, pp. 183–198.

Gristo, D. 2019. Google AI beats top human players at strategy game StarCraft II. Cham: Springer Nature.

Grossberg, S. 1982. Studies of mind and brain: Neural principles of learning, perception, development, cognition and motor control. Boston: Reidel Press.

Harnad, S. 1990. The symbol grounding problem, Physica D, 42, pp 335-346.

Haugeland, J. 1985. Artificial intelligence: The very idea. Cambridge/Bradford, MA: MIT Press.

Haugeland, J., ed. 1997. Mind design: Philosophy, psychology, artificial intelligence, 2nd edn. Cambridge, MA: MIT Press.

Hawking, S. and Mlodinow, L., 2010. The grand design. New York: Bantam Books.

Hayes, J.R. and Simon, H.A. 1974. Understanding written problem instructions. In Knowledge and cognition, L.W. Gregg (Ed.) Hillside, NJ: Erlbaum.

Heaven, W.D. (2020a). OpenAI's new language generator GPT-3 is shockingly good—And completely mindless. In *MIT Technology Review*, July.

Heaven, W.D. (2020b). The way we train AI is fundamentally flawed. In *MIT Technology Review*, November.

Hebb, D.O. 1949. The organization of behavior. New York: Wiley.

Hecht-Nielsen, R. 1989. Theory of the backpropagation neural network. Proceedings of the international joint conference on neural networks, I, pp. 593–611. New York: IEEE Press.

Hecht-Nielsen, R. 1990. Neurocomputing. New York: Addison-Wesley.

Heidegger, M. 1962. Being and time. Translated by J. Masquarrie and E. Robinson. New York: Harper & Row.

Heisenberg, W. 2000. Physics and philosophy. New York: Penguin Books.

Helmers, L., Horn, F., Biegler, F, Oppermann, T, and Muller, K-R. 2019. Automating the search for a patent's prior art with a full text similarity search. PLoS One 14 (3).

Hightower, R. 1992. *The Devore universal computer constructor.* Presentation at the Third Workshop on Artificial Life, Santa Fe, NM.

Hilbert, D. 1902. Open Court edition, 1971. In *Foundations of Geometry (Grundlagen der Geometrie)*, (1862–1943).

Hinton, G.E., 2007. Learning multiple layers of representation. Trends in Cognitive Sciences, 11 (10), 428-434.

Hinton, G.E., & Sejnowski, T.J. 1983. Analyzing cooperative computation. In Proceedings of the 5th Annual Congress of the Cognitive Science Society, Rochester, New York.

Hinton, G.E., Osindero, S., Teh, Y.W. 2006. A fast learning algorithm for deep belief nets. Neural Computation 18 (7): 1527–1554.

Hirschfeld, L.A. and Gelman, S.A., ed. 1994. Mapping the mind: Domain specificity in cognition and culture. Cambridge: Cambridge University Press.

Hobbes, T. 1651. Leviathan. London: Printed for A. Crooke.

Hofstadter, D. 1995. Fluid concepts and creative analogies, New York: Basic Books.

Holland, J.H. 1975. Adaptation in natural and artificial systems. Michigan, University of Michigan Press.

Holland, J.H. 1986. Escaping brittleness: The possibilities of general purpose learning algorithms applied to parallel rule-based systems. In Michalski et al. 1986.

Holland, J.H. 1995. Hidden order: How adaptation builds complexity. Reading, MA: Addison-Wesley

Hopfield, J.J. 1984. Neural networks and physical systems with emergent collective computational abilities. Proceedings of the National Academy of Sciences, 79: 2554-2558.

Hsu, F.-H. 2002. Behind deep blue: Building the computer that defeated the world chess champion. Princeton, NJ: Princeton University Press

Hubel, D.H, and Wiesel, T.N. 1959. Receptive fields of single neurones in the cat's striate cortex. The Journal of Physiology, 148, pp. 574-591.

Hugdahl, K. and Davidson, R.J. (eds) 2003. The asymmetrical brain. Cambridge: MIT Press.

Hume, D. 1739/1978. A treatise on human nature. L.A. Selby-Bigge (ed.), 2nd edn. London: Oxford University Press.

Hume, D. 1748/1975. Inquiries concerning human understanding and concerning the principles of morals. L.A. Selby-Bigge (ed.), 3rd edn. London: Oxford University Press.

Husserl, E. 1970. The crisis of European sciences and transcendental phenomenology. Translated by D. Carr. Evanston, IL: Northwestern University Press.

Iyer, R., Li, Y., Li, H., Lewis, M., Sundar, R., & Sycara, K. (2018). *Transparency and explanation in deep reinforcement learning neural networks.* AAAI, https://arxiv.org/abs/1809.06061.

Jaderberg, M., Czarnecki, W.M., Dunning, I., Marris, L., Lever, G., Castañeda, A.G., Beattie, C., Rabinowitz, N.C., Morcos, A.S., Ruderman, A., Sonnerat, N., Green, T., Deason, L., Leibo, J.Z., Silver, D., Demis Hassabis, D., Kavukcuoglu, K., and Graepel, T. 2019. Human-level performance in 3D multiplayer games with population-based reinforcement learning. Science 364 859-865.

James, W. 1902. The varieties of religious experience. London: Longmans Green and Co.

James, W. 1909. The meaning of truth: A sequel to "Pragmatism". Buffalo, NY: Prometheus Books.

James, W. 1981. Pragmatism. B. Kuklick, ed. Indianapolis, IN: Hackett.

Johnson, M. 1987. The body in the mind: The bodily basis of meaning, imagination and reason. Chicago: University of Chicago Press.

Jones, T.J., Darling, M.C., Groth, K.M., Denman, M.R., & Luger, G.F. 2016. A dynamic Bayesian network for diagnosing nuclear power plant accidents. In Proceedings J. Experiments in Chess FLAIRS Conference-16, New York: AAAI Press.

Jurasky, D., & Martin, J.H. (2020). Speech and language processing, 3rd edn, Upper Saddle River, NJ: Prentice Hall-Pearson.

Kant, I. 1781/1964. Immanuel Kant's critique of pure reason, Smith, N.K. translator. New York: St. Martin's Press.

Karmiloff-Smith, A. 1992. Beyond modularity: A developmental perspective on cognitive science. Cambridge, MA: MIT Press.

Kavraki, L. E., Svestka, P., Latombe, J.-C., and Overmars, M. H. 1996, Probabilistic roadmaps for path planning in high-dimensional configuration spaces, IEEE Transactions on Robotics and Automation, 12 (4): 566–580.

Kister, J., Stein, P., Ulam, S., Walden, W., & Wells, M. (1956). Experiments in chess. In Feigenbaum, E.A., Collected Papers, 1950–2007, Stanford University Libraries. Department of Special Collections and University Archives.

Klahr, D., Langley, P. and Neches, R. (eds.) 1987. Production system models of learning and development. Cambridge, MA: MIT Press.

Klein, W.B., Westervelt, R.T., and Luger, G.F. 1999. A general-purpose intelligent control system for particle accelerators. Journal of intelligent & fuzzy systems. New York: John Wiley.

Klein, W.B., Stern, C.R., Luger, G.F., and Pless, D. 2000. Teleo-reactive control for accelerator beamline tuning. Artificial intelligence and soft computing: Proceedings of the IASTED international conference. Anaheim: IASTED/ACTA Press.

Knill, D.C. and Pouget, A., 2004. The Bayesian brain: The role of uncertainty in neural coding and computation. Trends in Neurosciences, 27 (12) pp. 712-719

Kolmogorov, A.N. 1957. On the representation of continuous functions of one variable and addition. DOKL.Akad.Nauk USSR, 114, pp. 953-956.

Kolmogorov, A.N. 1965. Three approaches to the quantitative definition of information. Problems in Information Transmission, 1(1):1-7.

Kolodner, J.L. 1993. Case-based reasoning. San Mateo, CA: Morgan Kaufmann.

Koza, J.R. 1992. Genetic programming: On the programming of computers by means of natural selection. Cambridge, MA: MIT Press.

Koza, J.R. 1994. Genetic programming II: Automatic discovery of reusable programs. Cambridge, MA: MIT Press.

Krizhevsky, A., Sutskever, I., and Hinton, G.E. 2017. ImageNet classification with deep convolutional neural networks. Communications of the ACM. 60(6): 84

Kuhn, T.S. 1962. The structure of scientific revolutions. Chicago: University of Chicago Press.

Kushnir, T., Gopnik, A., Lucas, C., & Schulz, L. 2010. Inferring hidden causal structure. Cognitive Science 34:148-160.

Laird, J.E. 2012. The soar cognitive architecture. Cambridge, MA: MIT Press.

Lakoff, G, and Johnson, M., 1999. Philosophy in the flesh, New York: Basic Books.

Langley, P., Simon, H.A. and Bradshaw, G.L. 1987a. In Computational models of learning, E. Bloc (ed.), Berlin: Springer Verlag.

Langley, P., Simon, H. A., Bradshaw, G. L., & Zytkow, J. M. 1987b. Scientific discovery: Computational explorations of the creative processes. Cambridge, MA: MIT Press.

Langton, C.G. 1995. Artificial life: An overview. Cambridge, MA: MIT Press.

Lave, J. 1988. Cognition in practice. Cambridge: Cambridge University Press.

LeCun, Y. 1989. Generalization and network design strategies. In Pfeifer, S., Fogelman, S. (eds.), Connectionism in perspective, Elsevier, Amsterdam.

LeCun, Y., & Bengio, Y. 1995. Convolutional networks for images, speech, and time series. *The Handbook for Brain theory and Neural Networks* (10).

Leibniz, G.W. 1887. *Philosophische Schriften*. Berlin.

Levy, S. 2010. Hackers. Sebastopol, CA: O'Reilly.

Levy, D., & Newborn, M. 1991. How computers play chess. *Computer Science Press*.

Lewis, J.A. 2001. *Adaptive representation in a behavior-based robot: An extension of the copycat architecture*. PhD Dissertation, Computer Science Department, University of New Mexico, Albuquerque NM.

Lewis, J.A., & Luger, G.F. 2000. A constructivist model of robot perception and performance. In Proceedings of the Twenty Second Annual Conference of the Cognitive Science Society. Hillsdale, NJ: Erlbaum.

Locke, J. 1689. *An essay concerning human understanding*.

Lonergan, B.J.F. 1957. Insight: A study of human understanding. New York: Longmans.

Lovelace, A. 1961. *Notes upon L.F. Menabrea's sketch of the analytical engine invented by Charles Babbage*. In Morrison and Morrison (1961).

Luck, S.J. 1998. Cognitive and neural mechanisms in visual search. In Squire and Kosslyn (1998).

Luger, G. 1978. A state-space description of transfer effects in isomorphic problem situations International Journal Man-Machine Studies. London: Academic Press 10, p. 613-623.

Luger, G.F. 1981. Mathematical model building in the solution of mechanics problems: Human protocols and the MECHO trace. Cognitive Science, 5 (1), p. 55-77. New Jersey: Ablex Publishing.

Luger, G.F. (ed.) 1995. Computation and intelligence. Menlo Park: AAAI/MIT Press.

Luger, G.F. 2009a. Artificial intelligence: Structures and strategies for complex problem solving. New York: Addison Wesley-Pearson.

Luger, G.F. 2009b. AI algorithms, data structures, and idioms in prolog, lisp, and java. New York: Addison Wesley-Pearson.

Luger, G.F. and Bauer, M.A. 1978. Transfer effects in isomorphic problem solving. Acta Psychologica, 42, 121-131.

Luger, G.F., & Chakrabarti, C. 2008. Chapter 23: Expert systems. Tamas Rudas (Ed.) Handbook of probability: Theory and applications. Los Angeles, CA: Sage Publications.

Luger, G.F., & Chakrabarti, C., 2016. From Alan turing to modern AI: Practical solutions and an implicit epistemic stance. AI and Society: Knowledge, Culture and Communication, Springer. 31(1): 1-18.

Luger, G.F., & Goldin, G.A. 1973. *The use of artificial intelligence techniques for the study of problem-solving behavior*. Free session on research in problem solving and psychology. Third International Joint Conference on Artificial Intelligence, Stanford University.

Luger, G.F., Bower, T.G.R, and Wishart, J.G. (1983). A computational description of the stages of development of object identity in infants. In Proceedings of the fifth annual conference of the cognitive science society. Rochester, NY: The Cognitive Science Society.

Luger, G.F., Wishart, J.G., and Bower, T.G.R., 1984. Modeling the stages of the identity theory of object-concept development in infancy. Perception, 13, p. 97-115. Englewood Cliffs, NJ: Prentice Hall.

Luger, G.F., Lewis, J. and Stern, C. 2002. Problem solving as model refinement: Towards a constructivist epistemology. Brain, Behavior and Evolution. 59(1–2), pp. 87-100. Basel: Karger.

Mao, J., Gan, C., Kohli, P., Tenenbaum, J.B., & Wu, J. 2019. *The neuro-symbolic concept learner: Interpreting scenes, words, and sentences from natural supervision*.

Marechal, E. 2008. Chemogenomics: A discipline at the crossroad of high throughput technologies, biomarker research, combinatorial chemistry, genomics, cheminformatics, bioinformatics and artificial intelligence. Combinatorial Chemistry and High Throughput Screening, 11(8): 583-586.

Masterman, M. 1961. Semantic message detection for machine translation, using interlingua. *Proceedings of the 1961 International Conference on Machine Translation.*

Maturana, H.R. and Varela, F.J. 1987. The tree of knowledge: The biological roots of human understanding. Boston, MA: Shambhala Publications, Inc.

McCarthy, J. 1968. Programs with common sense. Minsky 1968, pp. 403–418.

McCarthy, J., & Hayes, P.J. 1969. Some philosophical problems from the standpoint of artificial intelligence. In *Meltzer and Michie*

McClelland, J.L. and Rumelhart, D.E., 1981. An interactive activation model of cortex effects in letter perception: 1. An account of basic findings. Psychological Review 88 (5) pp. 375-405.

McCorduck, P. 2004. Machines who think: A personal inquiry into the history and prospects of artificial intelligence. Taylor and Francis Group LLC.

McCulloch, W.S. and Pitts, W. 1943. A logical calculus of the ideas immanent in nervous activity. Bulletin of Mathematical Biophysics, 5:115–133.

McGonigle, B.O. and Chalmers, M. 2002. The growth of cognitive structure in monkeys and men. In Fountain, B., Danks, M. Animal cognition and sequential behaviour: Behavioral, biological, and computational perspectives. Boston: Kluwer Academic, 269-314.

Meltzer, B. and Michie, D. 1969. Machine intelligence 4. Edinburgh: Edinburgh University Press.

Michalski, R.S., Carbonell, J.G., and Mitchell, T.M. 1986. Machine learning: An artificial intelligence approach. Vol. 2. Los Altos, CA: Morgan Kaufmann.

Mikolov, T., Sutskever, I., Chen, K., Corrado, G., & Dean, J. (2013). Distributed representations of words and phrases and their compositionality. In *Advances in neural Information Processing Systems.*

Miller, G.A. 2003. The cognitive revolution: A historical perspective. Trends in Cognitive Science, 7, 141-145.

Miller, G. A., Galanter, E., & Pribram, K.H. 1960. Plans and the structure of behavior. New York: Holt, Rhinehart, and Winston, Inc.

Miller, G.A, Beckwith, R., Fellbaum, C.D., Gross, D., and Miller, K. 1990. WordNet: An online lexical database. International Journal of Lexicography 3, 4, pp. 235–244.

Minsky, M., ed. 1968. Semantic information processing. Cambridge, MA: MIT Press.

Minsky, M. 1975 A framework for representing knowledge. In *Brachman and Levesque* (1985).

Minsky, M. 1985. The society of mind, New York: Simon and Schuster.

Minsky, M. and Papert, S. 1969. Perceptrons: An introduction to computational geometry. Cambridge, MA: MIT Press.

Mitchell, M. 1996. An introduction to genetic algorithms. Cambridge, MA: The MIT Press.

Mithen, S. 1996. The prehistory of the mind. London: Thames & Hudson.

Morrison, P. and Morrison, E.. 1961. Charles Babbage and his calculating machines. NY: Dover.

Mosteller, F. and Wallace D.L. 1963. Inference in an Authorship Problem. Journal of the American Statistical Association vol. 58, (302) pp. 275-309.

Murphy, K. P. 2002. *Dynamic Bayesian networks: Representation, inference and learning.* PhD Dissertation, Computer Science Department, University of California, Berkeley.

Newell, A. 1990. Unified theories of cognition. Cambridge, MA: Harvard University Press.

Newell, A. and Simon, H.A. 1956. The logic theory machine. IRE Transactions of Information Theory, 2:61–79.

Newell, A., & Simon, H.A. 1963.GPS: A program that simulates human thought. In *Feigenbaum and Feldman* 1963.

Newell, A. and Simon, H.A. 1972. Human problem solving. Englewood Cliffs, NJ: Prentice Hall.

Newell, A. and Simon, H.A. 1976. Computer science as empirical inquiry: Symbols and search. Communications of the ACM, 19(3): 113–126.

Newell, A., Shaw, J.C., and Simon, H.A. 1958. Elements of a theory of human problem solving. Psychological Review, 65:151–166.

Nilsson, N.J. 1971. Problem-solving methods in artificial intelligence. New York: McGraw-Hill.

Nilsson, N.J. 1980. Principles of artificial intelligence. Palo Alto, CA: Tioga.

Nilsson, N.J. 1994. Teleo-reactive programs for agent control. The Journal of Artificial Intelligence Research, 1. 139-158.

Nilsson, N.J. 1997. Artificial intelligence: A new synthesis. San Francisco: Morgan Kaufmann.

Norman, D.A., Rumelhart, D.E., and the LNR Research Group (1975). Explorations in cognition. San Francisco: Freeman.

Olazaran, M. 1996. A sociological study of the official history of the perceptions controversy. Social Studies of Science, 26 (3): 611-659.

Oliver, I.M., Smith, D.J., and Holland, J.R.C. 1987. A study of permutation crossover operators on the traveling salesman problem. Proceedings of the Second International Conference on Genetic Algorithms, pp. 224–230. Hillsdale, NJ: Erlbaum & Assoc.

Oyen, D. 2013. *Interactive exploration of multitask dependency networks*. PhD Thesis, Department of Computer Science, University of New Mexico.

Papert, S. 1980. Mindstorms. New York: Basic Books.

Parisi, G.I., Kemker, R., Part, J.L., Kanan, C., & Wermter, S., 2019. Continual lifelong learning with neural networks: A review. *Neural Networks*. https://arxiv.org/abs/1802.07569.

Pascal, B. 1670. Pensees de M. pascal sur la religion et sur quelques autre Sujets. Paris: Chez Guillaume Desprez.

Paun, G. 1998. Computing with membranes. Journal of Computer and System Sciences, 61, 108–143.

Pearl, J. 1984. Heuristics: Intelligent strategies for computer problem solving. Reading, MA: Addison-Wesley.

Pearl, J. 1988. Probabilistic reasoning in intelligent systems: Networks of plausible inference. Los Altos, CA: Morgan Kaufmann.

Pearl, J. 2000. Causality. New York: Cambridge University Press.

Peirce, C.S. (1931–1958). Collected papers: 1931–1958. Cambridge: Harvard University Press.

Pesavento, U. 1995. An implementation of von Neumann's self-reproducing machine. Artificial Life 2: 337-354, Cambridge: MIT Press.

Piaget, J. 1954. The construction of reality in the child. New York: Basic Books.

Piaget, J., 1965. The child's conception of number. New York: W. Norton Company.

Piaget, J. 1970. Structuralism. New York: Basic Books.

Piaget, J., 1983. Piaget's theory. Handbook of Child Psychology, 1983: 1.

Plato. 1961. The collected dialogues of Plato, Hamilton, E., & Cairns, H. eds. Princeton: Princeton University Press

Plato. 2008. *The Republic*, translated by B. Jowett. Digireads.com Publishing.

Pless, D., & Luger, G.F. (2001). Towards general analysis of recursive probability models. In Proceedings of unncertainty in artificial conference—2001. San Francisco: Morgan Kaufmann.

Pless, D., & Luger, G.F. (2003). EM learning of product distributions in a first-order stochastic logic language. Artificial intelligence and soft computing: Proceedings of the IASTED international conference. Anaheim: IASTED/ACTA Press.

Polya, G. 1945. How to solve it. Princeton, NJ: Princeton University Press.

Popper, K.R. 1959. The logic of scientific discovery. London: Hutchinson.

Porphyry. (1887). Isagoge et in Aristotelis categorias commentarium. In A. Busse (Ed), *Commentaria in Aristotelem Graeca*, 4(1).

Post, E. 1943. Formal reductions of the general combinatorial problem. American Journal of Mathematics, 65:197–268.

Poundstone, W. 1985. The recursive universe: Cosmic complexity and the limits of scientific knowledge. New York: William Morrow and Company.

Proctor, R.W. and Vu, K.P.L. 2006. The cognitive revolution at age 50: Has the promise of the information processing approach been fulfilled? Journal of Human-Computer Interaction, 23: 253-284.

Purcell, O. and Lu, T.K. 2014. Synthetic analog and digital circuits for cellular computation and memory. Current Opinion in Biotechnology, Cell and Pathway Engineering, 29: 146-155.

Putnam, H. 1987. The many faces of realism. Chicago, IL: Open Court.

Putnam, H. 1994. Words and Life. Cambridge MA: Harvard University Press.

Quillian, M.R. 1967. Word concepts: A theory and simulation of some basic semantic capabilities. In *Brachman and Levesque* (1985)

Quine, W.V.O., 2013. Word and object. Cambridge, MA: MIT Press.

Quinlan, J.R., 1986. Induction of decision trees. Machine Learning, 1(1): 81-106.

Rammohan, R. (2010). *Three Algorithms for Causal Learning*. PhD Thesis, Department of Computer Science, University of New Mexico.

Rao, R.P.N. and Ballard, D.H., 1999. Predictive coding in the visual cortex: A functional interpretation of some extra-classical receptive-field effects. Nature Neuroscience. Nature America Inc. 1999: 79-87.

Raphael, B. (1968). SIR: A computer program for semantic information retrieval. In Minsky (1968).

Ray, T.S. (1991). Evolution and optimization of digital organisms. In Billingsley, K.R. et al. (eds.) Scientific excellence in supercomputing: The IBM 1990 contest papers. Athens, GA: The Baldwin Press.

Reitman, W.R., 1965. Cognition and thought. New York: Wiley.

Ribeiro, M.T., Singh, S., & Guestrin, C. (2016). *Model-agnostic interpretability of machine learning*. https://arxiv.org/abs/1606.05386.

Roberts, D.D. 1973. The existential graphs of Charles S. Pierce. The Hague: Mouton.

Rorty, R. 1979. Philosophy as the mirror of nature. Princeton, NJ: Princeton University Press.

Rorty, R. 1989. Contingency, irony, and solidarity. Cambridge: The University Press.

Rorty, R. 2007. The fire of life. Poetry. Chicago, IL: The Poetry Foundation.

Rosch, E. (1978). *Principles of categorization*. In Rosch and Lloyd (1978).

Rosch, E. and Lloyd, B.B., ed. 1978. Cognition and categorization, Hillsdale, NJ: Erlbaum.

Rosenblatt, F. 1958. The perceptron: A probabilistic model for information storage and organization in the Brain. Psychological Review, 65 (6): 386-408.

Rosenblatt, F. 1962. Principles of neurodynamics. New York: Spartan.

Rumelhart, D.E., McClelland, J.L., & The PDP Research Group. (1986a). Parallel distributed processing. Cambridge, MA: MIT Press.

Rumelhart, D.E., Hinton G.E., and Williams, R.J. 1986b. Learning representations by representing errors. Nature 323, pp. 533-536.

Russell, S.J. 2019. Human compatible. New York: Viking Press. (Penguin Random House).

Russell, S.J. and Norvig, P. 2010. Artificial intelligence: A modern approach, 3rd edn Englewood Cliffs, NJ: Prentice-Hall.

Ryle, G. 1949. The concept of mind. London: Hutchinson.

Sakhanenko, N.A., Rammohan, R.R., Luger, G.F., & Stern, C.R. (2008). A new approach to model-based diagnosis using probabilistic logic. *Proceedings of the 21st Florida International Artificial Intelligence Research Society Conference (FLAIRS-21)*.

Samek, W., Montavon, G., Vadeldi, A., Hansen, L.K., & Muller, K.R. (eds.) 2019. Explainable AI: Interpreting, explaining and visualizing deep learning. New York: Springer.

Samuel, A.L. 1959. Some studies in machine learning using the game of checkers, IBM Journal of R& D, 3:211–229.

Schank, R.C, and Tesler, L. 1969. A Conceptual Dependency Parser for Natural Language. In proceedings of the International Conference on Computational Linguistics (COLING). Stockholm: Research Group for Quantitative Linguistics.

Schank, R.C. 1980. Language and memory. Cognitive Science, 4, 243-284.

Schank, R.C. 1982. Dynamic memory: A theory of reminding and learning in computers and people. London: Cambridge University Press.

Schank, R.C. and Abelson, R. 1977. Scripts, plans, goals and understanding. Hillsdale, NJ: Erlbaum.

Schank, R.C. and Colby, K.M., ed. 1973. Computer models of thought and language. San Francisco: Freeman.

Searle, J. 1969. Speech acts. London: Cambridge University Press.

Searle, J.R. 1980. Minds, brains and programs. The Behavioral and Brain Sciences, 3: p. 417–424.

Searle, J.R. 1990. Is the brain's mind a computer program? Scientific American, 262, p. 26-31.

Sebeok, T.A. 1985. Contributions to the doctrine of signs. Lanham, MD: University of Press of America.

Sejnowski, T.J., and Rosenberg, C.R. 1987. Parallel networks that learn to pronounce English text. Complex Systems, 1, 145-168.

Selz, O. 1913. Uber die Gesetze des Geordneten Denkverlaufs. Stuttgart: Spemann.

Selz, O. 1922. Zur Psychologie des Produktiven Denkens und des Irrtums. Bonn: Friedrich Cohen.

Shannon, C. (1948). A mathematical theory of communication. *Bell System Technical Journal.*

Shapiro, S.C., 1971. A net structure for semantic information storage, deduction, and retrieval. Proceedings of the Second International Joint Conference of Artificial Intelligence, 1971: 512-523.

Shephard, G.M. 2004. The synaptic organization of the Brain, 5th edn. New York: Oxford University of Press.

Siegelman, H. and Sontag, E.D. 1991. Neural networks are universal computing devices. Technical Report SYCON 91-08. New Jersey: Rutgers Center for Systems and Control.

Silver, D., Schrittwieser, J., Simonyan, K., Antonoglou, I., Huang, A., Guez, A., Hubert, T., Baker, L., Lai, M., Bolton, A., Chen, Y., Lillicrap, T., Hui, F., Sifre, L., van den Driessche, G., Graepel, T., and Hassabis, D. 2017. Mastering the game of Go without human knowledge, Nature, vol. 550, p. 354-359.

Silver, D., Schrittwieser, J., Simonyan, K., Antonoglou, I., Huang, A., Guez, A., Hubert, T., Baker, L., Lai, M., Bolton, A., Chen, Y., Lillicrap, T., Hui, F., Sifre, L., van den Driessche, G., Graepel, T., and Hassabis, D. 2018. A general reinforcement learning algorithm that masters chess, shogi, and go through self-play, Science, vol. 362, p. 1140-1144.

Simmons, R.F. 1966. Storage and retrieval of aspects of meaning in directed graph structures. Communications of the ACM, 9:211–216.

Simon, H.A. 1975. The functional equivalence of problem-solving skills. Cognitive Psychology, 7, 268.

Simon, H.A. 1981. The sciences of the artificial, 2nd edn. Cambridge, MA: MIT Press.

Simon, H.A. and Hayes, J.R. 1976. The understanding process: Problem isomorphs. Cognitive Psychology, 8, 165.

Singh, S. 2017. Learning to play Go from scratch. Nature, 550 p. 336-337. Macmillan.

Skinner, B.F. 1957. Verbal behavior. Acton, MA: Copley Publishing Group.

Smith, B.C. 1985. *Prologue to reflection and semantics in a procedural language.* In Brachman and Levesque (1985).

Smith, B.C. 2019. The promise of artificial intelligence: Reckoning and judgment. Cambridge, MA: MIT Press.

Sowa, J.F. 1984. Conceptual structures: Information processing in mind and machine. Reading, MA: Addison-Wesley.

Spinoza, B. 1670. *Tractatus theologico-politicus.*

Spinoza, B. 1677. *Ethica Ordine Geometrico Demonstrata.*

Squire, L.R., & Kosslyn, S.M. eds. 1998. Findings and current opinion in cognitive neuroscience, Cambridge: MIT Press.

Stern, C. and Lee, M. 2001. Proceedings of the International Conference on Accelerator and Large Experimental Physics Control Systems-99. Trieste, Italy.

Stern, C. and Luger, G. 1997. Abduction and abstraction in diagnosis: A schema based account. In K. Ford et al. eds. Situated cognition: Expertise in context. Cambridge, MA: MIT Press.

Sutton, R.S. and Barto, A.G. 2018. Reinforcement learning: An introduction, 2nd Edn. Cambridge, MA: MIT Press.

Tarski, A. 1944. The semantic conception of truth and the foundations of semantics. Philosophy and Phenomenological Research, 4:341–376.

Tarski, A. 1956. Logic, semantics, metamathematics. London: Oxford University Press.

Thrun, S., Brooks, R., and Durrant-Whyte, H. eds. 2007. Robotics Research: Results of the 12th International symposium. Tracts in Advanced Robotics, Vol 28. Heidelberg: Springer.

Tian, J., & Pearl, J. 2001. Causal discovery from changes: A Bayesian approach, *Proceedings of UAI 17*.

Turing, A.M. 1936. On computable numbers, with an application to the Entscheidungsproblem. Proceedings of the London Mathematical Society, 2nd Series, 42, p 433-460.

Turing, A.M. 1948. *Intelligent Machinery. Tech Report, National Physical Laboratory.*

Turing, A.A. 1950. Computing machinery and intelligence. Mind, 59: 433–460.

Urey, H.C. 1982. The Planets: Their Origin and Development. Yale University Press.

van Noord, N., & Postma, E. 2016. *Learning scale-variant and scale-invariant features for deep image classification.* https://arxiv.org/pdf/1602.01255.pdf.

Varela, F.J., Thompson, E., and Rosch, E. 1993. The embodied mind: Cognitive science and human experience. Cambridge, MA: MIT Press.

von Glaserfeld, E. 1978. An introduction to radical constructivism. The invented reality, Watzlawick P, ed., pp. 17–40, New York: Norton.

von Helmholtz, H. 1925. Psychological optics, Vol. III: The perceptions of vision. J.P. Southall, Trans, Rochester, NY: Optical Society of America.

von Neumann, J. 1928. Zur Theorie der Gesellschaftsspiele. Mathematische Annalen, 100, 295-320.

von Neumann, J. and Burks, A.W. 1966. Theory of self-reproducing automata. Urbana, IL: University of Illinois Press.

Wadler, P. 1990. Comprehending Monads. *Proceedings of the 1990 ACM Conference on LISP and Functional Programming, LFP '90.*

Wallace, I., Klahr, D., & Bluff, K. 1987. A self-modifying production system of cognitive development. Klahr, D., Langley, P. and Neches, R.. Production system models of learning and development. Cambridge, MA, MIT Press359–435

Wang, Z., Balestriero, R., & Baraniuk, R.G. 2019. A max-affine spline perspective of recurrent neural networks. *Proceedings of the Internal Conference on Learning Representations (ICLR).*

Weizenbaum, J. 1966. ELIZA—A computer program for the study of natural language communication between man and machine. Communications of the ACM, 9(1), 36-45.

Weizenbaum, J. 1976. Computer power and human reason. San Francisco: W. H. Freeman.

Wellhausen, R. and Oye, K. 2007. Intellectual property and the commons in synthetic biology: Strategies to facilitate an emerging technology. Atlanta conference on science, technology and innovation policy. New York: IEEE.

Whitehead, A.N. and Russell, B. 1950. Principia mathematica, 2nd edn. London: Cambridge University Press.

Widrow, B. and Hoff, M.E. 1960. Adaptive switching circuits. 1960 IRE WESTCON convention record,96–104. New York: IEEE.

Wilks, Y.A. 1972. Grammar, meaning and the machine analysis of language. London: Routledge & Kegan Paul

Williams, L.R. 2016. Programs as polypeptides. Artificial Life 22,451-482.

Williams, B.C. and Nayak, P.P. 1996. Immobile robots: AI in the new millennium. AI Magazine 17(3), 17–35. AAAI Press.

Williams, B.C. and Nayak, P.P. 1997. A reactive planner for a model-based executive. Proceedings of the International Joint Conference on Artificial Intelligence, Cambridge, MA: MIT Press.

Winograd, T. and Flores, F. 1986. Understanding computers and cognition. Norwood, NJ: Ablex.

Winston, P.H. 1977. Artificial intelligence. Reading, MA: Addison-Wesley.

Wittgenstein, L. 1922. Tractus logico-philosophicus. London: Kegan Paul.

Wittgenstein, L. 2009. Philosophical investigations. Malden, MA: Blackwell.

Woodger, M. 1986. A. M. Turing's ACE Report of 1946 and Other Papers. Cambridge MA: MIT Press.

Wos, L. 1988. Automated reasoning, 33 basic research problems. New Jersey: Prentice Hall.

Wos, L. 1995. The field of automated reasoning. Computers and Mathematics with Applications, 29(2): xi–xiv.

Wu, Y., Schuster, M., Chen Z., Le Q.V., & Norouzi, M. 2016. *Google's neural machine translation system: Bridging the gap between human and machine translation*. https://arxiv.org/pdf/1609.08144.pdf. Retrieved 20 January 2020.

Young, R.M. 1976. Seriation in children: An artificial intelligence analysis of a Piagetian task. Basel: Birkhauser.

Young, R.M. and O'Shea, T. 1981. Errors in children's subtraction. Cognitive Science 5, 153-177.

Zaman, M.M.A., & Mishu, S.Z. 2017. Convolutional recurrent neural networks for question answering. 3rd International Conference on Electrical Information and communication Technology: IEEE, New York.

URL References (All url references checked 16 June 2021)

url 3.1: http://raysolomonoff.com/dartmouth/boxa/dart564props.pdf and https://en.wikipedia.org/wiki/Dartmouth_workshop.

url 3.2: https://en.wikipedia.org/wiki/Deep_Blue_(chess_computer).

url 3.3: https://en.wikipedia.org/wiki/Watson_(computer).

url 3.4: https://deepmind.com/research/alphago/.

url 3.5: https://www.chessprogramming.org/Christopher_Strachey.

url 4.1: https://www.google.com/search?q=online+medical+diagnosis.

url 4.2: https://www.goarmy.com.

url 4.3: www.cs.unm.edu/~luger/. See reference to book cover and algorithms.

url 5.1: https://en.wikipedia.org/wiki/WordNet.

url 5.2: https://en.wikipedia.org/wiki/FrameNet.

url 5.3: https://medium.com/@ODSC/using-the-cnn-architecture-in-image-processing-65b9eb032bdc.

url 5.4: https://en.wikipedia.org/wiki/Deep_learning.

url 5.5: https://en.wikipedia.org/wiki/AlphaGo_Zero.

url 5.6: https://en.wikipedia.org/wiki/AlphaZero.

url 5.7: https://medium.com/@hugo.sjoberg88/using-reinforcement-learning-and-q-learning-to-play-snake-28423dd49e9b.

url 6.1: https://en.wikipedia.org/wiki/Artificial_life.

url 8.1: https://plato.stanford.edu/entries/epistemology-bayesian/.

url 8.2: www.cs.unm.edu/~luger/. See reference to generalized loopy logic.

url 9.1: https://en.wikipedia.org/wiki/Shakey_the_robot.

url 9.2: https://en.wikipedia.org/wiki/Turing_test.

url 9.3: https://www.youtube.com/watch?v=5nTRunosX8w.

Index

© Springer Nature Switzerland AG 2021
G. F. Luger, *Knowing our World*, https://doi.org/10.1007/978-3-030-71873-2

Printed in the United States
by Baker & Taylor Publisher Services